HON. THOMAS J. GARGAN, Boston, Mass.,
President-General of the Society.

THE JOURNAL

OF THE

AMERICAN-IRISH
HISTORICAL SOCIETY

BY

THOMAS HAMILTON MURRAY

Secretary-General

.

VOLUME II

BOSTON, MASS.
PUBLISHED BY THE SOCIETY
1899

- Notice -

The foxing, or discoloration with age, characteristic of old books, sometimes shows through to some extent in reprints such as this, especially when the foxing is very severe in the original book. We feel that the contents of this book warrant its reissue despite these blemishes, and hope you will agree and read it with pleasure.

Facsimile Reprint

Published 1991 By
HERITAGE BOOKS, INC.
1540 Pointer Ridge Place, Bowie, Maryland 20716
(301) 390-7709

ISBN 1-55613-433-9

INTRODUCTORY NOTE TO SECOND VOLUME.

────────

I take great pleasure in presenting the second volume of the JOURNAL to the Society. In so doing, I desire to acknowledge many courtesies received from various sources during its preparation. I have also been favored with ideas and suggestions regarding the work and, where practicable, have incorporated the same. The present volume, covering the year 1899, shows an increase in scope over the preceding one, a fact typifying the Society's growth in the field of American historical organizations.   T. H. M.

BOSTON, MASS., Dec. 30, 1899.

THE AMERICAN-IRISH HISTORICAL SOCIETY.

WHEN AND WHERE FOUNDED.

The American-Irish Historical Society was founded on the evening of Jan. 20, 1897, at a meeting called for that purpose, and held in the Revere House, Boston, Mass. Over forty gentlemen were present. The Hon. Thomas J. Gargan of Boston presided. Thomas Hamilton Murray, then editor of the *Daily Sun*, Lawrence, Mass., was secretary of the meeting.

THE PRELIMINARY WORK.

The provisional committee that had attended to the preliminary work included Mr. Murray, just mentioned; James Jeffrey Roche, editor of the *Boston Pilot*; Joseph Smith, secretary of the police commission, Lowell, Mass.; Thomas B. Lawler of the publishing house, Ginn & Company, Boston, Mass., and Hon. John C. Linehan, state insurance commissioner, Concord, N. H.

OBJECTS AND PURPOSES.

The Society is organized for the special study of the Irish element in the composition of the American people; to investigate and record the influence of this element in the upbuilding of the nation, and to collect and publish facts relating to and illustrating that influence. The Society aims to correct erroneous, distorted and false views of history, where they are known, and to substitute therefor the truth of history, based on documentary evidence and the best and most reasonable tradition, in relation to the Irish in America.

SPEAKING MORE IN DETAIL.

Speaking more in detail, it may be stated that the objects and purposes of the Society are : The study of American history generally; to investigate, specially, the Irish immigration to this country, determine its numbers, examine the sources, learn the places of its settlement, and estimate its influence on contemporary events in war, legislation, religion, education, and other departments of activity; to place the result of its historical investigations and researches in acceptable literary form ; to print, publish, and distribute its documents to libraries, educational institutions, and among its members, in order that the widest dissemination of historical truth may be obtained ; to do its work without passion or prejudice, to view accomplished facts in the true scientific historical spirit, and having reached the truth to give it to the world.

MEMBERSHIP REQUIREMENTS.

Any male person of good moral character, who is interested in the special work of the Society, shall be deemed eligible for membership in the same. No tests other than that of character and devotion to the Society's objects shall be applied to membership. Application blanks may be obtained of the secretary-general.

THE MODE OF ADMISSION.

The Society believes that for the present as little red tape as possible should prevail in the admission of applicants. A large membership is desired. Consequently, a request to be enrolled addressed to the secretary-general, to any of the members of the Executive Council, or to a member of the Society who is located in the neighborhood of the applicant, will generally be sufficient to effect the desired result. It is recommended, however, that persons desiring admission shall obtain the blanks provided by the Society, for applicants.

THE FEES OF MEMBERS.

Life members pay $50 in advance at one time ; they are exempt from further membership dues. Annual members pay three dollars per year each. In the case of new members, of the annual class, their first payment should be made upon being officially notified of their admission.

NO LINES OF CREED OR POLITICS.

The Society is constructed on a broad and liberal basis. Being an American organization in spirit and principle, it greets and welcomes to its ranks Americans of whatever race descent, and of whatever creed, who take an interest in the special line of work for which the Society is organized. It at present includes Roman Catholics, Protestant Episcopalians, Methodists, Presbyterians, Unitarians, and members of other denominations. Catholic priests and Protestant ministers are on its roll. There are no creed lines and no politics in the policy of the organization.

OFFICERS OF THE SOCIETY.

The officers comprise a president-general, a vice-president-general, a secretary-general, a treasurer-general, a librarian and archivist, an historiographer (not yet elected), and an Executive Council. The constitution also provides for a vice-president for each state and territory and for the District of Columbia. It is proposed to eventually organize state and city chapters of the Society. A list of the present officers will be found contained herein.

THE FIRST PRESIDENT-GENERAL.

The first president-general of the Society was Richard Worsam Meade, 3d, rear-admiral, U. S. N. (retired). He was born in New York city, Oct. 9, 1837, at the home of his maternal grandfather, Judge Henry Meigs, which family has given many officers to the United States navy. He was the oldest son of the late Capt. Richard Worsam Meade, 2d, U. S. N., and was a nephew of the late Gen. George Gordon Meade, who for two years commanded the Army of the Potomac. President-General Meade died in Washington, D. C., May 4, 1897. His obsequies took place in that city. The Society contributed a floral harp. Among the mourners there were present from the Society Edward A. Moseley, secretary of the Interstate Commerce Commission; Paymaster John R. Carmody, U. S. N.; J. D. O'Connell of the U. S. Treasury Department, and Capt. John M. Tobin, all of Washington, D. C.

MEETINGS AND FIELD DAY.

Provision is made for quarterly meetings of the Society and monthly meetings of the Executive Council. As far as possible, each meeting, especially those of the Council, is held in a city or state different from the one where the preceding meeting was held. This prevents the Society from becoming merely local to any one state or city, and makes it what its founders intended it to be—a national body. A general field day of the organization is held annually in the summer or fall. The annual meeting for the election of officers is held in January.

DIPLOMA OF MEMBERSHIP.

Each member will be entitled to a diploma of membership, bearing the name of the Society, the date of his admission, and such other appropriate matter as may be decided upon. These certificates will be signed by the president-general, the secretary-general, the treasurer-general, and one or two other officers, and will be suitable for display in office, library, or study.

THE SOCIETY'S PUBLICATIONS.

The Society issues an annual volume, called the JOURNAL of the organization, handsomely printed and substantially bound in cloth. This volume is illustrated, contains a record of the Society's proceedings, papers contributed by the members as the result of original research, extracts from old documents bearing upon the Irish in this country, and matter of similar interest, much of it, indeed, of almost priceless value. A copy of the JOURNAL is annually given free to each member in good standing. The Society also issues special publications from time to time for the members.

OFFICERS OF THE SOCIETY, 1899.

President-General,
HON. THOMAS J. GARGAN,
Of the Law Firm, Gargan & Keating, Boston, Mass.

Vice-President-General,
HON. JOHN D. CRIMMINS,
40 East 68th St., New York City.

Secretary-General,
THOMAS HAMILTON MURRAY,
Editor *Evening Call*, 77 Main St., Woonsocket, R. I.

Treasurer-General,
HON. JOHN C. LINEHAN,
State Insurance Commissioner, Concord, N. H.

Librarian and Archivist,
THOMAS B. LAWLER,
New York City.
(With Ginn & Co., Publishers, Boston, New York, Chicago, London.)

EXECUTIVE COUNCIL.

The foregoing and

JAMES JEFFREY ROCHE, LL. D., Editor *The Pilot*, Boston, Mass.

MAURICE FRANCIS EGAN, LL. D., J. U. D., Professor of English Language and Literature, Catholic University, Washington, D. C.

ROBERT ELLIS THOMPSON, Ph. D., President Central High School, Philadelphia, Pa.

THOMAS ADDIS EMMET, M. D., LL. D., grand nephew of Robert Emmet, the Irish Patriot, New York City.

HON. THOMAS DUNN ENGLISH, the well known writer; ex-Member of Congress, Newark, N. J.

FRANCIS C. TRAVERS, President of Travers Brothers Co., 107 Duane St., New York City.

STEPHEN J. GEOGHEGAN, of the firm Gillis & Geoghegan, 537–539 West Broadway, New York City.

JOSEPH SMITH, Secretary of the Board of Police, Lowell, Mass.

AUGUSTUS ST. GAUDENS, Member of the National Academy of Design, New York City.

HON. MORGAN J. O'BRIEN, a Justice of the New York Supreme Court.

FRANCIS HIGGINS,.12 East 34th St., New York City.

JOHN CRANE, 307 West 103d St., New York City.

HON. JAMES S. COLEMAN, 38 East 69th St., New York City.

JOSEPH F. SWORDS, New York City; of the fourth American generation from Francis Dawson Swords, who was exiled from Ireland, 1760, and who served in the Patriot army throughout the American Revolution.

STATE VICE-PRESIDENTS.

Maine—JAMES CUNNINGHAM, Portland.
New Hampshire—JAMES F. BRENNAN, Peterborough.
Vermont—JOHN D. HANRAHAN, M. D., Rutland.
Massachusetts— OSBORNE HOWES, Boston.
Rhode Island—DENNIS H. SHEAHAN, Providence.
Connecticut—JOHN F. HAYES, M. D., Waterbury.
New York—GEN. JAMES R. O'BEIRNE, New York City.
New Jersey—HON. WILLIAM A. M. MACK, Elizabeth.
Pennsylvania—GEN. ST. CLAIR A. MULHOLLAND, Philadelphia.
Delaware—COL. JOHN P. DONAHOE, Wilmington.
Virginia—HON. JOSEPH T. LAWLESS, Richmond.
West Virginia—COL. O'BRIEN MOORE, Charleston.
South Carolina—HON. M. C. BUTLER, Edgefield.
Georgia—HON. PATRICK WALSH, Augusta. (Died March 19, 1899.)
Ohio—REV. GEORGE W. PEPPER, Cleveland. (Died August 6, 1899.)
Indiana—VERY REV. ANDREW MORRISSEY, C. S. C., Notre Dame.
Illinois—P. T. BARRY, Chicago.
Iowa—REV. M. C. LENIHAN, Marshalltown.
Minnesota—JOHN D. O'BRIEN, St. Paul.

Michigan—Hon. T. A. E. Weadock, Detroit.
Missouri—Julius L. Foy, St. Louis.
Tennessee—Michael Gavin, Memphis.
Kentucky—Edward Fitzpatrick, Louisville.
Kansas—Patrick H. Coney, Topeka.
Colorado—J. E. Lowery, M. D., Sopris.
Nebraska—M. D. Long, O'Neill.
Utah—Joseph Geoghegan, Salt Lake City.
Texas—Gen. A. G. Malloy, El Paso.
Oregon—Henry E. Reed, Portland.
California—James Connolly, Coronado.

District of Columbia—Patrick O'Farrell, Washington.

CHRONOLOGICAL RECORD OF THE SOCIETY.

1896. Dec. 26. Call issued at Boston, Mass., for a meeting to organize the Society.

1897. Jan. 20. The meeting was held on this date at the Revere House, Boston, Mass.; the Society was organized, and a Constitution and a code of By-Laws adopted. Hon. Thomas J. Gargan presided at the meeting, and Thomas Hamilton Murray was secretary.

1897. Jan. 20. At this first meeting addresses were delivered by Hon. John C. Linehan, Concord, N. H.; Joseph Smith, Lowell, Mass.; Hon. Hugh J. Carroll, Pawtucket, R. I.; Charles A. De Courcy, Lawrence, Mass.; George H. Moses, Concord, N. H.; Rev. John J. McCoy, Chicopee, Mass.; Osborne Howes, Boston, Mass.; P. J. Flatley, Boston, Mass., and one or two other gentlemen.

1897. Jan. 20. Paul B. Du Chaillu, the famous explorer, author of "The Land of the Midnight Sun," "The Viking Age," etc., was present at the meeting as the guest of the chairman, Thomas J. Gargan, and made an address. George H. Moses, mentioned in the preceding minute, was present as the guest of Hon. John C. Linehan, and took so much interest in the movement that he signed the agreement of association. Mr. Moses is editor of the *Concord* (N. H.) *Monitor*.

1897. Jan. 20. Rear Admiral Richard W. Meade, U. S. N. (retired), was elected as the first president-general of the Society.

1897. Jan. 20. Thomas Hamilton Murray was elected secretary-general; Hon. John C. Linehan, treasurer-general, and Thomas B. Lawler, librarian and archivist. Of these, Mr. Murray then resided in Lawrence, Mass.; Mr. Linehan is state insurance commissioner of New Hampshire, and resides in Concord, while Mr. Lawler was, at the time, a resident of Worcester, Mass.

1897. Jan. 20. The following were chosen to be members of the Executive Council of the Society: James Jeffrey Roche, Boston, Mass.; Robert Ellis Thompson, Philadelphia, Pa.; Theodore Roosevelt, New York city; Thomas J. Gargan, Boston, Mass.; Augustus St. Gaudens, New York city; Joseph Smith, Lowell, Mass.; Thomas Dunn English, Newark, N. J.; Maurice F. Egan, Washington, D. C.; Edward A. Moseley, Washington, D. C., and T. Russell Sullivan, Boston, Mass. A list of state vice-presidents was also submitted and adopted. Osborne Howes, Boston, vice-president for Massachusetts, is a descendant of David O'Killia (O'Kelly), who settled on Cape Cod as early as 1657, and who is mentioned in the old Yarmouth, Mass., records as "the Irishman." The records show that at the close of King Philip's War, O'Killia was assessed his proportionate part towards defraying the expenses of that struggle.

1897. Jan. 20. Secretary-General T. H. Murray announced at this first meeting that letters expressive of interest in the new organization, acknowledging an invitation, or giving an expression of opinion, had been received from Rear Admiral Richard W. Meade, U. S. N., Germantown, Pa.; Governor Hastings of Pennsylvania; United States Senator Hoar of Worcester, Mass.; Rev. Cyrus Townsend Brady, Protestant Episcopal archdeacon of Pennsylvania; Dr. Thomas Addis Emmet, New York city; Edward A. Moseley, secretary of the Interstate Commerce Commission, Washington,

D. C.; Joseph F. Swords, Hartford, Conn.; **Ex-United States Senator Patrick Walsh, Augusta, Ga.;** Gen. John Cochrane, president of the New York Society of the Cincinnati; Ex-Governor Waller of Connecticut; Rt. Rev. Thomas J. Conaty, later rector of the Catholic University, Washington, D. C.; Gen. Francis A. Walker, Boston, Mass.; Rev. George W. Pepper (Methodist), Cleveland, O.; Rev; J. Gray Bolton (Presbyterian), Philadelphia, Pa.; Ex-Congressman T. A. E. Weadock, Detroit, Mich., and John P. Donahoe, Wilmington, Del.

1897. Jan. 20.   Secretary-General Murray also announced letters from Prof. William M. Sloane, of Columbia University, New York; President Tyler of the College of William and Mary, Virginia; President Lee of Washington and Lee University, Virginia; Provost Harrison, of the University of Pennsylvania; Rev. Thomas J. Shahan of the Catholic University, Washington, D. C.; Very Rev. Andrew Morrissey, president of the University of Notre Dame, Indiana; H. B. Adams, professor of American and Institutional history, Johns Hopkins University, Maryland; Henry Stoddard Ruggles, Wakefield, Mass.; Samuel Swett Green, of the American Antiquarian Society, Worcester, Mass.; Theodore Roosevelt, New York city; Thomas Dunn English, Newark, N. J.; Judge Smith of the Superior court, Pennsylvania; Col. D. S. Lamson, Weston, Mass.; Rev. George C. Betts (Protestant Episcopalian), Goshen, N. Y., and Hon. Emmet O'Neal, United States attorney for the northern district of Alabama.

1897. Jan. 21.   *The Boston Globe, Herald*, and other papers contained reports concerning the formation of the Society. *The Springfield* (Mass.) *Republican* said : "The American-Irish Historical society, organized at Boston yesterday with a remarkable list of officers and the assurance of a charter membership as noteworthy, will prove without

question a body of real public importance.
. . . Among those present at the meeting
mostly from Massachusetts, New Hampshire, and
Rhode Island, was Edward A. Hall of this city,
whose history of the Irish in Hampden county
has grown into a history of the Irish in Western
Massachusetts, where, in fact, they settled a great
number of the hill towns, and their descendants
live to this day. . . . It will be the work of
the Society to show what a vast influence the
Irish element had in building our free commonwealths whose alliance made the first great country of the people, in which with all its faults
reposes the hope of the progress of the world into
a world of the people instead of one of warring
dynasties and vicious religious hatreds, setting
nation against nation. We look to this Society
for active, earnest, ardent work for the enlightenment, brotherhood and unity of this people first,
and of all other peoples in the long event. God
hath made of one blood all the nations of the
earth."

1897. Jan. 21. Rev. Edmund B. Palmer, Jamaica Plain, Mass.,
writes a congratulatory letter to Treasurer-General
Linehan. Mr. Palmer states that he is a great
grandson of Barnabas Palmer of Rochester, N. H.,
who was born in Cork or Limerick, 1725, and
who emigrated from there with two brothers, and
enlisted under Sir William Pepperill. Barnabas
sailed from Portsmouth, N. H.,—one of the force
of 3,000 men, 1745, and on the Isle of Cape
Breton, under Fort Louisburg, left his right arm.
Subsequently he settled in Rochester, N. H.,
married, had fourteen children, and was a member of the general court of New Hampshire that
ratified the Constitution of the United States.

1897. Jan. 21. Col. D. L. Lamson, Weston, Mass., writes desiring to become a member. He was lieutenant-
colonel commanding Sixteenth regiment (Mass.),
1861 ; A. A. G., Norfolk, 1862 ; served on staff

of General Hooker; is a member of the Society of Colonial Wars, Sons of the American Revolution, and Military Order of the Loyal Legion; one of his ancestors landed at Ipswich, Mass., in 1632, and received a grant of 350 acres which still remains in the family; another ancestor, Samuel, of Reading, Mass., participated in King Philip's War and had a son in the expedition of 1711. Another member of the family, Samuel, of Weston, commanded a company at Concord, Mass., April 19, 1775, and was major and colonel of the Third Middlesex regiment for many years, dying in 1795.

1897.   Jan.   21.   William Halley, editor of *The Vindicator*, Austin, Ill., writes a congratulatory letter. Mr. Halley came to this country from Ireland, in 1842, as a fellow voyager with Thomas D'Arcy McGee.

1897.   Jan.   23.   Lieutenant Commander J. D. Jerrold Kelley, U. S. N., attached to the battleship *Texas*, expresses a request to be admitted to membership.

1897.   Jan.   26.   Rear Admiral Richard W. Meade, U. S. N., writes from Germantown, Pa., accepting the office of president-general.

1897.   Jan.   26.   T. Russell Sullivan, Boston, Mass., a descendant of Governor James Sullivan of Massachusetts, acknowledges his election as a member of the Executive Council of the Society.

1897.   Feb.   3.   Hon. John C. Linehan, Concord, N. H., presents to the Society a copy of the volume issued by the state of New Hampshire and descriptive of the exercises attending the dedication, Sept. 27, 1894, at Durham, N. H., of the monument to Gen. John Sullivan of the Revolution.

1897.   Feb.   4.   N. C. Steele, M. D., Chattanooga, Tenn., writes interestingly relative to the Society. He says, " I am four generations removed from Ireland."

189 .   Feb.   6.   O'Brien Moore, Washington, D. C., writes, expressing his desire to become a life member.

1897. Feb. 8. Hugh McCaffrey, Philadelphia, Pa., writes, enclosing fifty dollars in payment of life membership fee.

1897. Feb. 9. Hon. William McAdoo, assistant secretary of the U. S. navy, Washington, D. C., thanks the Society for having elected him vice-president for New Jersey, his residential state.

1897. Feb. 10. Hon. Edwin D. McGuinness, mayor of Providence, R. I., and ex-secretary of state of Rhode Island, writes that he is entirely in accord with the purposes of the Society, and wishes to become a member.

1897. Feb. 11. The editor of the *Rosary Magazine*, through Rev. J. L. O'Neil, O. P., New York city, becomes a life member. This life membership is to stand to the credit of "The Editor of *The Rosary Magazine*." It is so arranged in order that successive editors of the publication may enjoy the rights and privileges of the Society. Father O'Neil was the first to represent the magazine in the organization.

1897. Feb. 16. Paymaster Mitchell C. McDonald, U. S. N., attached to the battleship *Texas*, cordially accepts an invitation to join the Society.

1897. Feb. 19. Arthur H. Chase, state librarian of New Hampshire, expresses a desire to receive the publications of the Society for the state library. He says: "I assure you the publications will be of great value to us."

1897. Feb. 23. Henry Carey Baird, Philadelphia, Pa., writes. His grandfather was a founder of the Hibernian Society of Philadelphia (1790).

1897. March 3. Hon. Ignatius Donnelly, author of "The Great Cryptogram," is admitted to the Society.

1897. March 6. Rev. Michael O'Brien, Lowell, Mass., becomes a life member.

1897. March 9. Heman W. Chaplin, Boston, Mass., writes desiring to become a member of the Society. He is a

descendant of the O'Briens of Machias, Me.,
patriots of the Revolution.

1897. March 15. Hon. Daniel H. Hastings, governor of Pennsylvania, expresses regrets at his inability to attend
the meeting on the 19th prox.

1897. March 17. Joseph Smith, Lowell, Mass., a member of the
Executive Council of the Society, reads a paper
before the Irish Society of that city on "The
Irish Element Among the Founders of Lowell."

1897. March 26. C. H. Meade, Germantown, Pa., writes informing
the Society of the serious illness of President-
General Meade.

1897. April   5. Call issued for the second meeting of the Society
(to be held on the 19th inst.).

1897. April   9. Letter from Gen. John Cochrane, New York city,
a descendant of an officer of the Revolution.

1897. April 10. Letter written by Charles E. Brown, town clerk of
historic Concord, Mass.

1897. April 17. Letter written by Leonard A. Saville, town clerk
of Lexington, Mass., acknowledging, on behalf of
the selectmen and himself, an invitation to be
present as guests on the 19th inst. They are
unable to attend owing to a home celebration.

1897. April 19. The second meeting of the Society. Held in the
Revere House, Boston, Mass. Thomas J. Gar-
gan of Boston presides. Four papers read.

1897. April 19. The first paper at this meeting was by Thomas
Hamilton Murray, the secretary-general, on "The
Irish Bacons who Settled at Dedham, Mass., in
1640," one of whose descendants, John Bacon,
was killed April 19, 1775, in the fight at West
Cambridge (battle of Lexington).

1897. April 19. The second paper at the meeting was by John C.
Linehan, treasurer-general, on "The Seizure of
the Powder at Fort William and Mary," by Maj.
John Sullivan and his associates, some of which
powder was later dealt out to the patriots at
Bunker Hill.

1897. April 19. The third paper was by Edward J. Brandon, city clerk of Cambridge, Mass., on "The Battle of Lexington, Concord, and Cambridge," during which he read a list of Irish names borne by minute men or militia in the battle of the nineteenth of April, 1775.

1897. April 19. The fourth paper was by Joseph Smith, member of the Executive Council, on "The Irishman Ethnologically Considered."

1897. April 21. Henry A. May, Roslindale, Mass., writes for information concerning the Society. He states that he is a descendant through his mother, Roxanna Butler of Pelham, N. H., from James Butler, the planter of Lancaster, Mass. (1653), who came from Ireland, and was the largest land owner in what is now Worcester county. He owned land in Dunstable, Woburn, and Billerica, where he died in 1681. His son, Deacon John Butler, was the first child of Irish parentage born in Woburn, Mass., and John was the first settler of what is now Pelham, N. H., and lies buried there. A monument was erected to his memory on "Pelham Green," in the centre of the town of Pelham, in 1886, by his descendants, some 1,200 being present at the dedication in June of that year.

1897. April 29. Death of Col. Jeremiah W. Coveney, postmaster of Boston, the first member of the Society to pass away.

1897. April 30. C. H. Meade states that his father, the president-general, is in a critical condition.

1897. May 4. Death at Washington, D. C., of the president-general of the Society, Rear Admiral Richard W. Meade, U. S. N.

1897. May 5. Edward A. Moseley, Washington, D. C., a member of the Executive Council of the Society, pens a letter of condolence to Richard W. Meade, Jr., on the death of the latter's father, the Society's president-general.

1897. May 6.   Edward A. Moseley, just mentioned, writes to Secretary-General Murray relative to the obsequies of the president-general.   Mr. Moseley states that the matter of a floral tribute from the Society has been arranged.

1897. May 7.   Letter from Richard W. Meade, Jr., to Mr. Moseley, thanking the Society, through him, for the floral emblem contributed, and stating that it " now rests on my father's grave."

1897. May 15.   First meeting of the Executive Council of the Society held, Boston, Mass.   Present : Thomas J. Gargan, Boston, Mass. ; John C. Linehan, Concord, N. H. ; Thomas Hamilton Murray, Lawrence, Mass. ; Joseph Smith, Lowell, Mass. ; James Jeffrey Roche, Boston, Mass., and Thomas B. Lawler, Worcester, Mass.   Mr. Gargan presided.

1897. May 15.   At this first meeting of the Council, Edward A. Moseley of Washington, D. C., was chosen president-general of the Society, to fill the unexpired term of the late Admiral Meade.   Mr. Moseley is secretary of the Interstate Commerce Commission, Washington, D. C.   He was born in 1846, at Newburyport, Mass.   He is a member of the Society of Colonial Wars, a member of the Society of the Sons of the American Revolution, a member of the Society of the Sons of the Revolution, a member of the Bunker Hill Monument Society (his great-grandfather fought there as captain in General Putnam's brigade from Connecticut) ; has received the thanks of the commonwealth of Massachusetts " for distinguished services in the cause of humanity " ; is the great-great-grandson of Col. Jonathan Buck ; great-grandson of Col. Ebenezer Buck ; also claims descent from Col. William Gilmore of New Hampshire, formerly of Coleraine, Ireland — all Revolutionary heroes.

1897. May 24.   Hon. John D. Crimmins, New York city, becomes a life member of the Society.

1897. June.   Among the cities officially visited this month by
                 the secretary-general was Lynn, Mass., where
                 special courtesies were extended him by Daniel
                 Donovan and Capt. P. S. Curry, both of that
                 city.

1897. June 6.   Secretary-General Murray addresses a meeting at
                 Portland, Me., in behalf of the Society. James
                 Cunningham of Portland presides.

1897. June 14.   President-General Moseley writes to James Cun-
                 ningham of Portland, Me., thanking the latter for
                 his interest in getting up the meeting in that city
                 on the 6th inst.

1897. June 14.   Prof. Maurice Francis Egan of the Catholic Uni-
                 versity, Washington, D. C., becomes a member of
                 the Society.

1897. June 24.   John R. Alley of Boston, Mass., forwards check
                 for $50. Life membership fee.

1897. June 30.   Second meeting of the Council of the Society.
                 Held in the Parker House, Boston, Mass. James
                 Jeffrey Roche of Boston presided. Treasurer-
                 General Linehan was authorized to make arrange-
                 ments for the first annual field day of the Society,
                 the same to be held at Newcastle, N. H.

1897. July.   The secretary-general visited Peabody and Salem,
                 Mass., this month, being assisted in obtaining
                 members there by Thomas Carroll of the former
                 place.

1897. July 20.   Capt. John Drum, Tenth U. S. Infantry, admitted
                 to membership.

1897. July 28.   Third meeting of the Council of the Society.
                 Held at Salisbury Beach, Mass. President-Gen-
                 eral Moseley occupied the chair. Mr. Moseley
                 had earlier in the day entertained the council at
                 lunch in the Wolfe Tavern, Newburyport, Mass.

1897. Aug. 4.   Death of Henry V. Donovan, M. D., Lawrence,
                 Mass., a member of the Society and a graduate
                 of Harvard University.

1897. Aug. 30.   Rear Admiral Belknap, U. S. N. (retired), writes
                 from Newport, R. I., regretting his inability to be

present at the meeting to be held in Pawtucket, R. I., on the 1st prox.

1897.   September. An article descriptive of the Society's purposes appears in the current issue of the *Granite Monthly*, Concord, N. H.   It is from the pen of Treasurer-General Linehan.

1897.   Sept.   1.   Fourth meeting of the Council takes place at the Benedict House, Pawtucket, R. I.   James Jeffrey Roche of Boston, Mass., presided.   Secretary-General Murray read extracts from old Rhode Island documents containing mention of early Irish settlers.

1897.   Sept.   1.   The Council was entertained at a banquet this evening by the Rhode Island members of the Society.   The event took place at the Benedict House, Pawtucket.   Hon. Hugh J. Carroll, ex-mayor of the city, presided.   Secretary-General Murray, then a resident of Pawtucket, delivered an address of welcome.

1897.   Sept. 18.   Fifth meeting of the Council.   Held in the Parker House, Boston, Mass.   James Jeffrey Roche of Boston presides.   A gift to the library of the Society from Gen. St. Clair A. Mulholland, Philadelphia, Pa., is announced.   It comprises a copy of the " History of the Friendly Sons of St. Patrick and of the Hibernian Society," of that city.

1897.   Sept. 21.   Hon. John C. Linehan, treasurer-general of the Society, presents the library a copy of the "Addresses at the Dedication of the Monument Erected to the Memory of Matthew Thornton at Merrimack, N. H., September 29, 1892."

1897.   Sept. 24.   William McConway, Pittsburg, Pa., writes to President-General Moseley, enclosing life membership fee.

1897.   Sept. 28.   Edward Fitzpatrick, a member of the organization, contributes an article to the *Louisville* (Ky.) *Times*, on " Irish Settlers in Louisville and Vicinity."

1897. Sept. 28.   Hon. Joseph T. Lawless, secretary of state of Virginia, writes a cordial letter, and desires to be admitted to membership.

1897. Oct. 7.   Death of Gen. John Cochrane, a member of the Society, New York city.

1897. Oct. 23.   Hon. Elisha Dyer, governor of Rhode Island, writes accepting an invitation extended him to join the Society.

1897. Oct. 23.   Death of Laurence J. Smith, Lowell, Mass., a member of the Society.

1897. Nov. 10.   Governor Dyer of Rhode Island writes, regretting that he will be unable to attend the meeting of the Society on the 16th.

1897. Nov. 10.   E. Benjamin Andrews, D. D., LL. D., president of Brown University, sends a letter in which he cordially expresses his appreciation of the purposes of the Society. On another occasion, he writes of the organization : " I wish it success with all my heart."

1897. Nov. 15.   The Friendly Sons of St. Patrick, New York city, in session this evening, send fraternal greetings to the Society, the bearer thereof being Thomas B. Lawler, the Society's librarian and archivist.

1897. Nov. 16.   The third meeting of the Society was held this evening in Young's Hotel, Boston, Mass. Gen. James R. O'Beirne, New York, presided at the business session and Thomas J. Gargan, Boston, at the banquet immediately following.

1897. Nov. 16.   At this meeting an address was delivered by John Mackinnon Robertson of London, England, author of " The Saxon and the Celt." Dennis Harvey Sheahan, ex-clerk of the Rhode Island house of representatives, read a paper on " The Need of an Organization Such as the A. I. H. S., and Its Scope."

1897. Dec. 7.   Secretary-General Murray addressed the Churchmen's Club of Rhode Island, at Providence, on "Five Colonial Rhode Islanders." Mr. Justice Stiness of the Rhode Island supreme court presided.   The five treated by Mr. Murray were all of Irish birth or extraction.

1897. Dec. 11. Sixth meeting of the Council of the Society is held in the Parker House, Boston, Mass. Thomas J. Gargan of Boston presides. It is voted to prepare for publication, and publish, the first volume of the Journal of the Society's Proceedings. The volume thus authorized was issued some months later. There is received from Dr. J. C. O'Connell, Washington, D. C., a copy of his work on "The Irish in the Revolution and in the Civil War."

1897. Dec. 18. Death of Hon. Owen A. Galvin, a member of the Society, Boston, Mass.

1898. Jan. 14. Joseph F. Swords, of Hartford, the Society's state vice-president for Connecticut at this time, contributes a letter to the *Boston Pilot* treating of the origin of the family name Swords in Ireland.

1898. Jan. 25. Death of Hon. Charles B. Gafney, a member of the Society, Rochester, N. H.

1898. Jan. 29. Seventh meeting of the Council of the Society. Held in the Parker House, Boston, Mass., Thomas J. Gargan presiding. It was decided to hold the annual meeting and banquet of the Society at the Hotel San Remo, New York city, on the evening of the 17th prox.

1898. Feb. 7. Hon. Thomas M. Waller, ex-governor of Connecticut, qualifies as a member of the Society.

1898. Feb. 17. Eighth meeting of the Council, held at the Hotel San Remo, New York city, Thomas J. Gargan, of Boston, presiding.

1898. Feb. 17. Annual meeting of the Society at the San Remo, New York city, following the meeting of the Council. Gen. James R. O'Beirne of New York presides.   Edward A. Moseley, Washington, D. C., is reëlected president-general.

1898. Feb. 17. Annual banquet of the Society at the San Remo, immediately following the annual meeting. General O'Beirne also presided at the banquet.

Resolutions of sorrow adopted on the loss of the U. S. battleship *Maine*, in Havana harbor, and copies of the resolutions ordered transmitted to the president of the United States, and to the secretary of the navy.

1898. Feb. 17. At this annual banquet, Joseph Smith of Lowell, Mass., a member of the Council of the Society, contributed a paper on "Some Ways in which American History is Falsified." Addresses were delivered by Hon. Thomas Dunn English of Newark, N. J.; Dr. Thomas Addis Emmet, New York city; Judge Wauhope Lynn, New York city, and other gentlemen.

1898. Feb. 18. Hon. John D. Crimmins, of New York city, gives a reception to the Society and entertains the latter at lunch at his residence, 40 East 68th St.

1898. Feb. 24. John Goodwin, New York city, forwards check for $50 in payment of life membership fee.

1898. Feb. 25. The navy department, Washington, D. C., acknowledges receipt of the resolutions of condolence on the loss of the battleship *Maine*, adopted by the Society on the 17th instant, and returns thanks "in the name of the officers and men of the navy."

1898. March 3. Hon. Robert T. Davis, Fall River, Mass., ex-mayor of Fall River, and ex-member of congress, becomes a member of the Society.

1898. March 5. Andrew Athy, Worcester, Mass., joins the Society as a life member.

1898. March 13. Edward Fitzpatrick, Louisville, Ky., a member of the Society, contributes an article to the *Louisville* (Ky.) *Courier-Journal*, on "The Lost State of Clark." He mentions Thomas Connolly, who was a fifer in Clark's regiment.

1898. March 14. Hon. Patrick J. Boyle, mayor of Newport, R. I., admitted to the Society.

1898. March 17. Secretary-General Murray and Treasurer-General Linehan are guests at a banquet of the Irish

Society of Lowell, Mass. Joseph Smith of that city presides.

1898. March 27. Thomas J. Gargan, of the Society's Council, and Thomas Hamilton Murray, secretary-general of the Society, contribute to a symposium in the *Boston Sunday Globe* on the subject of an Anglo-American alliance. Both strongly oppose the idea.

1898. April 18. President Andrews of Brown University writes, accepting invitation to attend the meeting in Providence, R. I., on the 21st instant.

1898. April 19. Letter written by Harvey Wheeler, chairman of the selectmen of historic Concord, Mass., sending hearty greetings to the participants in the meeting under the auspices of the Society on the 21st instant.

1898. April 20. Hon. John H. Stiness, a justice of the Rhode Island supreme court, sends regrets that he cannot attend the meeting on the 21st instant.

1898. April 21. Ninth meeting of the Society's Council is held at the Narragansett Hotel, Providence, R. I. Letter read from Hon. Eli Thayer, Worcester, Mass.

1898. April 21. In the evening, following this Council meeting, a reception and banquet was given the Council by the Rhode Island members of the Society, at the Narragansett, Providence. Dennis Harvey Sheahan of Providence presided.

1898. April 21. The post-prandial exercises at this banquet included a paper by Thomas Hamilton Murray, the secretary-general, on "Matthew Watson, an Irish Settler of Barrington, R. I., 1722." There were addresses by President Andrews of Brown University; Prof. Alonzo Williams of Brown; Hon. John C. Linehan, Concord, N. H.; Rev. Arthur J. Teeling, Lynn, Mass.; Joseph Smith, Lowell, Mass.; Capt. E. O'Meagher Condon, New York city; James Jeffrey Roche and Thomas J. Gargan, Boston, Mass., and other gentlemen.

1898. April 21. Prof. William M. Sloane of Columbia University, New York, admitted to membership.

1898. April 28. James G. Hickey, manager of the United States Hotel, Boston, Mass., becomes a life member of the Society.

1898. May 15. Death of Andrew Athy, Worcester, Mass., a life member.

1898. May 15. Secretary-General Murray addressed a meeting at Bangor, Me., in the interests of the Society. William F. Curran of Bangor, presided.

1898. May 21. Secretary-General Murray visits Springfield,Mass., to enlarge the Society's membership, and receives valuable assistance from Edward A. Hall and Dr. Philip Kilroy, both of that city.

1898. June. Secretary-General Murray this month visited Portsmouth and Dover, N. H.; New Haven, Conn.; New Bedford and Holyoke, Mass. Special courtesies were shown him at Portsmouth by John Griffin; at Dover, by John A. Hoye; and at New Bedford by Edmund O'Keefe and Rev. James F. Clark.

1898. June 3. Edward Fitzpatrick, Louisville, Ky., contributes an article to *The Times* of that city on " Early Irish Settlers in Kentucky."

1898. June 21. Death of John R. Alley, Boston, Mass., a life member of the Society.

1898. June 22. The secretary-general addresses a meeting at Chicopee, Mass., Rev. John J. McCoy, P. R., of Chicopee, presiding.

1898. June 25. Death of Joseph H. Fay, M. D., Fall River, Mass., a member of the Society and graduate of the University of Vermont.

1898. June 30. First field day of the Society. Held at Newcastle, N. H., with headquarters at the Hotel Wentworth. The exercises in the evening were presided over by Hon. John C. Linehan, Concord, N. H. Bernard Corr of Boston, Mass., read a paper on " The Ancestors of Gen. John Sullivan." Addresses were delivered by Mayor

Tilton of Portsmouth, N. H.; Dr. William D. Collins, Haverhill, Mass.; John F. Doyle, New York city; James F. Brennan, Peterborough, N. H.; William J. Kelly, Kittery, Me.; Dr. W. H. A. Lyons, Portsmouth, N. H.; Joseph Smith, Lowell, Mass.; Capt. E. O'Meagher Condon, New York city; James Jeffrey Roche, Boston, Mass.; Charles H. Clary, Hallowell, Me.; John Griffin, Portsmouth, N. H.; James H. McGlinchy, Portland, Me.; Secretary-General Murray and other gentlemen.

1898.   June 30.   Charles H. Clary of Hallowell, Me., who is here mentioned as making an address this evening, is a descendant of "John Clary of Newcastle, province of New Hampshire, who was published to Jane Mahoney of Georgetown, Me., 1750." John settled in Georgetown presumably about the time of his marriage. Four children were born before 1760.

1898.   June 30.   A communication from President-General Moseley was read at the exercises this evening by the secretary-general. Mr. Moseley called attention to the fact that Hon. John D. Long, secretary of the navy, had consented to name one of the new torpedo boats, soon to be constructed, the *O'Brien*, and to name two of the new torpedo-boat destroyers, respectively, *Barry* and *Macdonough*, these names to perpetuate three American patriots of Irish blood. The meeting adopted a vote of thanks to Secretary Long.

1898.   June 30.   Secretary-General Murray, this evening, called attention to the fact that on Sept. 10 would occur the anniversary of the battle of Lake Erie when Commodore Perry, the son of an Irish mother, administered such a thorough defeat to the British. It was suggested that the anniversary be duly observed by the Society. Referred to the Council. The secretary-general also suggested that the anniversary of the surrender of the British General, Burgoyne, Oct. 17, and that of the surrender of Lord Cornwallis, Oct. 19, be celebrated by a public meeting in Boston or New York. Referred to the Council.

1898. July.   During this month Mr. Murray, the secretary-general, visited Lewiston, Augusta, Hallowell, and Gardiner, Me., in the interests of the Society, being greatly assisted in the three latter places by Thomas J. Lynch, a prominent lawyer of Augusta. Mr. Murray also visited Biddeford, Me., where he addressed a meeting, specially called, and presided over by Cornelius Horigan of that city. He was also materially assisted by Rev. T. P. Linehan of Biddeford. Secretary-General Murray likewise visited, this month, Manchester, N. H., and was introduced to prominent people there by Michael O'Dowd of Manchester. The object of the secretary-general's visit to these places was to explain the purposes of the organization and to obtain additional members for the latter.

1898. July   2.   Capt. John Drum, Tenth United States Infantry, a member of the Society, killed in battle before Santiago de Cuba.

1898. July 25–26.   Secretary-General Murray visits Nashua, N. H., and while there addresses a gathering of several gentlemen invited to meet him. Dr. T. A. McCarthy of Nashua presides.

1898. August.   The Society issued this month a pamphlet entitled : " Irish Schoolmasters in the American Colonies, 1640–1775, with a Continuation of the Subject During and After the War of the Revolution." The authors are Hon. John C. Linehan, the Society's treasurer-general, and Thomas Hamilton Murray, the secretary-general. An edition of 2,000 copies was printed.

1898. Aug.   4.   Secretary Murray addressed a meeting at Rutland, Vt., T. W. Maloney, a leading lawyer of that city, presiding. During his stay in Rutland, Mr. Murray also received valuable assistance from John D. Hanrahan, M. D., of that city.

1898. Aug. 18. Tenth meeting of the Council of the Society. It was held in the Parker House, Boston, Mass. President-General Moseley occupied the chair. A minute was adopted on the death of Capt. John Drum, Tenth United States Infantry. Capt. Drum's son, John D., of Boston, was elected to membership in the Society.

1898. Aug. 25. Death of City Marshal John E. Conner of Chicopee, Mass., a member of the Society.

1898. Aug. 30, 31; Sept. 1. Secretary-General Murray visits Waterbury, Conn., and obtains several new members for the Society. He receives courtesies from Dr. J. F. Hayes and other gentlemen of that city.

1898. September. The Society issued this month a pamphlet on "The 'Scotch-Irish' Shibboleth Analyzed and Rejected; with Some Reference to the Present 'Anglo-Saxon' Comedy." The author is Joseph Smith, Lowell, Mass. An edition of 1,500 copies was printed.

1898. Sept. 3. Obsequies in Boston, Mass., of Capt. John Drum, Tenth U. S. Infantry, his body having been brought home from Cuba. James Jeffrey Roche of Boston represented the Society as a pall bearer. The organization contributed a floral offering.

1898. Sept. 23. Death at Newport, R. I., of Rev. Philip Grace, D. D., a member of the Society.

1898. October. Secretary-General Murray visited this month, among other places, Philadelphia, Pa., and was assisted in his work there by Hugh McCaffrey of that city, a life member of the Society.

1898. Oct. 21. Henry Collins Walsh, a descendant of Gen. Stephen Moylan of the Revolution, becomes a member of the Society.

1898. Nov. 11. James Whitcomb Riley, the "Hoosier Poet," Indianapolis, Ind., admitted to membership.

1898. Nov. 14, 15, 16. Secretary-General Murray visits Albany, N. Y., in the interests of the organization.

1898. Dec. 3. Eleventh meeting of the Council. Held in the Parker House, Boston, Mass., Thomas J. Gargan of Boston presiding. Committees were appointed to take appropriate action on the death of City Marshal John E. Conner of Chicopee, Mass., and on that of Rev. Philip Grace, D. D., Newport, R. I.

1898. December. Death of Capt. John M. Tobin at Knoxville, Tenn., a member of the Society. He was a veteran of the Civil War, and in the war with Spain had been a quartermaster in the First Brigade, Second Division, First Army Corps.

1899. Jan. 14. Gen. George Bell, U. S. A. (retired), Washington, D. C., is admitted to membership.

1899. Jan. 19. Twelfth meeting of the Council of the Society. Held at Sherry's, 44th street and Fifth avenue, New York city. Thomas J. Gargan of Boston, Mass., presided. Among the members of the Council present were Hon. John D. Crimmins, New York; Joseph Smith, Lowell, Mass.; James Jeffrey Roche, Boston, Mass.; Francis C. Travers, New York; Hon. John C. Linehan, Concord, N. H.; Thomas B. Lawler, New York, and Thomas Hamilton Murray, Woonsocket, R. I.

1899. Jan. 19. Annual meeting of the Society held at Sherry's, New York city, immediately following the meeting of the Council. Gen. James R. O'Beirne, New York, in the absence of the president-general, presided. Thomas J. Gargan of Boston was chosen president-general of the Society for the ensuing year; Hon. John D. Crimmins, New York, was chosen vice-president-general; Thomas Hamilton Murray, Woonsocket, R. I., was reelected secretary-general; Hon. John C. Linehan, Concord, N. H., was reëlected treasurer-general; Thomas B. Lawler, New York, was reëlected librarian and archivist.

1899. Jan. 19. The annual banquet of the Society was held at Sherry's, New York, immediately after the annual meeting. Gen. James R. O'Beirne, New York, presided. The attendance numbered about 175 gentlemen, many cities and states being represented. The post-prandial exercises included the reading of four original papers, viz.: By Dr. Thomas Addis Emmet, New York, a paper on "Irish Emigration During the Seventeenth and Eighteenth Centuries"; by Hon. John C. Linehan, Concord, N. H., a paper on "Some Pre-Revolutionary Irishmen"; by Rev. John J. McCoy, P. R., Chicopee, Mass., a paper on "The Irish Element in the Second Massachusetts Volunteers in the Recent War" (with Spain); by James Jeffrey Roche, Boston, Mass., a paper on the general lines of the Society's work. There were also several addresses.

1899. Jan. 20.   Hon. Theodore Roosevelt, governor of New York state, gives a reception to the members of the Society at the residence of his sister, Mrs. Cowles, Madison avenue, New York city. He is assisted in receiving by Mrs. Cowles, and the members are presented by Gen. James R. O'Beirne, state vice-president of the Society for New York. Governor Roosevelt delivers an address. Following the reception, lunch is served.

1899. Jan. 20.   Subsequent to the reception by Governor Roosevelt, the members are received by Hon. John D. Crimmins, vice-president-general of the Society, at his New York residence, 40 East 68th street.

1899. Feb. 9.   Rev. Richard Henebry, Ph. D., professor of Keltic languages and literature, Catholic University, Washington, D. C., admitted to the Society.

1899. Feb. 15.   James McGovern, New York city, admitted to life membership.

1899. Feb. 19.   John J. Lenehan, New York city, admitted to life membership.

1899. March.   A work is issued this month on "The Irish Washingtons at Home and Abroad, Together with Some Mention of the Ancestry of the American Pater Patriæ." The authors are Thomas Hamilton Murray, secretary-general of the Society, and George Washington of Dublin, Ireland. The work is dedicated to the Society.

1899. March 9. Myles Tierney, New York city, enrolled as a life member of the organization.

1899. March 16. Communication written by Rev. William L. Ledwith, D. D., librarian of the Presbyterian Historical Society, Philadelphia, Pa., asking for information relative to the American-Irish Historical Society. He concludes : " The lines on which your Society and ours are working must often meet."

1899. March 19. Death of Hon. Patrick Walsh, mayor of Augusta, Ga., ex-United States senator, and member of the Society.

1899. March 30. Maj. William H. Donovan of the Ninth Massachusetts is commissioned colonel of the regiment. He was one of the majors of the command in the war with Spain, and participated in the gallant work of the regiment on Cuban soil. Colonel Donovan is one of our members in Lawrence, Mass.

1899. March 31. Death at Boston, Mass., of Col. Patrick T. Hanley, a veteran of the Civil War, and member of the Society.

1899. April 9. Death of Hon. John H. Sullivan, East Boston, Mass., a member of the Society.

1899. April 11. The selectmen and town clerk of Lexington, Mass., express regrets that they will not be able to attend the meeting at Providence, R. I., on the 19th inst. Their letter bears the official seal of the town.

1899. April 13. E. Benjamin Andrews, superintendent of public schools, Chicago, Ill., writes expressing his regret that he cannot attend the meeting on the 19th inst.

1899. April 15. Death of Hon. Eli Thayer, Worcester, Mass., a member of the organization.

1899. April 16. Death of William F. Cummings, M. D., Rutland, Vt., a graduate of the University of Vermont, and member of the Society.

1899. April 19. The thirteenth meeting of the Society's Council
is held in the Narragansett Hotel, Providence,
R. I., on this, the anniversary of the battle of
Lexington (1775). Thomas J. Gargan, president-
general of the Society, occupies the chair.
Stephen J. Richardson, New York city, is introduced, and explains the plan and scope of a projected " Encyclopædia Hibernica." The Council
approves the work. It is voted that the annual
field day of the Society, this year, be held at
Elizabeth, N. J., on the occasion of the launching of the U. S. torpedo-boat *O'Brien.*

1899. April 19. Hon. John D. Crimmins, New York city, vice-
president-general of the Society, at this meeting
of the Council personally subscribes five hundred
dollars for the general purposes of the organization. This is the largest individual gift the
Society has thus far received.

1899. April 19. Lieut. Martin L. Crimmins, 18th U. S. infantry,
is admitted to membership. Lieutenant Crim-
mins is at this date with his regiment in the
Philippines. He is a son of Hon. John D.
Crimmins, New York city.

1899. April 19. Thomas J. Gargan, Boston, Mass., and Stephen
J. Geoghegan, New York city, request to be
recorded as life members.

1899. April 19. Following the meeting of the Council the mem-
bers thereof are received and banqueted at the
Narragansett, in Providence, by the Rhode
Island members of the Society. M. J. Harson
of Providence presides. Addresses are made by
President-General Gargan, Vice-President-General
Crimmins, Treasurer-General Linehan; Thomas
F. O'Malley, Somerville, Mass.; Rev. S. Banks
Nelson (Presbyterian), Woonsocket, R. I.; Rev.
Frank L. Phalen (Unitarian), Concord, N. H.;
Capt. E. O'Meagher Condon, New York city, and
Joseph Smith, Lowell, Mass.

1899. April 20.   Miss Annetta O'Brien Walker, Portland, Me., writes to President-General Gargan, with reference to the forthcoming launching of the torpedo-boat *O'Brien*. She is a great-granddaughter of Captain O'Brien, brother to the patriot in whose honor the boat is named. Miss Walker desires to be present at the launching.

1899. April 29.   Death of Joseph J. Kelley, East Cambridge, Mass., a member of the Society.

1899. May 8.   William Gorman, Philadelphia, Pa., enrolled as a life member.

1899. May 17.   Order issued by the war department to Major William Quinton, 14th U. S. infantry, a member of the Society, to proceed from Boston to San Francisco, and thence to Manila, for service in the Philippines.

1899. May 19.   Dr. Thomas Addis Emmet, New York city, subscribes one hundred dollars for the publication fund of the Society.

1899. May 27.   Lewis Nixon, builder of the U. S. torpedo-boat *O'Brien*, writes from the Crescent shipyard, Elizabeth, N. J., that: "The uncertainty as to the delivery of certain forgings, making in Pennsylvania for the *O'Brien*, renders it impossible, at this time, for me to give you even an approximate date for the launching. I am endeavoring to get some information in this matter, and just as soon as I receive it I shall communicate with you." Mr. Nixon states that he takes pride in the fact that he is "building the *O'Brien*, which is a name honorably and valorously associated with the early history of our navy."

1899. May 30.   Secretary-General Murray attends a preliminary meeting held in Boston, Mass., to form a Franco-American Historical Society, and makes an address expressing good wishes on behalf of the American-Irish Historical body.

1899. July.   Announcement is made that a member of the Society, Rev. Cyrus Townsend Brady, Philadelphia, Pa., has writtten a novel entitled, " For the Freedom of the Sea," the same being a romance of the War of 1812.

1899. July 22. Death of William Slattery, a member of the Society; associate justice of the police court, Holyoke, Mass. ; graduate of Harvard University.

1899. Aug. 2. Rev. Frank L. Phalen, of the Society, is commis-missioned chaplain of the Second Regiment of Infantry (Massachusetts).

1899. Aug. 6. Death of Rev. George W. Pepper, D. D., Cleve-land, O., vice-president of the Society for that state.

1899. Aug. 18. The librarian of the University of Washington, Seattle, Wash., requests for the institution copies of the reports and other publications of the So-ciety. He says : " We are very anxious to obtain these, and will gladly pay all transportation."

1899. Aug. 20. Death of Rev. Denis Scannell, rector of St. Anne's church, Worcester, Mass., a member of the Society.

1899. Aug. 29. Fourteenth meeting of the Council. Place : Aquidneck House, Newport, R. I. Hon. John C. Linehan of Concord, N. H., presides. This is the anniversary of the battle of Rhode Island, 1778, in which the American forces were com-manded by Gen. John Sullivan.

1899. Aug. 29. Suggestion made at this Council meeting, and favorably considered, that the Society erect a bronze tablet to the memory of soldiers of Irish birth or lineage who were at the battle of Bunker Hill, 1775, fighting in behalf of American liberty. A committee is appointed to further consider the matter.

1899. Aug. 29. This evening, subsequent to the Council meet-ing, dinner was partaken of at the Aquidneck by some 25 gentlemen including members of the Society and prominent citizens of Newport who had been invited to be present. The post-pran-dial exercises were presided over by Hon. Charles.

E. Gorman of Providence, R. I. Hon. Patrick
J. Boyle, mayor of Newport, R. I., delivered an
address of welcome, as a member of the Society
and as mayor of the city. The paper of the
evening was by Thomas Hamilton Murray,
secretary-general of the Society, on "The Battle
of Rhode Island, 1778." Addresses were made
by Hon. John C. Linehan, treasurer-general of
the Society; by Rev. L. J. Deady of Newport,
R. I.; by Dennis H. Tierney of Waterbury,
Conn.; by P. J. McCarthy of Providence, R. I.,
and by J. Stacy Brown, city solicitor of Newport.
An original letter written by Gen. John Sullivan
in 1778, was read and exhibited.

1899. Sept. 9. In answer to an inquiry on behalf of the Society,
the United States navy department replies, giving
information as to the percentage of completion
attained by the torpedo boats *Blakely* and
O'Brien and the torpedo boat destroyers *Barry*
and *Macdonough*.

1899. Oct. 2. J. F. Hayes, M. D., the Society's state vice-president for Connecticut, is reëlected to the Water-
bury, Conn., board of education.

1899. October. Reitz, secretary of state for the Transvaal,
announces the appointment of Gen. James R.
O'Beirne, New York city, as commissioner extraordinary to represent the Transvaal's interests in
the United States. General O'Beirne is our
Society's state vice-president for New York.

1899. Oct. 7. Fifteenth meeting of the Council of the Society
is held in Boston, Mass. President-General
Gargan occupies the chair. There are also
present Messrs. Linehan, Smith, Murray and
Roche. It is voted to invite Sir Thomas Lipton, owner of the yacht *Shamrock*, to be a guest
of the Society on such date as may suit his con-
venience. A letter is received from Hon. John
D. Crimmins, New York city, proposing Hon.
Thomas H. Carter, United States senator from
Montana, and Thomas J. Cummins, of New York

city, for membership in the Society.   Both gentlemen are admitted.

1899.   Oct.   11.   Sir Thomas Lipton, owner of the yacht *Shamrock*,
challenger for the America's cup, writes to
Secretary-General Murray, cordially acknowledging the invitation to be a guest of the Society.
Sir Thomas's letter is dated " Steam Yacht *Erin*,
Sandy Hook."   He says : " Nothing would give
me greater pleasure than to avail myself of their
[the members'] hospitality but under the present
uncertain conditions of weather it is doubtful
when the contest will be finished, which renders
it impossible for me, meantime, to make any
arrangements of the nature you are good enough
to suggest."

1899.   Oct.   12.   Letter received stating that James F. Brennan,
Peterborough, N. H., has recently been appointed
by the governor and council of New Hampshire
to be a member of the board of state library
commissioners.   Mr. Brennan is our Society's
vice-president for New Hampshire.

1899.   Nov.   7.   Hon. Patrick J. Boyle, of the Society, is elected
mayor of Newport, R. I., for the sixth consecu-
tive time.

1899.   Nov.   15.   Reception and banquet at the Bellevue, Beacon
street, Boston, Mass., under the auspices of the
Society.   President-General Gargan presided.
Among the guests was William Ludwig, the Irish
baritone.   The paper of the evening was by
Michael E. Hennessy of the Boston *Daily Globe*,
his topic being, " Men of Irish Blood Who Have
Attained Eminence in American Journalism."

1899.   Nov.   17.   Letter received from Col. James Armstrong,
Charleston, S. C.   Colonel Armstrong is an editor on the Charleston *News and Courier* ; harbor
master of the port.   He served on the staff of
Governor Wade Hampton, and is of Irish parentage.

1899. Nov. 20. Hon. Patrick A. Collins, a member of the Society, is nominated for mayor of Boston, Mass., by the Democratic convention. He is an ex-member of congress and ex-United States consul-general to London, England.

1899. Nov. 20. President-General Gargan delivered an address before the Charitable Irish Society in Boston, Mass., this evening. His subject was, " Naval Heroes of the Revolutionary War." In the course of his address he paid a tribute to the patriotic O'Briens of Machias, Me., who bravely figured in that struggle.

1899. Nov. 21. Letter received from Henry E. Reed, Portland, Ore., state vice-president of the Society for Oregon. He regrets that he has not been able to give more attention to the Society, but his duties for the past two years having taken him up and down the Pacific coast from Alaska to the Mexican boundary, he has been pressed for time. However, he has interested a number of Oregon people in the Society, and requests to be supplied with membership application blanks.

1899. Nov. 26. Dr. Stephen J. Maher of New Haven, Conn., a member of the Society, presided at a public reception in the Hyperion, that city, to Lord Mayor Tallon of Dublin, and Hon. John E. Redmond, M. P. Col. John G. Healy, another member of the Society, opened the exercises.

1899. Nov. 27. An official declaration in behalf of the Society is issued in Boston to-night, endorsing the project to bring the remains of John Paul Jones back to this country from France, where he died in 1799.

1899. Nov. 28. The *News and Courier*, Charleston, S. C., contains an editorial to-day, speaking highly of the Society and its work.

1899. Nov. 29. Death of Edmund Phelan, a member of the Society, at his home, 32 Adams street, Roxbury (Boston), Mass.

1899.   Dec.   2.   Col. James Gadsden Holmes, Charleston, S. C.,
                    presents to the Society a copy of the "History
                    of the Calhoun Monument" in that city. This
                    monument was erected in honor of Hon. John C.
                    Calhoun, whose father was an Irishman by birth,
                    and was dedicated April 26, 1887.

1899.   Dec.   7.   Henry Stoddard Ruggles of Wakefield, Mass.,
                    calls the Society's attention to a work recently
                    published by the Massachusetts chapter, Daugh-
                    ters of the American Revolution. It is entitled,
                    "Honor Roll of Massachusetts Patriots, Hereto-
                    fore Unknown; being a List of Men and Women
                    who Loaned Money to the Federal Government,
                    1777–1779." Among the names in this list are
                    Daniel McCarthy, Dennis Tracy, Patrick Wade
                    and Daniel Ryan.

1899.   Dec. 12.   Hon. Jeremiah Crowley, of the Society, is re-
                    elected mayor of Lowell, Mass.

1899.   Dec. 13.   Thomas Carroll of Peabody, Mass., a member of
                    the Society, delivers an historical address at the
                    twenty-fifth anniversary celebration of St. John's
                    Catholic parish in Peabody.

1899.   Dec. 19.   Thomas F. O'Malley, Somerville, Mass., a mem-
                    ber of the Society, delivers an historical lecture
                    on "The Colonial Irish" before the St. Peter's
                    Catholic Association, Cambridge, Mass.

1899.   Dec. 30.   The *Boston Pilot* of this date contains an article
                    from Joseph Smith, Lowell, Mass., of the Society,
                    on "The Irish Brigade of Rochambeau's Army,"
                    giving an account of its services in behalf of
                    American independence.

PROCEEDINGS OF THE SOCIETY, 1899.

The annual meeting of the Society for 1899 was held on Thursday evening, Jan. 19, at Sherry's, Forty-fourth street and Fifth avenue, New York city. Gen. James R. O'Beirne, the Society's state vice-president for New York, presided, and Thomas Hamilton Murray of Woonsocket, R. I., was secretary.

A letter was received from President-General Moseley, Washington, D. C., in which he expressed regret at his inability to be present. The notice for the meeting was as follows:

THE AMERICAN-IRISH HISTORICAL SOCIETY.

NOTICE OF MEETING AND BANQUET.

DEAR SIR: You are hereby notified that the annual meeting and banquet of the American-Irish Historical Society will be held at Sherry's, Forty-fourth street and Fifth avenue, New York city, on Thursday evening, Jan. 19, 1899.

The business session will be called to order at 6:30 o'clock. Gen. James R. O'Beirne, our state vice-president for New York, will preside. Officers will be chosen for the ensuing year, the annual reports presented and such other business transacted as may properly come before the meeting.

The banquet will take place at 8 o'clock. Tickets for the same will be three dollars each. They are now ready, and may be obtained of the secretary-general, whose address is given below.

The post-prandial exercises will include addresses by the following members of the Society:

The Hon. Theodore Roosevelt, governor of New York; the Hon. Morgan J. O'Brien, a justice of the New York supreme court; the

Hon. William McAdoo, recently assistant secretary of the navy; the Hon. John C. Linehan, state insurance commissioner of New Hampshire; the Hon. John D. Crimmins, New York city; the Hon. Thomas J. Gargan, Boston, Mass.; the Rev. John J. McCoy, Roman Catholic rector, Chicopee, Mass.; the Rev. Cyrus T. Brady, Protestant Episcopal archdeacon of Pennsylvania; James Jeffrey Roche, LL. D., editor of the *Boston Pilot;* Mr. John P. Holland, inventor of the submarine torpedo boat; Mr. Joseph Smith, secretary of the police commission, Lowell, Mass., and Thomas Addis Emmet, M. D., LL. D., a grand nephew of the Irish patriot, Robert Emmet.

The occasion will be of great interest, and it is hoped that at least five hundred members and friends will be present at the banquet. Each member is at liberty to bring with him as many personal guests as he chooses. A large attendance is desired.

It is necessary to know as soon as possible how many will attend the banquet, in order that proper arrangements can be made with the hotel people. To this end, therefore, kindly notify the secretary-general if you intend to be present.

Fraternally,

EDWARD A. MOSELEY,
President-General.

THOMAS HAMILTON MURRAY,
Secretary-General.

Secretary's address: 77 Main street, Woonsocket, R. I.

Upon the business session being called to order, the ticket placed in nomination by the Council of the Society was presented for action.

It was unanimously accepted, adopted and declared the Society's choice for the ensuing year. The personnel of the ticket is set forth on pages 9, 10 and 11 of this volume.

Many new members were proposed and elected to the Society.

The annual report of the secretary-general, Thomas Hamilton Murray, was presented. It was as follows:

THE SECRETARY-GENERAL'S REPORT.

The American-Irish Historical society has become a permanent institution. We are now entering the third year of our existence.

Success has attended our efforts from the start, and the future is bright with prospect for continued good work.

The society already has a membership of close to 1,000, and the material will compare favorably with that of any historical organization in this country. Among our members are representatives of the Society of Colonial Wars, the Society of the Cincinnati, the Sons of the Revolution, the Military Order of Foreign Wars, the United States Medal of Honor Legion, the Society of Tammany, the Bunker Hill Monument society, the Military Order of the Loyal Legion and several other patriotic bodies.

We have also in our membership representatives of literary and educational organizations such as the Papyrus club of Boston, the Twentieth Century club of that city, the American Oriental society, the New England Historic-Genealogical society, the Royal Society of Northern Antiquarians, Denmark, and the Archæological Institute of America. Relative to the great American universities, we number in our ranks alumni of Harvard, Yale, Dartmouth, Boston, Johns Hopkins, Bowdoin, Brown, Notre Dame, the University of Vermont, the University of Pennsylvania and the University of Virginia. The Catholic University at the national capital is represented on our roll by its rector, its vice-rector and three of the faculty.

We have among our associates descendants of David O'Killia (O'Kelly), the Irishman who located on Cape Cod, Mass., as early as 1657; of Barnabas Palmer, an Irishman, born in 1725, who was present at the capture of Louisburg, and of Gen. Stephen Molyan of the American Revolution. Three great societies composed mainly of men of Irish lineage are likewise represented in our organization. I refer to the Charitable Irish Society of Boston, founded in 1737; the Friendly Sons of St. Patrick of Philadelphia, and the Friendly Sons of St. Patrick of New York city.

We have with us, too, many people who are prominent in law, medicine, and journalism, and many who have attained eminence on the bench, in science and art, and in mercantile pursuits. With this composition, the American-Irish Historical society can legitimately claim to be well equipped in personnel for the work it has in view.

In the war with Spain, just closed, our Society was well represented, and one of our members perished in battle before Santiago de Cuba. Of the Society there fought on Cuban soil: Theodore

Roosevelt of the Rough Riders; Capt. John Drum of the Tenth
U. S. Infantry, Major W. H. Donovan of the Ninth Massachusetts,
and Sergt. E. F. O'Sullivan, also of the Ninth.

Gen. M. C. Butler of the Cuban Evacuation Commission is of us,
while in the Sixty-ninth New York we are also represented.

Since our last annual meeting seven members have died.   They
were: Dr. Joseph H. Fay, Fall River, Mass.; Mr. Andrew Athy,
Worcester, Mass.;   Mr. John R. Alley, Boston, Mass.; City Marshal
John E. Conner, Chicopee, Mass.; Rev. Philip Grace, D. D., New-
port, R. I.; Capt. John Drum, U. S. A., and Capt. John M. Tobin,
Washington, D. C.

Captain Drum, of the Tenth U. S. Infantry, was killed in battle
near Santiago, Cuba, July 2, 1898.   A braver soldier never lived.
His obsequies took place in Boston, our Society contributing
an appropriate floral offering.   Captain Tobin died in December,
last, at Knoxville, Tenn.   Up to within a short time before his
death he had been assistant quartermaster, First Brigade, Second
Division, First Army Corps.   During the Civil War he served
gallantly in the Ninth Massachusetts regiment, particularly dis-
tinguishing himself at Malvern Hill, and being wounded at the
Wilderness.

In June, last, the Society observed its first field day, the exercises
taking place at historic Newcastle, N. H.   The occasion proved of
great interest to all participating.   The place for the field day event
this year has not yet been selected.

Since our last annual meeting a gathering under the auspices of
our Rhode Island members has been held in Providence.   It was
presided over by Dennis H. Sheahan, recently clerk of the General
Assembly of Rhode Island, and was an unlimited success.   Among
the guests were President Andrews of Brown University, Prof. Alonzo Williams of that institution, and other prominent gentlemen.

The Society is to be congratulated upon the issuance of its first
bound volume of Proceedings.   The edition numbered 1,100 copies
and has been distributed among the members, while copies have also
been sent to public libraries, colleges, and historical societies.   Of
the pamphlet, "Irish Schoolmasters in the American Colonies,"
2,000 copies were issued and disposed of in like manner.   The
pamphlet on "The Scotch-Irish Shibboleth" numbered 1,500 copies.

The Society has on hand and is constantly accumulating much
valuable material relating to the Irish chapter in American history.

We are hampered to some extent, however, by the absence of a publication fund. I hope that sooner or later methods will be devised and steps taken to provide for this deficiency. At present the only income the Society has is from the membership fees. The prompt payment of these when due, therefore, becomes a matter of no little importance.

Largely owing to the representations of our friends at Washington, the secretary of the navy has selected the names of three American naval officers of Irish blood for three of the new torpedo craft. These names are O'Brien, Barry and Macdonough. The first is to be applied to the torpedo boat now building at Elizabethport, N. J., and the two others to torpedo-boat destroyers. The *Macdonough* is now under construction at Weymouth, Mass. The *O'Brien* is to be launched at Elizabethport probably the coming May.[1] I would suggest that the occasion and the place be appropriate for our field day celebration this year.

I cannot close without calling the attention of the society to the continued good offices of Gen. James R. O'Beirne and Hon. John D. Crimmins, both of New York. This year, as last, these gentlemen have been indefatigable in arranging for our annual meeting here, and have spared no effort to make the occasion a thoroughly successful one. Mr. Francis C. Travers, Dr. Thomas Addis Emmet and other gentlemen residing in New York have also shown much active interest, and deserve the gratitude of the society.

The report of the secretary-general, thus presented, was accepted and adopted.

Hon. John C. Linehan, of Concord, N. H., submitted his report for the year. It showed the following aggregates:

RECEIPTS.

Balance on hand as per last report	$672.96
Three life membership fees at $50	150.00
615 annual membership fees	1,845.00
From dinner tickets at Providence, R. I. . . .	80.00
From dinner tickets at New York city	160.00
	$2,907.96

[1] It was so thought at the time of this meeting, but the launching has been unavoidably delayed.

EXPENDITURES.

Various (as set forth in detail) $2,389.36

    Balance on hand $518.60

An auditing committee, consisting of Secretary-General Murray, James Jeffrey Roche of Boston and Joseph Smith of Lowell, Mass., reported having examined the books and vouchers of the treasurer-general, and found the same correct.

The treasurer-general's report was thereupon unanimously accepted and adopted.

The importance of raising a fund to forward the work of the Society, especially in the matter of publications, was discussed, Judge Wauhope Lynn of New York city and other gentlemen talking to the question. The matter was finally referred to the Council for action. The business meeting then adjourned.

THE ANNUAL BANQUET.

Upon the adjournment of the business meeting, the company formed in line and proceeded to the annual banquet. Gen. James R. O'Beirne of New York city presided.

Back of the presiding officer's chair were displayed an American and an Irish flag. An orchestra was stationed in the balcony.

Grace was said by Rev. Joshua P. Bodfish of Canton, Mass.

Among those seated at the tables were noted the following:

      Gen. James R. O'Beirne, New York city.
      Rev. Joshua P. Bodfish, Canton, Mass.
      Hon. Thomas J. Gargan, Boston, Mass.
      Hon. John D. Crimmins, New York city.
      Hon. Joseph F. Daly, New York city.
      Hon. Thomas Dunn English, Newark, N. J.
      Hon. John C. Linehan, Concord, N. H.
      Hon. Wauhope Lynn, New York city.
      Hon. Franklin M. Danaher, Albany, N. Y.

Hon. Thomas F. Gilroy, New York city.
Hon. William McAdoo, New York city.
Hon. Patrick Garvan, Hartford, Conn.
Hon. James A. O'Gorman, New York city.
Hon. Joseph P. Fallon, New York city.
Hon. Maurice J. Power, New York city.
Hon. Andrew J. White, New York city.
Hon. James S. Coleman, New York city.
Hon. John E. Fitzgerald, New York city.
Rev. John J. McCoy, P. R., Chicopee, Mass.
Rev. Thomas Smyth, Springfield, Mass.
Rev. M. J. Lavelle, New York city.
Rev. Richard Neagle, Malden, Mass.
Rev. T. W. Wallace, New York city.
Rev. Martin Murphy, Great Barrington, Mass.
Rev. J. J. Howard, Worcester, Mass.
Rev. John W. McMahon, D. D., Boston, Mass.
Rev. Philip J. Gormley, Boston, Mass.
Rev. J. T. Danahy, Newton, Mass.
Dr. Thomas Addis Emmet, New York city.
Dr. Philip Kilroy, Springfield, Mass.
Dr. Stephen J. Maher, New Haven, Conn.
Dr. Farquhar Ferguson, New York city.
Dr. J. F. Hayes, Waterbury, Conn.
Dr. P. J. Cassidy, Norwich, Conn.
Dr. T. F. Harrington, Lowell, Mass.
Dr. Thomas J. Dillon, Boston, Mass.
Dr. J. Duncan Emmet, New York city.
Dr. C. E. Nammack, New York city.
Dr. D. B. Lovell, Worcester, Mass.
Dr. Francis J. Quinlan, New York city.
Dr. W. M. E. Mellen, Chicopee, Mass.
Dr. J. J. Morrissey, New York city.
James Jeffrey Roche, Boston, Mass.
Thomas Hamilton Murray, Woonsocket, R. I.
Joseph Smith, Lowell, Mass.
Thomas B. Lawler, New York city.
John T. F. Mac Donnell, Holyoke, Mass.
Pierce Kent, New York city.
M. A. Toland, Boston, Mass.

John F. McAlevy, Pawtucket, R. I.
Stephen J. Geoghegan, New York city.
Thomas B. Fitzpatrick, Boston, Mass.
T. A. Emmet, Jr., New York city.
John Crane, New York city.
Edmund Reardon, Cambridge, Mass.
Col. John McManus, Providence, R. I.
P. T. Barry, Chicago, Ill.
Capt. Wm. J. Carlton, New York city.
Thomas F. Somers, New York city.
R. Walter Powell, St. Joseph, Mo.
Patrick Kilroy, Springfield, Mass.
Capt. E. O'Meagher Condon, New York city.
Charles F. Coburn, Lowell, Mass.
Dennis H. Tierney, Waterbury, Conn.
John Goodwin, New York city.
Michael Brennan, New York city.
M. A. O'Byrne, New York city.
Humphrey O'Sullivan, Lowell, Mass.
Col. John G. Healy, New Haven, Conn.
Daniel Donovan, Lynn, Mass.
Florence G. Donovan, Brooklyn, N. Y.
William Lane, Brooklyn, N. Y.
John J. Rooney, New York city.
Joseph I. C. Clarke, New York city.
Richard Healey, Worcester, Mass.
James A. Fogarty, New Haven, Conn.
J. Francis Jones, New York city.
R. E. Danvers, New York city.
M. E. Hennessy, Boston, Mass.
Francis C. Travers, New York city.
Vincent P. Travers, New York city.
Joseph F. Swords, New York city.
Col. Henry L. Swords, New York city.
John F. Doyle, New York city.
Col. John F. Doyle, Jr., New York city.
Alfred L. Doyle, New York city.
James Curran, New York city.
Michael Gavin, 2d, New York city.
Thomas S. Brennan, New York city.

T. St. John Gaffney, New York city.
E. A. McQuade, Lowell, Mass.
Edmund O'Keefe, New Bedford, Mass.
William Lyman, New York city.
Edward O'Flaherty, New York city.
Louis V. O'Donohue, New York city.
Michael J. Dowd, Lowell, Mass.
Francis W. Foley, New Haven, Ct.
M. J. Drummond, New York city.
E. J. O'Shaughnessy, New York city.
John J. Pulleyn, New York city.
Patrick Gilbride, Lowell, Mass.
Thomas H. Boyle, Lowell, Mass.
William P. Mellon, New York city.

The following gentlemen, all of New York city, were likewise present:

Richard Deeves.
John G. O'Keefe.
James J. Phelan.
David A. Brien.
James G. Johnson.
John Vincent.
B. Moynahan.
Mark P. Brennan.
Edmund M. Brennan.
Thomas F. Brennan.
Joseph J. Ryan.
R. M. Walters.
Edward J. McGuire.
John H. McCarthy.

Michael E. Bannin.
Thomas S. Bannin.
J. P. Callahan.
E. J. Farrell.
John Vesey.
Andrew Little.
P. Gallagher.
James Flynn.
John D. Moore.
N. J. Barrett.
John O'Connell.
Isaac Bell Brennan.
George Coleman.

In addition to the foregoing, the following were also present. Residence is not given, but a majority are believed to be of New York city:

A. Fred Brown.
Thomas R. Hall.
William H. Hume.
Frederick T. Hume.
John Connelly.
James F. Minturn.

John C. McGuire.
John Kirkpatrick.
William J. Farrell.
T. S. Danahy.
C. H. Conway.
John P. Kelly.

4

Wm. H. Kelly.
A. B. Carlton.
J. J. Gleason.
F. C. O'Reilly.
J. J. Clingen.
George E. Kilgore.
J. DeM. Thompson.
J. F. Slevin.
Charles Black.
Owen J. Carney.
Patrick C. Meehan.
Theodore Meehan.
M. D. Greene.

Wm. J. Fanning.
John McKean.
R. W. Powell.
John Callaghan.
Austin Finnegan.
George F. Crowley.
P. A. Moynahan.
Arthur B. Waring.
F. C. Hodgdon.
Richard Dixon.
T. T. Tomlinson.
G. B. Warriner.
Thomas F. Glynn.

Upon the cigars being lighted, Gen. James R. O'Beirne, the presiding officer, arose and in a neat speech opened the after-dinner exercises.

He first introduced Dr. Thomas Addis Emmet of New York city, who read a paper on "Irish Emigration During the Seventeenth and Eighteenth Centuries."

Hon. John C. Linehan of Concord, N. H., followed with a paper on "Some Pre-Revolutionary Irishmen," which was well received, and proved of much value and interest.

Rev. John J. McCoy of Chicopee, Mass., read an able paper on "The Irish Element in the Second Massachusetts Volunteers in the Recent War" (with Spain).

James Jeffrey Roche, editor of *The Pilot*, Boston, Mass., entertained the company with a paper touching upon the work of the Society, and was frequently applauded.

John Jerome Rooney of New York city recited a fine poem on "The Irish Name," and elicited the plaudits of the company.

Thomas J. Gargan of Boston, Mass., the new president-general, delivered a stirring address relative to the Society's mission.

Joseph Smith of Lowell, Mass., made a short address, urging the establishment of a fund to assist the organization in carrying on its work. He also read a letter from Jeremiah Curtin, the author, who was then visiting Russia.

During the evening an address from Edward A. Moseley of Washington, D. C., the retiring president-general, was presented, Mr. Moseley not being able to attend in person.

Capt. E. O'Meagher Condon of New York city made a brief address, which was well received.

At intervals during the evening the company joined in singing patriotic American and Irish selections, accompanied by the orchestra.

There were also addresses by Hon. Thomas Dunn English of Newark, N. J., and Hon. William McAdoo, recently assistant secretary of the United States navy, whose remarks aroused much enthusiasm.

Letters regretting their inability to attend the gathering were received from Hon. Theodore Roosevelt, governor of New York; Hon. George F. Hoar, Washington, D. C.; Hon. George Fred Williams, Boston, Mass.; E. Benjamin Andrews, superintendent of public schools, Chicago, Ill., and from other gentlemen.

Before adjourning, General O'Beirne reminded the members that Hon. Theodore Roosevelt, who had expected to be present to-night but was unable, would give the Society a reception the next afternoon (Jan. 20) at 4 o'clock. The reception would take place at the residence of the governor's sister, Mrs. Cowles, Madison avenue. General O'Beirne requested the members to meet at the Hotel Savoy at 3 : 30 p. m., in order that they might proceed to the governor's reception in a body. The company then adjourned.

GOVERNOR ROOSEVELT'S RECEPTION.

Pursuant to the agreement made at the meeting the previous evening, a large number of the members of the Society met at the Hotel Savoy, New York, on the afternoon of Jan. 20, 1899. About half an hour later they formed in line and walked to the residence of Mrs. Cowles, the governor's sister, on Madison avenue.

They were received by Governor Roosevelt, assisted by Mrs. Cowles. Each member of the Society present was introduced by General O'Beirne, and was cordially greeted.

After all had been introduced, Governor Roosevelt made a charming little speech, expressing his pleasure at meeting the Society's representatives. He also expressed regret at having been unable to attend the Society's dinner last night, but official duties had prevented.

He complimented the Society on the work in which it is engaged, and said that such historical bodies are capable of a great deal of good. He paid an eloquent tribute to the soldier of Irish extraction in American military life, and recalled special instances where this element's valor had been displayed. The governor spoke feelingly of Capt. "Bucky" O'Neill, one of the officers who had served under him in the "Rough Riders" during the war with Spain, and said that he was one of the best captains in the regiment.

Upon the conclusion of his address, the governor invited those present to partake of a lunch that had been prepared, and the invitation was cordially accepted.

After bidding adieu to the governor and his sister, many of the members accepted an invitation from Hon. John D. Crimmins and participated in a reception at the latter's residence, 40 East 68th street, New York. It proved a most enjoyable occasion.

The leading addresses made, papers read, etc., at the annual meeting here follow:

ADDRESSES MADE AND PAPERS READ

At the Annual Meeting, Thursday Evening, January 19, 1899.

LETTER FROM EDWARD A. MOSELEY, THE RETIR-ING PRESIDENT–GENERAL.

Edward A. Moseley, Washington, D. C., the retiring president-general of the Society, wrote as follows:

To the Members of the American-Irish Historical Society:

BROTHERS :—I regret very much that it will be impossible for me to attend the annual meeting of our Society on the 19th instant. I have been under medical treatment during the past ten days, and I am still far from well, and am advised by my physician that it would be very unwise for me to leave the city for some time to come.

It would be an exceeding pleasure to me to be with you, and to meet so many of the distinguished gentlemen of our Society who will be present, and who will, no doubt, illuminate with their wit and eloquence the banquet hall at Sherry's on the evening of the 19th. I shall be with you in spirit, but as I cannot be there in person, would you kindly make a few suggestions for me at the meeting.

I have received the copy of Volume I of the *Journal*. It is a handsome volume, and a publication creditable to its editors and our Society. My only regret is that we cannot afford to publish such works extensively, and place one in the household of every American who boasts of his supposed Anglo-Saxon ancestry, and especially in the hands of our dear brethren, the "Scotch-Irish" advocates, who take so much pains to distinguish themselves from the mere Irish element.

In these days, when the brotherhood of man does not count for so much as in the early days of the republic, and when some are dividing themselves into classes and races and assuming superiority for the so-called "Anglo-Saxon race" over all the other races of men created by Almighty God, it seems to me that, as we do not claim to be of the "Anglo-Saxon race," we should not submit to the implication contained in the term that all other peoples, including the Irish, are inferiors in race.

It is, therefore, high time for us to reassert and emphasize our protest against the claim that the American people belong to the "Anglo-Saxon race," or that any of the Caucasian peoples are in any degree inferior in race to any other. Where differences exist it is a question of environment. After two or three generations, no one can perceive any radical distinctions between Americans descended from ancestors who were Englishmen, Irishmen, Scotchmen, Welshmen, Dutchmen, Germans, Scandinavians or of any other European nationality.

As there never was an "Anglo-Saxon" race—that being a term which designated two German tribes—we repudiate any suggestion that American civilization or progress is materially indebted to any supposed Anglo-Saxon element in our composition. On the contrary, we assert that all European nationalities have contributed to our advancement and magnificent citizenship.

The purpose of our Society is not to attribute all our splendid traits and achievements alone to the Irish element in our composition. Unlike our Anglomaniac brethren, who contend that everything great and good must be Anglo-Saxon, we merely claim credit for a just share in the upbuilding of the nation.

I would like the learned gentlemen of our Society to enlighten the average American, from time to time, in his local newspaper or on the rostrum, in respect to this Anglo-Saxon fetish. This has already been done for the American student by many distinguished ethnologists. It is easy to give object lessons on this line by the color of the hair and the eyes, and the shape of the skull, features which demonstrate beyond question that men of the supposed Anglo-Saxon type are the rare exceptions in our make-up, and are often very far from being at the top of the scale in any respect; while on the other hand, men of the received Celtic type compose the overwhelming majority in this country and in the British Isles— even in England itself, and in every part of England. They are in the vast majority all over the world wherever the English tongue prevails.

Many of the gentlemen of our Society can write just such admirable papers as Mr. Bocock contributed to the *Cosmopolitan* magazine of this month (who confined himself, however, to instances of Irishmen who achieved great fame). No one has done more in this direction than our respected vice-president for the District of Columbia, Mr. J. D. O'Connell, whose pen has ever been at the service of his countrymen, particularly in this respect.

Whenever an Irishmen attains to fame or distinction in war, literature, art, law, or statesmanship in the British Empire, he is immediately claimed to be an Englishman, and, consequently, as displaying " Anglo-Saxon " pluck and " Anglo-Saxon " intellect.

The truth is, that among all those who have achieved great prominence in the English-speaking world, the Anglo-Saxon type is conspicuous by its absence. Nine times in ten, when a man boasts of " Anglo-Saxon " pluck, enterprise, ability, and progress, he himself is not of that type of man, and nine-tenths of the incidents he cites were brought about through the pluck, enterprise, ability and progress which came from mixed blood.

I can only liken this misrepresentation of the truth of history to the rattling of peas in a bladder, shaken by one of Shakespeare's clowns. Puncture the bladder, my friends, whenever and wherever it is shaken. Tell the clown who calls himself an "Anglo-Saxon" that he is an ass! and prove to him by the color of his hair, the color of his eyes, and the shape of his skull that he is a Celt, a Milesian, a Latin, or anything but an " Anglo-Saxon," and that if it was ever true that the English people were Anglo-Saxon, and that the Anglo-Saxons were ever, at any time, the greatest people on earth—superior to all other races—that time has so long since passed away that no one now remembers it, and no true history chronicles when and where they flourished.

*   *   *   *   *   *   *

But I have already trespassed too far on this line. Permit me to wish you all, if not too late, a very happy and prosperous New Year, and also to say to you that, as I have been twice honored by election to the presidency of the Society—and that is, I think, sufficient honor for any member—I beg to invoke the national rule against a third term. Therefore, if any friend of mine should be so indiscreet as to nominate me for that office, I request and urge you to ask him to immediately withdraw the nomination.

Fraternally yours,

EDWARD A. MOSELEY,
President-General.

WASHINGTON, D. C., Jan. 17, 1899.

IRISH EMIGRATION DURING THE SEVENTEENTH AND EIGHTEENTH CENTURIES.

BY THOMAS ADDIS EMMET, M. D., NEW YORK CITY.

Irish people were among the pioneers in this country from almost the first settlement on the Atlantic coast, and continued until the line of immigration had crossed the continent to the Pacific.

The Colonial records bear testimony that Irish people were here at an early period, and so many hamlets on the frontier were designated by distinctive Irish names that had we no other proof than these facts, we could not honestly divest ourselves of the conviction that Ireland contributed more in numbers for the development of this country than came from any other one source.

Great injustice has been done the Irish people by depriving them of credit so justly due them. This has resulted partially from ignorance, but to a greater extent it is due to an influence exerted prior to the first settlement in this country. The purpose which prompts this injustice has been maintained through English influence, and has always been wanting so much in charity to the Irish people, that we can hope to accomplish little in any effort to establish the truth so long as individuals in this country are willing to have their judgment influenced by the policy of a foreign power.

The same influence has been as actively engaged in claiming that we are English; that this country is consequently "a worthy daughter of a more worthy mother!" Yet my investigations have impressed me with the belief that of the seventy-five millions forming our present population, there are a far greater number of individuals who could be more certain of their African origin, than there are those who could prove a direct English descent.

It is not sufficient to show proof of an ancestor sailing from an English port, as all such were rated during the seventeenth century as English, without reference to their nationality. Moreover the bearing of an English name would be no more conclusive, as we shall show that a large proportion of the "Wild Irish" were compelled by law to assume English surnames, which their descendants bear at the present time.

I have no precise data bearing directly upon the earliest immigration of the Irish to this country, for none exists. On the other hand, the assertion that they were among the first settlers, and the most numerous afterwards, cannot be rejected or disproved. I will now very clearly show, as circumstantial evidence, that throughout the greater portion of the seventeenth century a dire provocation existed, and that the Catholics were driven out of Ireland by a persecution which has never been equaled. The world to-day is in ignorance of the fact, since a complete history of Ireland, and of the suffering borne by a majority of the people, has yet to be written.

Whenever an advantage was to be gained by falsifying an historical event in connection with Ireland, the English government has never hesitated, in the past, to exercise its influence for that purpose. Yet with a strange inconsistency every record in the keeping of the government bearing upon its own immediate history, is zealously preserved, notwithstanding the most damning testimony is thus furnished of corruption, double dealing and crime.

As an American I would gladly have laid aside all religious appellations if it had been possible otherwise to have done justice to my subject, but unfortunately, as a consequence of the prejudices of centuries, not a few people regard the "Protestant Irishman," the "Presbyterian Irishman," and the "Catholic Irishman" as so many distinct species of the human family. The necessity, therefore, exists in doing justice to Ireland, that all at least in relation to the Catholic portion should be made prominent, as this precludes the plea of being either English or "Scotch-Irish."

But as regards the race, the fact is that even within the period of which we shall treat in regard to the forced emigration, there remained in Ireland but little of the pure old Celtic stock. The inhabitants of Ireland had been gradually becoming a mixed people, and were as much of an aggregation as the population of the United States is a conglomeration of all other races. Yet there is something in the Irish climate and surroundings, which, even within a generation, exercises a powerful influence in bringing the descendants of all foreigners to a type possessing much in common, and with characteristics unlike any other people.

It was not until near the close of the reign of Charles the First,

that the Irish people were forced to emigrate.   Therefore, I propose
to begin with a brief reference to the so-called " Rebellion of 1641."

In this movement Charles the First of England was the active
spirit, and if ever a man richly deserved his fate through retributive
justice, Charles rightly suffered.   His inhuman treatment of the
Irish people, who had been most loyal to him, would have justified
his execution if no other cause existed.   No historical event, which
antedates the testimony of living witnesses, can be more clearly established in all its details than the history of this forced outbreak in
1641, and this can be done notwithstanding there are few instances
in history which have been more distorted by falsehood.

It would not be germane to my subject to enter into detail at
greater length than to establish the provocation, or necessity existing at this time, for a large emigration of the Irish people.   The
English government had long held for the crown an absurd claim
which involved the title of every estate in Connaught.   The Catholics held nine tenths of the land and they bore in numbers about
the same proportion to the population.   During the reign of James
an effort had been made to clear off this claimed lien, and large
sums of money had been paid by the owners to the English government for this purpose, with the understanding that these transac-
tions should be made a public record.

When Charles came to the throne it was found that James had
appropriated this money for his own use, and the only record existing was one in which only the title of estates held by Protestants
was established.

For an additional sum Charles promised, among many other
promises which he did not keep, to have the title of the estates held
by the Catholics cleared of all government claims, wherever the
holder could prove his right of possession.   For this ostensible
purpose a commission was appointed, at the head of which was
the Lord Chief Justice and the chief prosecuting officer for the
crown in Ireland.

It is now known that the real object of the commission was to
obtain some pretext for a general confiscation of the land, and to
make a plantation of Catholic Connaught, after the people had
been disposed of.   As a stimulus to the zeal of these officers an
additional bonus of two shillings on the pound was granted from
the value of each estate confiscated to the crown, when made on the
plea of a defective title.   The owner was generally made foreman of

the jury and whenever the verdict was a " Prevarication on the evidence," as it was termed, and not for the crown, he was fined to bankruptcy, his estate confiscated " legally," and the jurymen were both fined and imprisoned.

But this semblance of justice proved to be too slow a process, so the country was suddenly overrun with English troops to force an extended outbreak. Additional instructions were given to exterminate, if possible, the whole Catholic population, English as well as Irish, as is clearly proved by the writings of Leland, Clarendon, Warner, Carte, and other writers, who had no sympathy for the Irish people.

The cattle and all available property were seized ; persons in all stations of life were imprisoned, without having charges .preferred against them, or they were wilfully murdered without provocation ; the wives and daughters of the Catholic Irish were subjected to unspeakable brutality, and it was a frequent boast that no woman was spared ; the well and the sick, the young and the old were indiscriminately turned adrift, their houses were burned, and all provisions and stores which could not be used by the troops were wantonly destroyed.

No less than three thousand heads of families, constituting the Catholic nobility and gentry, and the owners of the land in the west of Ireland were imprisoned, charged with treason, and their property was seized.

A new commission was now formed, consisting of judge and jurymen in English interests, yet who were sworn, it is supposed, to investigate with some pretext to honesty the charge of treason against these individuals. As a result of their labors *over one thousand indictments were drawn up by this commission in two days*, by which each individual was found guilty of treason, thus losing his life, and his property was seized for the crown! If it be assumed that this jury worked continuously each day for twelve hours, the average would be about one indictment for a little less than every minute and a half. During which time it was supposed that witnesses duly sworn were examined as to the guilt of each individual, and after due deliberation, and after giving the prisoner the benefit of all doubt, where the testimony was deemed unreliable, the verdict had been rendered.

Is it possible to conceive of a more complete travesty on justice ? The prisoners knew nothing of the proceedings, and the average time

for conviction of less than one minute and a half was scarcely sufficient to add the signatures necessary to give each death warrant a
semblance of legality.

By this one transaction the British crown came into possession of
some ten millions of acres, which was a little more than one half of
all the available land in Ireland.

Between five and six hundred thousand men, women, and children were slaughtered, or died from starvation. Many thousand
were sent to the West Indies, or to the American colonies, and sold
as slaves. A limited number escaped to the mountains, where many
died from starvation, and the remainder lived for years a life in
common with the wild beasts, with a price upon their heads, and
were hunted as such. The whole and entire population of this
great tract of country disappeared, and was literally wiped out.

Shortly after, Cromwell overran the south and southwestern
portion of Ireland which was also chiefly settled by Catholics, and
they received as little mercy from his army as had been meted out
to those of their creed in Connaught. When Cromwell had completed his work at least two thirds of the landed property in Ireland
had been confiscated ; and after the greater portion of the Catholic
Irish men, women, and children had been put to the sword, or
driven into exile, the whole country became resettled with his soldiers, or by persons devoted to the English interest. Over one
hundred thousand young children, who had been made orphans, or
who were taken from their Catholic parents, were sent to the West
Indies, to Virginia, or to New England, that they might thus lose
their faith, as well as all knowledge of their nationality.

During this period thousands of Irishmen were driven into exile, to
enter the armies of European nations, or to emigrate and settle on the
frontiers of the American colonies, as a bulwark against the Indians,
for the protection of the more favored settlers on the coast.

In addition, a host of both men and women who were taken
prisoners, were sold in Virginia and New England as slaves, and
without respect to their former station in life.

In later years, certain writers have attempted to pervert the truth
by claiming that these men and women, who were refined and
educated, and who had been the owners of the confiscated lands,
were convicts. But I have not been able to obtain any reliable
evidence to prove that Virginia or any of the American colonies
were ever made penal settlements.

The Catholics of Ireland were the only people of Europe who had at this time so great a necessity for leaving their country. It is a well established fact that during the greater part of the eighteenth century thousands of able-bodied male Catholics, in the south and western portion of Ireland, left the country at an early period of life for some European port, and very few ever returned. This is corroborated by the circumstance that the Catholic population of Ireland steadily decreased during this period, and at one time it was less than half a million of individuals scattered through the bogs and wilds of the country.

The wealthy English people invested their money freely in the early settlement of the West Indies and in Virginia, but they remained at home. The middle and lower classes, who were more likely to have emigrated to a new country, were, to a great extent, contented at home. They had no cause to leave it, as the political changes which occurred in England during the seventeenth century had a decided tendency to better their condition.

I believe that with the exception of some among the first settlers in Virginia and New England, the far greater portion of the English who did emigrate during the seventeenth and the first half of the eighteenth century, went to Bermuda, Barbadoes, Jamaica, and the other West India Islands, and did not come to this country. The American colonies were mostly settled under a grant to some proprietor or corporation, with more restrictions on business pursuits than were made by the English government for the West India Islands. Consequently the field for individual enterprise was greater on the Islands.

Those of English birth who settled on the main land did so largely in Virginia and Carolina, and as a rule their business was confined to the seaport towns. I believe that a larger proportion of the English than of any other people, when successful in business, returned in after life to their native country, or went with their families to Barbadoes or Jamaica to invest their money in sugar plantations. It is from this circumstance that these islands have always been more English in character than any American colony now within the territory of the United States.

For an Irishman without means there was no opening in any of the West India Islands but as a common laborer. In the American colonies, however, he could easily reach the frontiers, free from all restriction after he had served out the time necessary to pay for his passage, and could there establish his independence with the labor of clearing off the forest from the land selected by himself.

In consequence of the restrictions made by England to destroy Irish commerce, it is well known that for several centuries the intercourse between Ireland and different continental countries, by means of vessels engaged in smuggling, was far greater than by any communication with England, which was almost an unknown land to the west coast Irishman.

It is not possible to form even an estimate as to the numbers of Irish who went by means of these smugglers chiefly to France and Spain. We only know the fact that a steady current of impoverished Irishmen passed over to the continent year after year. We also know that a very large number served in the armies of those countries, but it is doubtful, under any circumstances, if more than a comparatively small proportion of the number could have been thus provided for. Of the remaining portion but few could have had any other means of support, and no other explanation presents itself but emigration to America from necessity, and on their arrival in a foreign vessel their nationality would have been overlooked.

The English government during the eighteenth century allowed no vessel, knowingly, to sail from Ireland direct, but it was necessary by law first to visit an English port before clearance papers could be obtained for the voyage. A record was also kept for the purpose of collecting a head tax on every individual thus leaving an English port for the colonies. I have gone carefully over this register, and to my surprise scarcely a name appears which could be identified with Ireland. Notwithstanding this fact the official register has been cited in proof that there was no emigration from Ireland but those who were sent abroad in servitude, and consequently that this country for a century, at least, was settled chiefly by English people.

But we must remember that every Irishman in Ireland within reach of English authority was at that time governed by the following law: "An act that Irishmen dwelling in the counties of, etc. . . . . go appareled like Englishmen and wear their beards after the English manner, swear allegiance, and take English sirnames; which sirnames shall be of one town, as Sutton, Chester, Trim, Skryne, Corke, Kinsale; or colours, as white, black, brown; or arts or sciences, as smith or carpenter; or office, as cook, butler, etc., and it is enacted that he and his issue shall use this name under pain of forfeyting of his goods yearly, etc." As a consequence, every Irish emigrant crossing in an Irish or English vessel and from either England or Ireland, appeared in, the official record as English, for the voyage did not begin according to law until cleared from an English port.

By this circumstance we prove the converse, that a large Irish emigration did reach this country by some route which was not under English control. How otherwise can we explain the presence of undoubted Irish surnames unchanged, as found in early records of the country? And on the other hand we find to-day Irishmen and their descendants in this country, bearing the names of Sutton, Chester, Kinsale, White, Black, Brown, Smith, Carpenter, Cook, Butler, etc., proving thereby that this law was enforced, by which they were deprived of their pure Irish names, and that they did not change these names after coming to this country.

Virginia was undoubtedly first settled by the English, but at an early period the Irish began to come in, bound to serve a stated term in payment for their passage money, but eventually these people became free men, settling down on the frontier, and their descendants in the next generation, as indicated by their names appearing in the records, began to take part in the affairs of the colony.

Maryland was largely settled by Irish Catholics, and Calvert himself received his title of Lord Baltimore from a place in the southwest of Ireland.

William Penn spent a portion of his life in Ireland before he received his grant in America. A number of his followers were Irish, and the most prominent person next to Penn himself was James Logan, an Irishman, who acted as governor of the province for a number of years. He was most tolerant to the Irish Catholics, who were allowed free exercise of their religion, and they received protection in this colony from the first settlement.

Many of those who first settled in New Jersey were from Ireland, and there were undoubtedly some Irish in New Amsterdam. In the Jesuit Relations it is shown that Father Jogues, who afterwards suffered the death of a martyr among the Indians of Central New York, came about 1642 from Canada to administer to some of his faith then living among the Dutch and in New Jersey.

In 1634 the General Court of Massachusetts Bay granted lands on the Merrimac river for an Irish settlement, and there were many

Irishmen who served in King Philip's Indian War, whose names
are still preserved in the colonial records. I have a record of the
fact, but neglected to note the authority, of a reference to a contem-
poraneous account of a fearful storm which occurred in the winter
of 1634–'35, off the north coast of Ireland.[1] As one of the incidents mention is made of the shipwreck of a vessel filled with Irish
emigrants, on the second day out of their voyage to join, as was
stated, the Merrimac river settlement in New England.

This straw of information is a valuable indication in our current
of circumstantial evidence. It establishes the fact by another
source that an Irish settlement was planned on the Merrimac river
as early as 1634. It also shows that however intolerant the New
England Puritans were sometimes to the Irish in their immediate
surroundings, they did tolerate in this instance and likely in many
others, the "fighting Irish," as they were termed. In fact they
gave little thought to their religious belief so long as they remained
on the frontier to fight the Indians. This incident shows that
emigrants sailed from the north of Ireland for this settlement, notwithstanding it may have been necessary to have officially com-
menced their voyage from an English port. The fact as to their
religion is established by a knowledge of the condition of the country at that particular time, which I have attempted to describe.
The Catholics were fleeing in all directions from the districts of
country which had been laid waste, and in some instances they had
to subsist on the dead bodies of those who had preceded them, and
who had died on the way from starvation. Comparatively few but
Catholics left Ireland at this time, as individuals in sympathy with
the English were then busy in bettering their condition by securing
a portion of the spoils.

There were a number of adult Catholics, as I have stated, sent
out to New England through the efforts of Cromwell, and, although
they may not have come at that time as willing emigrants, they were
not likely to have lost their faith under the circumstances, and
their descendants must afterwards have become identified with the
country.

Prendergast in "The Cromwellian Settlement of Ireland," states
the following: "As one instance out of many: Captain Vernon was

---

[1] Thomas D'Arcy McGee in his "History of the Irish Settlers in North America" says
that "in 1636, the *Eagle Wing*, with one hundred and forty passengers, sailed from Car-
rickfergus to found an Irish colony on the Merrimac, but had to put back owing to stress of
weather, and the project was for many years abandoned."

employed by the commissioners for Ireland into [from] England, and contracted in their behalf with Mr. David Selleck and Mr. Leader, under his hand, bearing date of 14th of September, 1653, to supply them with two hundred and fifty women of the Irish nation, above twelve years and under the age of forty-five, also three hundred men above twelve years of age and under fifty, to be found in the country within twenty miles of Cork . . . to transplant them into New England." These men and women were seized and sold in New England at a profit for the English commissioners. Prendergast further states in this connection : " How many girls of gentle birth must have been caught and hurried to the private prisons of these men-catchers none can tell." " But at last the evil became too shocking and notorious, particularly when these dealers in Irish flesh began to seize the daughters and children of the English themselves, and to force them on board their slave ships ; then, indeed, the orders, at the end of four years, were revoked."

If we take into consideration the total number of " Puritan Fathers " in New England at this time, it would seem not improbable that these two hundred and fifty young Irish women, with many others sent over from Ireland about the same time, must have all eventually been transformed at least into Irish Puritans. If so their progeny must in time have given quite a Hibernian tint to the blue blood of the descendants from the *Mayflower.* I have not found that the New England writers have noted these facts, but probably they failed to do so on evidence that they were not " Scotch-Irish " women.

From the time that William of Orange possessed himself of the British crown and until the beginning of our Revolution, a steady stream of emigrants passed out of Ireland to this country. The English government manifested a determination to destroy utterly every Irish industry, and this policy was maintained until the Volunteer movement, when for a period a portion at least of the Irish people had charge of their own affairs.

William, of " Blessed Memory," in consequence of his hatred of the Irish people, both Catholic and Protestant, caused the destruction of all woolen manufactories, and other industries of the north of Ireland. The so-called " Scotch-Irish " were chiefly the sufferers at this time, and as a consequence thousands of them emigrated to France, where, with the assistance of the French government, these people established in that country woolen and silk industries which,

5

for nearly two hundred years, have been a constant menace to England's trade.

After the departure of a large portion of these people from Ulster, the country became again gradually settled up from England, and by Catholic, Presbyterian, and Protestant Irish from different parts of Ireland, who were not Scotch.

In a few years later a large proportion of the Irish Presbyterians, with a limited number of Catholics in Ulster, became engaged in commerce and various manufacturing interests.   But all these people were ultimately ruined by England's policy, that Ireland should not prosper, and they were gradually forced to leave the country to better their condition by emigration to the American colonies.

The Presbyterians who settled in the north of Ireland, after the early part of the eighteenth century, had come chiefly from the central portion of England, and as a rule represented the better element among the new settlers. They, like Cromwell, hated the Scotch, and would never have accepted the term "Scotch-Irish" for themselves.   After "the Restoration" these people in common with the Catholics, were only tolerated as non-conformists, and were not allowed by the Protestant authorities to take any part in public affairs.

From adversity these people became in time more tolerant towards their fellow sufferers, the Catholic portion of the population, and were finally moulded into a remarkably fine and self-reliant type of men.   Those who emigrated to the colonies were well fitted to help lay the foundation of the American Republic, and those who remained behind proved sturdy patriots.   A little more than one hundred years ago they originated in Belfast the United Irishmen movement, and they were the first to make the demand for religious tolerance in Ireland, that their Catholic countrymen might be free to worship God according to the dictates of their conscience.

During the last century, Maine, New Hampshire, the greater part of Vermont and west Massachusetts, west Pennsylvania, a large portion of Maryland, the western part of Virginia, between the Blue Ridge and the Alleghany mountains, into North Carolina, along the French Broad river, to the upper part of South Carolina, and into the territory now forming Tennessee and Kentucky, with a part of the northwest territory, to the north of the Ohio river, and which then belonged to Virginia, was largely, and in some sections was entirely, settled by Irish, who did not change their names before or after leaving Ireland. From the latter circumstance the course of settlement can be traced by the surnames of the first settlers, and the indications are rendered all the stronger by the names of so many settlements which clearly indicate the localities in Ireland whence these people came.

It can be claimed that some of these Irish emigrants were of English descent from some period more or less remote. This was doubtless true, but they became Irish by birth, and were no longer in sympathy with English interests, or they would not have left the country. Notwithstanding the severe penalties, which were so long in operation, for "taking up with the Irishy," the fate of many of the invaders was the same after each invasion. In time they yielded to the charms of the Irish women, and their progeny became often more Irish than those from the original Celtic stock. The descendants of many a Cromwellian soldier can be found in Ireland and abroad, who are to-day bitter and uncompromising foes to England's rule in Ireland, and are a potent check to her influence elsewhere.

I have found reported among the debates in the Irish Parliament, a speech by the Hon. Luke Gardiner, delivered April 2d, 1784, on Irish Commerce, and from which I quote: "America was lost by Irish emigrants. These emigrations are fresh in the recollection of every gentleman in this house. I am assured, from the best authority, the major part of the American army was composed of Irish, and that the Irish language was as commonly spoken in the American ranks as English. I am also informed it was their valor determined the contest, so that England had America detached from her by force of Irish emigrants, etc."

I find in Marmion's work, "The Ancient and Modern History of the Maritime Ports of Ireland," some interesting facts bearing upon a portion of the exodus to this country.

In 1771, 1772, and 1773, over twenty-five thousand emigrants left Belfast, and other ports in that immediate neighborhood, for the American colonies, in consequence of having been evicted from one of the estates of the Marquis of Donegal, in Antrim.

Marmion states, "The emigrants were chiefly farmers and manufacturers who, it was calculated, by converting their property into specie, which they took with them abroad, deprived Ulster of one fourth of its circulating medium, which then consisted altogether of specie; and also a portion equal thereto to the most valuable part of its population."

Could Robert Morris, the financier of the Revolution, enlighten us as to the effect from bringing this amount of specie into the country, we would realize that the benefit was an incalculable one, and it is a matter of surprise that writers of our history have not noted so important a circumstance.

What credit we had in this country after the paper money had depreciated, was based upon this specie throughout the greater part of the Revolution. Among many instances to this purpose was its use in moving the army to Virginia with such expedition as to ensure the capture of Cornwallis, which event contributed more to the termination of the war than any other; and without the credit based on this specie the struggle would have terminated long before the alliance was made with France.

The Irish people throughout this country were with few exceptions in sympathy with the cause of the colonies, and immediately after the battle of Bunker Hill thousands among them entered the army, but particularly such was the case with these emigrants from the north of Ireland, who, from their continuous service and discipline, became a mainstay of the organization until the end of the war. These Irishmen, who had settled in Pennsylvania, turned out chiefly under the command of Col. Edward Hand and Col. William Irving. They were both Irishmen, and had served as surgeons in the British service, the first in the army and the latter in the navy.

Hand was certainly of Catholic parents from the north of Ireland, and his command, composed largely of Presbyterians, joined the army before Boston shortly after Washington took command. But the arrival of Hand's troops, it is claimed, had been preceded a few days by a body of Catholic Irishmen from Maryland and lower Pennsylvania, under the command of Col. Stephen Moylan, who was a personal friend of Washington, an aide on his staff, and an active officer throughout the war. Moylan was a brother of the Catholic bishop of Cork, Ireland, who was a devoted friend to the American cause.

Joseph Galloway, a native of Maryland, but long a resident of Pennsylvania before the Revolution, was one of the best informed men in the colonies, and probably, with the exception of Franklin, had no equal as to his accurate knowledge relating to the general condition of affairs in the country. He was an early and active sympathizer in the American cause until the Declaration of Independence, when he became a Loyalist. During a visit to England he was examined in June, 1779, before an investigating committee of the House of Commons, and his testimony has been frequently published. When asked as to the composition of the Rebel army— his answer was—" The names and places of their nativity being taken down I can answer the question with precision,—there were scarcely one fourth natives of America; about one half Irish,—the other fourth were English and Scotch." He might have stated more in detail, that the fourth part was composed of some English, very few Scotch, and more Germans, or Dutch, as they were called, from Pennsylvania and the valley of Virginia, who formed the brigade under the command of Muhlenberg, and the Eighth Virginia regiment.

Galloway's testimony was in relation to his experience while superintendent of the police in Philadelphia during the British occupancy. It is but just to state that to a subsequent question, " Do you know anything of the army of the Rebels in general, how that is composed—of what country people ? " His answer was, " I judge of that by the deserters that came over." Had we no other testimony to corroborate Galloway's first statement it would be to the discredit of the Irish, but taken as a whole it is shown that no larger proportion of them deserted than of any other nationality ; and if the proportion of native born from Irish parents could be ascertained, the number of deserters among those of Irish blood would be shown to have been less than any other.

I have estimated that about one fourth of all the American officers were Irish by birth or descent.

A large number of Irish were in the Continental Congress or prominent as leaders in every station of life. I may mention that even Washington was possibly descended on his father's side from a Washington who had lived in Ireland, and his mother's family, the Balls, beyond doubt came from the neighborhood of Dublin. Walford in his " Country Families of the United Kingdom " shows that at the present time the only families with any property bearing the name of Ball, are to be found in Ireland. The family, it is stated, came to Ireland in the Fourteenth century as Flemish emigrants. The De Wessyngtons, it is also claimed, were Flemish, who settled about the same time in both England and Ireland. But the head of the English family, it seems, died some years before the planting of Jamestown, Va. The members of the Irish branch[1] have

---

[1] See " The Irish Washingtons at Home and Abroad ; together with Some Mention of the Ancestry of the American Pater Patriæ. By George Washington of Dublin, Ireland, and Thomas Hamilton Murray, Boston, Mass." Boston : The Carrollton Press, 1898.

all been traced and some of them to this country.   One, a son of
Henry Washington, who was a prominent man, disappeared from
Ireland during the troubles I have described.   He probably escaped
to Bermuda, where many vessels first stopped on their way to the
American colonies.

During a visit to Bermuda in 1852, I had occasion to examine
some of the early church records.   I there saw several references
made in the minutes of the Vestry meetings to one Washington,
"a sojourner," who was several times fined for not conforming by
attending the service of the Established church.   He seemed to
have proved incorrigible as he was finally ordered "to go his way."
He probably did so to Virginia, from the known fact that his father
had been a friend of Lord Baltimore, and others who were connected
with the Virginia settlements.

The Irish Presbyterians and Catholics were in full sympathy with
this country during the Revolution, while in Ireland or elsewhere
there were very few Scotch who favored the American cause.   A
noted exception to the rule was John Witherspoon, a signer of the
Declaration of Independence from New Jersey, who was a devoted
patriot.   The only large settlement of Scotch in the colonies was
formed in North Carolina by the British government, after the battle of Culloden, by transplanting the Highlanders.   Among them
was Flora McDonald, whose husband, with every other man in the
settlement, espoused the English cause and fought against the
Americans.

It is full time that we divest ourselves of English influence in
this country.   Until this be done we will remain in ignorance of the
truth relating to a large portion of our history, which has yet to be
written in strict accord with the facts.

HON. MORGAN J. O'BRIEN,
A Justice of the New York Supreme Court.

MR. JOHN CRANE,
NEW YORK CITY.

MR. STEPHEN J. GEOGHEGAN,
NEW YORK CITY.

MR. JOSEPH FORSYTH SWORDS,
NEW YORK CITY.

FOUR MEMBERS OF THE EXECUTIVE COUNCIL.

SOME PRE-REVOLUTIONARY IRISHMEN.

BY HON. JOHN C. LINEHAN, CONCORD, N. H.

Two hundred and fifty years ago, the Five Nations, better known later as the Six Nations, was the most powerful confederacy of Indians in North America. The governor of the province of New York, in a communication to the committee of trade dated February 22, 1687, said, " The Five Nations are the most warlike people in America. They go as far as the South sea, the Northwest passage, and Florida to war. They are so considerable that all the Indians in these parts of America are tributary to them." To gain the friendship of these people, was the constant aim of the French in Canada, and the English in New York and New England.

The latter at the outset had an advantage from the fact, well-known, that the former under Champlain, had antagonized the confederacy, by forming an alliance with the Hurons whom it had not, up to that time, subjected to its rule. This advantage, however, there is good reason to believe, would not have inured to the benefit of the English, were it not for the influence of two men of Irish blood, who by their tact, discretion, and humanity, secured the alliance of the Six Nations for the British government. The union thus created was of the greatest possible benefit to the English colonies, and existed until the power of the confederacy was destroyed forever, and the Indians themselves, connected with it, almost swept from the face of the earth.

This deed was performed by troops under the command of another man of Irish blood, who is credited with being the first in the English colonies to commit an overt act against the British government by leading a body of armed men against the Royal troops at Newcastle, N. H., on Dec. 14, 1774. Thus will the names of three men, Thomas Dongan, William Johnson, and John Sullivan, be forever inseparably connected with the annals of the Six Nations, and the records of the province and state of New York.

The ferocity, the cruelty, and the barbarism of the Indians comprising the Six Nations, are described at length on the pages of the various works written by Francis Parkman.   Their very name terrorized the other Indian tribes, almost from the Gulf of St. Lawrence to the Mississippi, and in their efforts to dominate all others, they devastated the entire country.   It was not, therefore, surprising that their enmity was feared, and their friendship sought.   After the conquest of New York, and during the dominion of the three first governors appointed by the English government, no effort had been made to secure the latter.

The appointment, however, by James II, of Col. Thomas Dongan, placed at the head of affairs in New York a man of distinguished character as a soldier, and, as events subsequently proved, possessed of abilities in civil affairs that entitle him to the rank of a statesman.   He was a native of Ireland, a Catholic in religion, and had been, through weal and woe, a stanch adherent of his royal master. He had seen service in the French army, and in both Britain and France was looked upon as a brave and skilful officer.

He was commissioned governor on Sept. 30, 1682.   Under his administration the first legislative assembly met in the colony and under it a law was enacted granting religious toleration to the members of all Christian churches.   He had not been long in his new position before he realized the importance of securing for his government the good will of the Five Nations.   It goes without saying that, in their intercourse with the American Indians, the French, for one reason or another, had been able to get along with them better than did the English, and up to the time of Colonel Dongan's arrival, they were doing all in their power to secure an alliance with the Indians whose prowess they feared as well as respected.   He saw that action, immediate action, was necessary to counteract the influence being exercised by the French.

One of the first steps taken by him was to oblige the Jesuit missionaries who were among them to return to Canada ; thus proving that his religion was no obstacle in the way of loyalty to his government.   For this, and for other similar acts, he was complained of by the Canadian authorities, who wrote at length to the king of France, who in turn complained to the king of England in relation to the matter.

This did not deter Dongan, however, and during his entire administration, extending over a period of nearly six years, he labored incessantly to effect a union between his government and the Indians, which, through his tact, and his good judgment, was finally effected to his satisfaction before his departure. No man of British birth or of the Protestant religion, labored more diligently, zealously, or successfully for his government, than did this Irish-born Catholic. His address to the Indian Nations in City hall, Albany, on Aug. 5, 1687, near the close of his administration, as published in the documentary history of New York, is most interesting reading, as well as a good illustration of the condition of affairs then existing between the French and the English nations on this continent.

Dongan was so fair, honorable, and equitable in his dealings with all men, that, to this day, none of New York's rulers, before or since the Revolution, stands higher with historical writers. An unpublished life of him, written more than seventy-five years ago, by ex-Governor Plumer, of New Hampshire, is now in possession of the New Hampshire Historical Society. During Dongan's term as governor, all the New England governors looked to him for counsel and advice. It was not uncommon in those days to appeal to him to send the Mohawks to their aid in repelling the attacks of the French and Indians. It can safely be said that from the settlement of New Amsterdam down to the day of his departure, no one man had done more than he in shaping the course of events which ultimately led to the success of the English government, and the final establishment, in consequence, of the republic. It is not too much to say that, had the French been successful thus early in securing the coöperation of the Indians mentioned, the result to the English colonies would be easy to conjecture.

From 1688 to 1746 it is safe to say that the colony of New York contained no man who can be considered equal to Dongan in the capacity of either a soldier or a statesman. In the latter year, however, a young man arrived in America, commissioned by the royal government as "colonial agent and sole superintendent of all the affairs of the Six Nations and other Northern Indians," who became in time his legitimate successor. For nearly thirty years he was the greatest power in New York, and his reputation extended far beyond its borders.

His name was William Johnson. He was the son of Christopher Johnson, of Smithtown, County Meath, Ireland, who was descended from a distinguished Irish family. His mother was Anne Warren, daughter of Michael Warren, of the same county, and sister of Admiral Sir Peter Warren, who was second in command, under Admiral Lord Boscawen, at the reduction of Louisburg, Cape Breton. Christopher Johnson was the son of William McShane, afterwards anglicized to Johnson, and of Anne Fitzsimmons, of Westmeath, Ireland.

William McShane was the son of Thomas McShane, and Thomas McShane was the son of John O'Neill, who was a descendant of the O'Neills of Ulster.   Four steps backward, consequently, places William Johnson where he properly belongs as a descendant of one of the greatest of the Northern Gaelic clans.   The Warrens, from whom his mother was descended, came to Ireland in 1170.   This record is taken from the order book of Sir John Johnson, the son of William, and a major-general in the British army during the Revolution.

William Johnson was adopted by his uncle Admiral Warren, and accompanied him to America in 1746, or thereabouts.   From the first he took an active part in the affairs of the province and it was not long before his reputation extended beyond it.   His services were duly recognized by the home government and a baronetcy was the expression of its satisfaction with his management of the affairs committed to his charge.

His power over the Indians of the Six Nations was unbounded. The union effected by Dongan was strengthened and perfected by him.   In the various conflicts occurring from his arrival in New York, until the final downfall of the French power in Canada, he was looked up to as a leader by all the eastern provincials.   He was commander-in-chief of the forces engaged in the expedition against Crown Point, to which soldiers were furnished by the four New England colonies and New York.

In consequence, his form and features became familiar to Rogers, Stark, and others from New Hampshire, who were with him at Lake George and Fort William Henry.   Of him it was said at this period by a well known historical writer, that " he was perhaps the most prominent man in the province of New York, during the decade that preceded the Declaration of Independence."

The sturdy Knickerbocker, Peter Van Shaak, in alluding to him, said, on July 24, 1774, " I own I consider him as the greatest character of the age."

Another writer said of him, "Coming to America at the age of twenty-three, although of good birth and family, he set out to make his own fortunes, and plunged into the forests. He opened a store, bought furs, and traded with the natives. He won their admiration, for he was athletic, brave and true-hearted. He won their confidence, for he always told the truth, and treated them with justice. He was made superintendent of Indian affairs, but he never took advantage of his place to rob his wards.

"He was made a baronet, but he never forgot his humble friends. For nearly thirty years he stood up as the advocate of the Six Nations, compelling a recognition of their rights. The struggle often was severe, for he encountered every obstacle that the greed or avarice of the whites could suggest, but he triumphed, enforced good faith towards the red men, and retained their friendship."

The correspondence between Sir William and the governors of the New England colonies, in those trying times, takes up considerable space in the Provincial records. In considering the present condition of New York, Massachusetts, Connecticut, Rhode Island and New Hampshire, so far as population and resources are concerned, it cannot but be of interest to make a comparison with the situation then. On the authority of Theodore Atkinson, provincial secretary of New Hampshire, in the spring of 1755, that province fitted out a regiment of 500 men for the Crown Point expedition and had them in the woods fully two months before the other provinces had their men on the Hudson river.

In addition, the province supplied its own troops with rations during that period. Colonel Blanchard of this regiment was post-commander at Fort Edward. The New York regiment was also under his command. Colonel Blanchard's regiment experienced hard service, and acquitted itself creditably. Sir William wrote Governor Wentworth, Nov. 4, 1755, and said : " The activity and usefulness of Colonel Blanchard's regiment would prejudice me in favor of any other from your province." In September of the same year a second regiment, numbering 300 men, was raised and placed under command of Colonel Gilman.

In the formation of this expedition the following apportionments were made for the colonies named : Massachusetts, 1,200 ; Connecticut, 1,000 ; New York, 800 ; Rhode Island, 500 ; New Hampshire, 600.

To this division, so far as the provinces of New Hampshire and Massachusetts were concerned, the New Hampshire officials objected.   Their proportion as a rule being one hundred, to Massachusetts, 1,000.   They were informed in reply that Massachusetts had raised four regiments, respectively, for Governor Shirley, Sir William Pepperell, and two for the Nova Scotia campaign, and in justice, this fact ought to be taken into consideration.

New Hampshire retorted in turn, that, while willing to give Massachusetts credit for raising the four regiments named, their province furnished more than half of the men ; a circumstance similar to that which occurred twenty years later at Bunker Hill, where New Hampshire furnished more than one half of the men, and Massachusetts took nearly all the honor.   A compromise was effected by reducing the number from 600 to 500.   It can be seen from this that the provinces of New York and New Hampshire were in close touch in those early days, and the record made in the Civil War by the descendants of the men who fought at Fort Edward and Fort William Henry, was fully equal to that made by their ancestors, as testified to by Sir William Johnson.   To the white settlers around him, he was always a kind friend as well as a wise counselor.

To his subordinates, he was a generous and liberal superior. When appointed to take command of the expedition in question, and while negotiating with the authorities of New Hampshire and Massachusetts for the appointment of white officers for the Indian troops, he insisted that as the service would be very severe, they must receive the same compensation as the officers in the regular service, and required what he called "solid satisfaction" instead of a verbal agreement as a guarantee for the payment of the same. He was surrounded on his estate by many of his own countrymen, and lived in the same style, so far as it could be done, as those of his rank did in Ireland.   It is fair to presume that the Gaelic tongue was not unknown in his family, for one of his daughters was alluded to as " Sheilia," and Sir Guy Johnson, his nephew and successor, was credited with being the possessor of a "genuine rich Irish brogue."

His son John succeeded to his estate and title.   As in the case of Colonel Dongan, Great Britain did not possess on the American continent a more loyal or devoted subject or a more faithful officer than it had in Sir William Johnson, and both, as the records show, in blood were Irish of the Irish.   It was not his fortune to live when the struggle began between the colonies and Great Britain for he died on June 24, 1774.

On Dec. 14, 1774, barely six months from the death of Johnson, the first rumble of the guns of the Revolution was heard. On that date an armed body of determined men, led by Major John Sullivan and Capt. John Langdon, stormed Fort William and Mary, at Newcastle, near Portsmouth, N. H. The garrison was captured, the munitions of war taken, and in broad daylight, the British flag was hauled down, and, so far as New Hampshire was concerned, remained down forever. This was the first overt act against the Royal government in the thirteen colonies. It was four months before the conflict at Concord and Lexington, and six months before the battle of Bunker Hill.

The powder captured at Newcastle was put to good use at Bunker Hill, and many of the men who handled it in both places had served their apprenticeship as soldiers under Johnson during the various Indian campaigns. John Sullivan was the grandson of Major Philip O'Sullivan, one of the defenders of Limerick, who went with his regiment to France after the surrender. His family was one of the most distinguished in the south of Ireland. His father was Owen O'Sullivan, who was a teacher in New Hampshire for over fifty years. He contributed four sons, all of whom became commissioned officers, to the Continental army. Two of these later became governors, respectively, of New Hampshire and Massachusetts. John Sullivan, when the troubles first began, was an attorney with an established reputation and with a lucrative practice. On the authority of John Adams, he was worth ten thousand pounds when he cast his lot with the advocates of independence. He held the commission of major in one of the Provincial regiments.

He had seen no active service, but possessed a good theoretical military education from a close study of all available works relating to the art of war. His ability was recognized by his associates. He was chosen delegate from his town to the first Provincial congress of New Hampshire, and was selected by that body to represent his native province in the first Continental congress which met in Philadelphia in 1774. He was reappointed January 25, 1775. He was the first person chosen to represent New Hampshire in Congress, and his name heads the first roll of delegates to that body. He was one of the eight brigadier-generals appointed by Congress in 1775, and in less than a year from the date of his commission was promoted to major-general.

His first appointment came to him for his leadership at New-

castle, and his promotion for the ability displayed in leading Montgomery's defeated army back from Canada, without, it is said, the
loss of a man or a gun. The Royal government recognized his
ability as it feared his influence. Realizing who was to be held
responsible for the storming of the fort at Newcastle, Peter Livius,
a Royalist refugee, who had been chief justice of New Hampshire,
wrote him in June, 1777 :

"You were the first man in active rebellion, and drew with you
the province you live in. You will be one of the first sacrifices to
the resentment and justice of the government. Your family will be
ruined, and you must die with ignominy." This was the man to
whom Washington turned for a leader when Congress determined,
in 1779, to organize an expedition for the destruction of the Six
Nations. When the Revolution began the colonial authorities sent
delegates to the great council of the Iroquois, to secure, if possible,
their neutrality in the coming contest. There was good reason to
expect it, for the Provincials had fought with them and for them
against the French for years. The confederacy could muster at
this time about 2,000 warriors. The delegates returned, confident
that an arrangement had been effected, but, as subsequent events
proved, any action by the Indians to that end was revoked, and fully
1,200 of them were secured for the British service.

It is not necessary, neither was it the intention, to describe here
the events occurring on the frontiers of New York and Pennsylvania during the years 1777 and 1778. The terrible atrocities
perpetrated on the defenceless settlers by Indians, Tories, British
regulars, and refugees, whose passions were inflamed with hatred
against the struggling patriots, were a disgrace to civilization and a
foul blot on the British government, which sought to crush the
Revolution by such horrible methods. A well-known New York
writer, a descendant of some of those who suffered at Cherry
Valley, while describing the massacres by the Indians said : "But,
after all, I blame much more the English monarch who incited the
fiendish warfare, than the red men, who took his gold and fought
after their fashion."

He could have truthfully added that but twenty years after, similar
deeds were committed without the aid of Indian auxiliaries, by
order of the same government, when it crushed, in Ireland, the
rebellion of 1798.

Many of those who then met their death by the bullet or bayonet, or swung from the gallows, were akin to hundreds who marched and fought under Sullivan in this campaign. A kinsman of one of them, Francis McKinley, who suffered death on the scaffold in Ireland at that time, is now president of the United States. The destruction of the thriving settlement of Wyoming and Cherry Valley, and the devastation along the banks of the Susquehanna, finally brought Congress to a realization of the situation.

That body adopted a resolution on February 27, 1779, authorizing General Washington to take the most effective measures for protecting the people and punishing the Indians, who were allies of the British. The commander-in-chief made no delay. An expedition consisting of four brigades, made up of some of the best troops in the Continental Army, was organized. Their composition was as follows: First Brigade, Brig.-Gen. William Maxwell, four regiments from New Jersey; Second Brigade, Brig.-Gen. Enoch Poor, three New Hampshire and one Massachusetts regiments. Third Brigade, Brig.-Gen. Edward Hand, three Pennsylvania regiments, a German battalion, three independent companies, and a battalion of Morgan's riflemen. Fourth Brigade, Brig.-Gen. James Clinton, four New York regiments and a section of artillery.

The command of the expedition was first offered to General Gates, the hero of Saratoga, as a matter of courtesy, with the request, in case he did not desire to assume command, to turn it over to General Sullivan. The expected happened; it was refused, and the army was placed under Sullivan's leadership. Washington's instructions were, in short, to devastate, and, if possible, destroy the Indian settlements totally, and to capture as many persons as possible. Sullivan had no easy task before him. Difficulties, which are needless to mention here, beset him on all sides. Some of the troops were discontented, almost to the point of mutiny, on account of the worthless character of the Continental paper money paid them; and delays in furnishing supplies were not among the least annoyances of the situation.

Sullivan's energetic disposition and tireless efforts, aided largely by Washington's sympathetic encouragement, finally overcame all obstacles, and on June 14, 1779, his command had reached Wyoming. It is not necessary to describe in detail this campaign, for it is too well known.

Washington's instructions were carried out to the letter. The powerful confederacy of the Indians, for more than a century the terror of the country and the peaceful settlers, was completely destroyed; their villages, orchards, and cornfields were devastated beyond reparation, and the greater part of themselves, not killed or captured, driven forever beyond the Canadian border. No repetitions of Wyoming and Cherry Valley were possible thereafter. For his conduct of the campaign, Sullivan was severely criticised. The destruction of property was cruel and needless, it was said, and the treatment of the Indians not in harmony with civilized warfare.

To these strictures no reply was made. Sullivan heard them in silence, and through life bore them uncomplainingly. He had obeyed the orders given him by General Washington, and time has done him justice. The great state of New York has ever held his name in grateful remembrance. It is borne by one of its counties. Nearly twenty years ago the people dwelling in the valleys through which marched his victorious troops, assembled at Newtown, Waterloo, Geneseo, and Aurora, to celebrate the first centennial of the campaign, which opened up the fertile lands of Central New York to the victors in the War of Independence.

The principal celebration was at Newtown. Among the participants were the governors of New York, Pennsylvania, and New Hampshire, the provinces furnishing full three quarters of Sullivan's soldiers; and Gen. William T. Sherman, then commander of the United States Army. In his address, he said : "Washington gave General Sullivan orders to come here and punish the Six Nations for their cruel massacre in the Valley of the Wyoming, and to make it so severe that it would not occur again, and he did so. General Sullivan obeyed his orders like a man and like a soldier."

As a recognition of what had been done, Sullivan and his troops received the thanks of Congress, and were complimented in General Orders by Washington. At the conclusion of his military service, John Sullivan returned to his native state, where he lived to the hour of his death, honored and respected by those who knew him best. He was its third governor, its first United States judge, appointed by Washington, and the organizer, and for a time commander, of the state militia.

He was attorney-general of his state for years, and was succeeded later in the same position by his son and grandson. His great great grandson, Captain John Sullivan, was an officer in the Thirteenth N. H. Regiment in the Civil War. From the entrenchments round Boston in the winter of 1775 he wrote to the Committee of

Safety of New Hampshire, in response to its request, giving his opinion of the kind of a government we ought to have for he was in favor of separation from the outset. On the line of his suggestions was drafted the State Constitution of 1776, which was the first to be adopted by any of the thirteen colonies, and this at a time when the minds of many, prominent in public affairs, were wavering on the question of independence. There was no intention to give, in this paper, any account in detail of the great events occurring between 1682 and 1779, save what is necessary to bring out as clearly as possible the characters and the deeds of a few men of Irish blood who aided largely in furnishing material for making American history, and as well to give the country which produced them the credit to which it is justly entitled.

The credit due Ireland for them, as well as for many others who have distinguished themselves here in years gone by, has not always been given. Our duty, as members of the American-Irish Historical Society, will be to right this great wrong and never cease our efforts until the errors of latter day historians, so far as they relate to the Irish in America, are corrected. This expedition against the Six Nations is in itself a great illustration of the prominent part taken by men of Irish birth or parentage in the War for Independence and the establishment of the Republic. Of the five generals holding command, the leader, Major-General John Sullivan, and Brigade-Commander James Clinton were born here of Irish parentage. Two of the other three, namely : General Edward Hand and General Wm. Maxwell, were born in Ireland. The fifth, General Enoch Poor, was a native of New Hampshire.

That there were many of Irish blood in the ranks with muskets on their shoulders, the rosters of each regiment will doubtless show. Among them was Timothy Murphy, who was one of the few of Lieutenant Boyd's scouting party escaping capture by the Indians. He was styled by Colonel Hubbley, commander of one of the Pennsylvania regiments, in his diary, as a noted marksman and a great soldier. On his authority Murphy killed, during the campaign, thirty-three Indians. His name is, in consequence, a household word in Pennsylvania and New York. Among those of Boyd's party killed or tortured to death were Lieut. Thomas Boyd, Corp. Michael Parker, John Conroy, William Faughey, James McElroy, Benjamin Curtin and Corporal Calahawn. Col. Thomas Proctor, who commanded the Pennsylvania artillery regiment, and Col.

6

William Butler, of the same brigade, were both born in Ireland.

As a native of Ireland I am proud of the record here spread forth of the deeds of Irishmen and the sons of Irishmen ; and as an adopted son of New Hampshire, I glory in the spirit of independence displayed by the people of that state from the very first, and believe that it is largely due to the liberal strain of Irish blood running in the veins of her sons. Her men were with Johnson at Crown Point, as they were with Stark at Bunker Hill, and Sullivan at Newtown. They never failed to go where duty called, and their service in the Civil War showed no degeneration, for the official records of the Union and Confederate armies give the Fifth New Hampshire credit for losing more men in action than any other infantry regiment in the Union army. Territorially, as well as in population, she does not cut a large figure to-day, but less than a century and a half ago, she sent as many men to Crown Point as the province of New York, and contributed nearly one quarter of the troops for Sullivan's expedition, besides furnishing its commander.

She contributed more than her quota of men to the Continental army, one hundred thousand dollars more than her proportion of money, and possessed within her borders fewer Tories than did any one of the original thirteen colonies. It has often and truthfully been said, "New Hampshire is a good state to hail from." She gave you here in New York one of your most distinguished governors, Gen. John A. Dix, who, when the shadow of secession hung like a cloud all over the country, penned the memorable sentence, " If any man attempts to haul down the American flag, shoot him on the spot." She sent to Massachusetts the only man, Gen. Benjamin F. Butler, who dared to execute the order ; only he thought shooting too honorable and hanged the man Mumford, who dared to disobey it. The record of her sons for bravery and honorable service has been second to none. One of her regimental commanders, Henry Dearborn, who was with Sullivan in his campaign, became afterwards commander-in-chief of the United States army. Another, Maj.-Gen. John G. Foster, was one of the defenders of Sumter, and a gallant soldier of the Civil War. Still another was Maj.-Gen. Fitz John Porter, who, like General Dix, became a resident of New York. The *Kearsarge*, built of New Hampshire timber and manned mainly by New Hampshire tars, met the *Alabama*, and under the direction of executive officer Capt. James S. Thornton, the grandson of New Hampshire's Irish-born signer of the Declaration of Independence, in a fair, open fight, sent the British-built and British-armed privateer to the bottom of the ocean.

In civil affairs, also, her sons have distinguished themselves. She sent to Massachusetts, Henry Wilson; to Maine, William Pitt Fessenden; to Iowa, James W. Grimes; to Michigan, Zachariah Chandler; and to Ohio, Salmon P. Chase. The latter was secretary of the treasury, and the others chairmen, respectively, during the Civil War, of the senate committees on military affairs, on finance and appropriations, on District of Columbia, and on committee on commerce. To represent herself during the same period, she sent to the United States senate John P. Hale and Daniel Clark. The former was chairman of the committee on naval affairs, the latter chairman of the committee on claims.

She contributed to New York, in addition to those named, Horace Greeley and Charles A. Dana. Of those here mentioned, John P. Hale, Daniel Clark, James W. Grimes and Horace Greeley were of Irish descent. Hale was the son of Mary O'Brien. Her father was Wm. O'Brien, the younger of the historic O'Brien brothers of Maine. While acting as second in command under his brother, Capt. John O'Brien, on the Hibernia ship of war during the Revolution, he was mortally wounded in an engagement with an English vessel, and died of his wounds at the age of twenty-two.

The reader of history to-day, if conversant with the events occurring in British and French America from the first settlement down to the outbreak of the Revolution, can see the wisdom of securing the friendship of the Six Nations. For a century they stood as a bulwark between the English and their northern rivals. Without their aid and with their enmity the former could not have prospered as they had; and, as a consequence, would not have been in condition to resist the unjust exactions of the home government. For this reason the names of Colonel Thomas Dongan and of Sir William Johnson ought to be held forever in remembrance in New York and in New England for what they had done in bringing this about. The ways of Providence are mysterious, and to mortals often beyond comprehension.

This powerful confederacy, for so many years the terror of the French, as it was the hope of the English settlements, outlived its usefulness; and its downfall was finally brought about by the men or the children of the men with whom it had been for so many years in alliance.   As in the first instance, the union between it and the English had been effected mainly through the influence of two men of Irish birth, so in the end it was broken forever by an army led by a man of Irish parentage.

If these conclusions are correct, Thomas Dongan, Wm. Johnson O'Neill, and John Sullivan ought to be assigned honorable positions among the pioneers and builders of the United States of America.

MR. JAMES F. BRENNAN,
Of New Hampshire, State Library Commissioner.
Residence, PETERBOROUGH.

JOHN D. HANRAHAN, M. D.,
Of Vermont, Ex-President Rutland County Medi-
cal and Surgical Society.
Residence, RUTLAND.

JOHN F. HAYES, M. D.,
Of Connecticut, Member Waterbury Board of
Education.
Residence, WATERBURY.

WILLIAM A. M. MACK, M. D.,
Of New Jersey.
Mayor of ELIZABETH, N. J.

FOUR STATE VICE-PRESIDENTS OF THE SOCIETY.

THE IRISH ELEMENT IN THE SECOND MASSA-CHUSETTS VOLUNTEERS IN THE RECENT WAR (WITH SPAIN).

BY REV. JOHN J. MCCOY, P. R., CHICOPEE, MASS.

" What have ye brought to our Nation-building, Sons of the Gael ?
 What is your burden or guerdon from old Innisfail ?
 Here build we higher and deeper than men ever built before;
 And we raise no Shinar tower, but a temple forevermore."
 —*John Boyle O'Reilly.*

Just after the Parnell investigation in 1885, when the Irish Parliamentary party came out of the fires of ill will and fraud, and was crowned with the world's credit, John Boyle O'Reilly said to a priest friend of mine, the Rev. Dr. O'Callaghan of Boston, " Father Denis, in the clubs of Boston to-night it is a glory to be an Irishman."

What the hot-hearted O'Reilly said that happy night of exclusive and scholarly Boston may as truthfully be said now of the whole state from the Cape to the Berkshires. Men who most love the Bay state's white flag, with its protecting shield and uplifted arm, are saying it is a glory in Massachusetts to-night to be an Irishman or an Irishman's son ; and they find their reason for this in the heroic showing of her citizen soldiers, who went out from a people that had not enervated under more than thirty years of softening peace, right into the zone of flame and blood at El Caney, San Juan, and Santiago, and bore themselves so gallantly there, and in the other fact that more than every second man in the Massachusetts contingent had the heart within him warmed by the red blood of the fighting Gael.

The Ninth Massachusetts Volunteers, though not entirely as is usually supposed of Irish blood, is yet so nearly so, that at home our people commonly speak of the splendid command, as " the Irish Ninth ; " while the Second, which has won imperishable renown in Cuba, and has awakened the honest pride of every patriotic heart at home, in the valley of the Connecticut, upon the Berkshire hills, and along the quiet Quinsigamond, is spoken of by press and people as the ideal Massachusetts regiment, and as made up from the best blood of liberty-loving New England.   This is true; and it is the best blood because most of it is Irish blood.   Many men appear to think that a man to be of Irish stock must be an O'Sullivan, an O'Brien, a McCarthy or an O'Neill.

Five young men of my near neighborhood went to the war. Their names were Tobin, Nesbett, McCullough, Braziel and Judd. Three, Tobin, Braziel and Judd, were of Irish parents, but American born, and a few months before were boys in my parish school. The two others, McCullough and Nesbitt, were Protestant boys born in Ireland.   Only one of the names would ordinarily be recognized as Irish.   Thinking that what was true in this case might be in others, and that many of the men of the regiment might be of Irish blood, I sought for the facts, believing that the facts when known would make for the credit of our people.   I sought the rosters of the companies, and asked the officers to mark the names of men of Irish blood, and from this excellent source have I the word which I say to-night.

In answer to a letter sent to the captains of companies, I received replies giving me the following figures :

Company A has 11, known to be of Irish blood, and then such names as Allison, Fay, Cardin and Young have not been counted in.

Company B has 33 men of Irish blood, and does not count Devine or Young. Company C has 9 men. Company D has 14 men. Company E has 6, and still we find such names as Doane, Leonard and Blake outside the count.   Company F has 14 men.

Company G has 40 Irish Catholics, 2 Irish Protestants, 2 Italians, 3 Germans, 3 Scots, 2 Swedes, 1 Nova Scotian, 7 French-Canadians, and 17 of old Yankee stock.

Company H has 13 men. Company I, 24 officers and men. Company K has 12, and still we are not counting such names as Verrily, Kelley, Carr and Crehy.

Company L has 13, and outside of that we find Barnes, Carney, Kingston, Norton and Raymond.

Company M has 22, and beyond that 22 there is a Simmons, a Carey, Daniels, Graham, Manning, Riley and Ward—all good old Irish names.

The count I have given you is in most cases that of the captains of companies, as far as received, and is as close as hasty work can hope to be. I am satisfied that with more time and kindly aid of officers and men, I shall be able to make the roll exact and the number of men of Irish stock much increased.

We may note, too, that our count to-night is only of men Irish born or in the first American generation. Many of the best in the regiment have it farther back, as for instance the gallant colonel himself, who writes me, "My great-grandfather was Patrick Clark who came from Ireland."

In the regiment was a young second lieutenant, whom the correspondents praised and the artists pictured, and who drew the eyes of Massachusetts to himself by his cool bravery and marvelous skill as a sharpshooter which he used in silencing the murderous Spaniards who fired from the trees at our wounded. A Spanish mauser ploughed through his shoulder, but he is alive and well, and to-day the gentlest and most unspoiled hero of the war is Lieut. Daniel Moynihan of Northampton.

"I myself am of Irish blood, and Second Lieut. Thomas F. Burke is of Irish blood also," writes the city marshal of Springfield, Henry McDonald, who was captain of Company B.

Of Irish blood, too, is the captain of Company G, who was acting major in the dangerous time, John J. Leonard. So, too, is his soldierly and capable first lieutenant, William G. Hayes. So, too, the second lieutenant, Edward J. Leyden, and Sergeants Scully, Ward, Murphy and Gibbons.

After a long and intimate knowledge of the regiment, and a closer acquaintance with its *personnel* than any other man could possess just now, its colonel, who is high sheriff of Hampden county and known for his conservativeness and thoughtfulness of speech, thus gives me his estimate, and writes it over his own hand: "If we go back for two generations, I think from one half to three fourths of the members of the Second Massachusetts Volunteers were of Irish blood."

This regiment had in the war the gratuitous services of a chaplain whose name is a benediction to-day in the Connecticut valley, Father Fitzgerald, chaplain of the Twenty-second Infantry, U. S. A. He is an Irishman born, and may fittingly be spoken of in this connection, and the world will honor us as well as him. Every man of the regiment, Catholic and Protestant alike, loves him, and can scarcely meet a priest to-day without claiming kindly right to speak

of him.   The gist of the general love is in the words of an enthusi-
astic captain, who writes me in this manner: "The Rev. E. A. Fitzgerald, chaplain Twenty-second Infantry, U. S. A., was as truly
chaplain of the First Brigade, Second Division of the Fifth Army
Corps, comprising the Eighth and Twenty-second Regular Infantry
and the Second Massachusetts Volunteers."

Chaplain Fitzgerald had the respect of all the officers and men of
the brigade for his earnest devotion to their interests and for his
unflinching courage during the progress of the battles at El Caney
and San Juan, where he confronted danger at every turn and amid
shot and shell attended to the needs of the wounded.   He won for
himself a name unequaled in bravery by that of any other chaplain
in the Santiago campaign.   While he was not wounded, his clothing
showed the effect of the mausers.

During the time of disease, a horror of war more trying than
battle, he was unceasing in his labors for the sick, going from one
end of the brigade to the other daily, and reeking with sweat during
the heat of the day.   His cheerful countenance and kindly disposition in his daily work brought comfort and true sunshine to many a
drooping soldier irrespective of creed or race.   Colonel Clark, Second Massachusetts Volunteers, says of him : " One of God's noble-
men," and Adjutant Hall, Twenty-second Infantry, in speaking of
him, said that he was the "salt of the earth."   The officers and men
of the brigade are unstinted in his praise, and his name will ever be
cherished with reverence, respect and good wishes by his comrades
in the Santiago campaign, the rank and file of the unassuming volunteers of the Second Massachusetts.   I am satisfied that a study
of the men who fought on land and on the sea in the war with Spain,
will be highly creditable to our people.

MR. JOHN D. O'BRIEN,
Of Minnesota.
Residence, ST. PAUL.

REV. M. C. LENIHAN,
Of Iowa.
Residence, MARSHALLTOWN.

MR. EDWARD FITZPATRICK,
Of Kentucky.
Staff of the *Louisville Daily Times*.

MR. MICHAEL GAVIN,
Of Tennessee.
Residence, MEMPHIS.

FOUR STATE VICE-PRESIDENTS.

THE "SCOTCH-IRISH" AND "ANGLO-SAXON" FALLACIES.

BY JAMES JEFFREY ROCHE, BOSTON, MASS.

MR. PRESIDENT AND GENTLEMEN OF THE AMERICAN-IRISH HISTORICAL SOCIETY:

A few weeks ago I attended a performance of Sheridan's comedy, " The Rivals," very ably interpreted by a new company of players.

One of them, an excellent performer, taking the part of Sir Lucius O'Trigger, interpolated a " gag," as it is called in theatrical parlance, to the effect that modesty is a word which has no equivalent in the Irish language. It was an interpolation to make the unthinking laugh—but to make the judicious grieve.

For the Irishman is not immodest, not as the word is meant to imply—impudent. Thackeray, the shrewd judge of character, rather condemns the Irishman for his national bashfulness.

The Irishman, at home and abroad, has ever been shamefully apologetic for his race and himself. He, the proudest of mortals, is always depreciating his nation's glory before the world.

The most successful of Irish soldiers, as we gauge success, was Wellington, a man of Irish birth, whose family had lived in Ireland for three hundred years. Yet, if we may believe biography, he always called himself an " Englishman." If he with three hundred years of Irish ancestry behind him was English, is there, on all this continent, such a being as an "American," since not many of us can call ourselves " natives " by much over one century of heritage ?

Quite recently, in Boston, a wise and patriotic Irishman, though not a Home Ruler, said, in presenting his case before an American audience, that his family was not exactly " Irish," since they had been in Ireland only six hundred years !

And the patriotic poet, Doctor Sigerson, of Dublin, talking with my dear lamented friend, the late Alfred Williams, himself a descendant of the great Roger Williams, of Rhode Island, remarked, incidentally, in regard to a mutual friend, that " there was an old feud between his family and mine—but we have agreed to forget it."

The "feud" dated back to the Danish invasion—many centuries ago—when Doctor Sigerson's ancestors fought against Brian Boru! I mention this incident merely to show that it is possible to go back —too far—in the path of genealogy.

Let us be content with reasonable research. If we can prove that St. Brendan was the first discoverer of America, and that a seaman named "Patrick Maguire" was the bow-oar who set the first foot on the strand of the New World, from the boat of Columbus—what of it? Any clumsy forger will come forward at once and declare that Brendan was a "Scotch-Irishman" and Maguire an "Anglo-Saxon," as their names imply. For have they not demonstrated, to their own entire satisfaction, that St. Patrick was not only a Scot, but also a Calvinist—centuries ere Calvin was born? We can afford to ignore the fables of what is, to us, comparative antiquity.

The point that I wish to make is this : I concede willingly, and, I may say, gladly, that the founders of the great Irish-American societies in America, a century or a century and a half ago, were not all of the distinctively Irish race whose faith was Catholic ; but of their nationality there was not the shadow of a doubt. They were Irish, and proud to call themselves such. They were not "Scotch-Irish," nor "Anglo-Irish."

If they belonged, for the most part, to the faith of Grattan and Tone and Emmet, does any true Irishman love their memory the less therefor? Not one! In all the history of this, our poor, crime-stained, unhappy world, there is no nation so free from the sin of persecution for conscience's sake as poor, persecuted Catholic Ireland. Our national saints and martyrs have been Catholic and Protestant. We have never discriminated against any man because of his religious belief, but, rather, have been proud of following our leaders who loved Ireland first.

But we are jealous in claiming our own. We do not want any man to be called "Scotch-Irish" or "Anglo-Saxon," because he did not happen to be of the same faith as Strongbow or Henry the Second, the Catholic invaders who first overran Ireland.

Emmet is ours as much as O'Connell ; Parnell belongs to Ireland as much as Owen Roe. We do not discriminate between Andrew Jackson and Phil Sheridan when we glory in the deeds of Irish-Americans.

We have only one living thought at present. Our faces are set against any alliance with the hereditary enemy of Ireland and of America. That feeling is not Irish alone; it is American. It is born of experience. On our part, seven hundred years old. On the part of America, over one hundred years old. But is not the experience of one century as valuable as that of seven when we have to deal with real things? It ought to be more valuable, even as the injury of yesterday is more stinging than one of seven years ago.

The danger of an Anglo-American alliance is imminent. Its effect on Ireland is comparatively trivial. Its effect on America is immeasurably disastrous. By it we should forfeit the friendship of France, whose men and money made our freedom possible, and of Russia, whose timely aid saved us from disintegration during the Civil War. "Republics are ungrateful," says the old adage. *This* republic must prove, at least, one exception to the rule, if it be a rule.

The American, and especially the Irish-American, who would favor an alliance with England, would be unworthy of Heaven, unwelcome in Purgatory, and lonesome in Perdition.

THE IRISH NAME.

John Jerome Rooney, of New York, read the following beautiful and stirring poem :

> Who fears to claim the Irish name?
> Who will forswear his blood?
> Who holds in shame the deeds and fame
> Of Emmet, Grattan, Flood?
> Their hearts held true through death and rue,
> Through death and sore disgrace,
> Then who 'll forget the boundless debt
> We owe our Irish race?
>
> Ere Learning's sun had found the road
> Above the Eastern hill,
> Her lamp of art and wisdom glowed
> By Irish lake and rill;
> To Scotia's crags it flashed a ray,
> And Albion spoke reply;
> From tower and shrine it beamed benign,
> A beacon in the sky!
>
> Where'er the rights of man were pressed
> Beneath the heel of wrong—
> Where'er, from utmost East to West,
> The helpless sought the strong—

There—there the son of Erin found
    His soul's appointed place—
When Freedom calls, oh, what appals
    The dauntless Irish race.

Within the mighty woods of Maine
    You hear their cheery word;
Upon the boundless Texan plain
    They drive their thundering herd;
They smite the veins of golden ore,
    They gird the earth with plans—
But first and most (their proudest boast),
    They're true Americans !

Then, who would shame the Irish name
    By one ignoble deed?
He—he alone we will not own
    Who would belie his seed!
We claim our line—your blood and mine—
    From out a sacred sod.
Then, hand in hand, we'll take our stand—
    True to ourselves and God !

THE WORK OF THE SOCIETY.

BY THOMAS J. GARGAN, BOSTON, MASS.

The new president-general of the Society, Thomas J. Gargan, said :

GENTLEMEN :—We may congratulate ourselves on the progress which this Society has made during the two years of its existence. On Jan. 20, 1897, in response to a call, signed by thirty gentlemen from several of the states of our republic, forty or more gentlemen assembled at Boston and organized the Society.

Among other statements, the call recited that a number of gentlemen, interested in the part taken in American history by people of Irish birth or lineage, are about to organize themselves into an historical society for the purpose of investigating and recording the influence of that element in the upbuilding of the nation ; also to place the Irish element in its true light in American history. To secure its correct perspective in relation to historic events on this soil is the final aim of the new Society. Its primal object will be to ascertain the facts, weigh them in relation to contemporary events, and estimate their historical value, avoiding in this process the exaggeration and extravagance of poorly-informed writers on the one hand, and the prejudice and misrepresentation of hostile writers on the other.

We further stated, the organization will be constructed on a broad and liberal plan. It will be non-political, and no religious test will be required for admission to membership or the holding of office. Being an American organization in spirit and principle, the Society will welcome to its ranks Americans of whatever race descent who evince an interest in the special line of research for which the Society is organized.

Established on this broad and liberal basis, the accessions to its roll of membership have been most encouraging, as we have now more than one thousand members, representatives in the truest sense of the intelligence and character of the descendants of the

Irish race in America, coming from all parts of this great country, a country which their forefathers, among the early colonists, took an active part in reclaiming from the wilderness and upbuilding into this great republic of the United States, of which we are no insignificant factor. A distinguished man, who wrote nearly a century ago, said that all history was a series of lies, which a few men agreed to consider facts. We all agree that much of the history that has been written in the past has been written by men who have preferred to see things through their prejudices rather than their eyes, and no people have suffered more from the ignorance and prejudice of writers—particularly English writers—than the Irish people.

Unfortunately, many New England writers inherited the prejudices of their English ancestors, and have either deliberately slurred the contributions of the Irish in our history, or have failed to record them. A discriminating and critical public demands that the searchlight shall be thrown upon the dark spots. We are now, in this scientific age, rewriting much of our history and revising our judgment of men. We cordially welcome this new era, confident that when all the facts are carefully scrutinized and critically examined, the Irish in the United States have nothing to fear, but, on the contrary, will gain immeasurably in the minds of all intelligent and impartial men.

In the first volume of the Journal of this Society, papers will be found treating of the early history of the Irish settlers in New England, by Messrs. Murray, Linehan, Smith, Brandon and Sheahan, members of our Society, thus preserving in permanent form facts useful to the future historian. The New England historian has never been noted for modesty in claiming a full share of the glory of our country for New Englanders, or, as he is prone to write it, descendants of the "Anglo-Saxon" race.

While honoring, as they deserve to be honored, the men of Boston and Massachusetts who initiated the War of the Revolution, we are not unmindful of what others have done to make our independence possible, and to establish this form of government of ours, founded upon the doctrine—not of the divine right of kings or of any other ruler, no matter what he may call himself—to rule people, but the divine right of the people to rule themselves, and lest we forget, in our hour of conquest, let us recall again the doctrine of the founders of this government: that all government ought to rest on the consent of the governed. In establishing this government, the Irish element was a very important factor. In the British House of Commons' Report, fifth session, fourteenth Parliament, Vol. xiii, page 303, we find the report of an investigation of the causes of defeat in the war with the colonies—the investigation was held in 1779—Major-General Robertson, who had served twenty-four years in America, was asked: "How are the provincial corps composed, mostly from native Americans, or from emigrants from various nations of Europe?" He answered: "Some of the corps mostly of natives, others, I believe the greatest number, are enlisted from such people as can be got in the country, and many of them may be emigrants. I remember General Lee telling me that he believed half the rebel army were from Ireland."

In Vol. xiii, British Commons' Reports, page 431, Joseph Galloway, a native of Pennsylvania, speaker of the assembly of the colony for twelve years, and a delegate to the First Continental Congress, who became a violent Tory in 1773, was examined for several days by members of the House of Commons. Among the questions asked was: "That part of the rebel army that enlisted in the service of congress, were they chiefly composed of natives of America, or were the greater part of them English, Scotch, or Irish?" Galloway answered: "The names and places of their nativity being taken down, I can answer the question with precision. There were scarcely one fourth natives of America, one half Irish, the other fourth English and Scotch."

The Irish contributed their full share in the War of 1812, in the war with Mexico, and in the war that kept the Union whole. All facts relating to the part borne by them should be carefully collected. In the late war with Spain we have a large field for investigation. From the state of Massachusetts, one fifth of her quota of soldiers were unmistakably of Irish ancestry; the Ninth regiment, Massachusetts volunteers, went into the field as an Irish-American regiment; of the four other regiments, and the large number of sailors, an impartial investigation would show a surprisingly large number of men of Irish ancestry, and what is true of Massachusetts is true of every state in the Union.

Gentlemen, while we are proud of our origin and our ancestry, we do not forget that, above all, we are Americans, that we earnestly desire that all the different elements that go to make up this nation shall be blended together.

This American republic is a mighty crucible into which are

thrown many elements. We have been, and shall be, tested by severe fires; we must separate the dross and the alloy, and the refined product will come forth purified by the severest tests. In our process of amalgamation, we shall eliminate from the different nationalities and races what is gross and bad, avoiding the vices and emulating the good traits and virtues, evolving, as the product of our American civilization, the highest type of manhood or womanhood to be found on the habitable globe.

COL. JOHN P. DONAHOE,
Of Delaware.
Residence, WILMINGTON.

CAPT. PATRICK O'FARRELL,
Of the District of Columbia.
Residence, WASHINGTON.

COL. C. C. SANDERS,
Of Georgia.
Residence, GAINESVILLE.

MR. P. T. BARRY,
Of Illinois.
Residence, CHICAGO.

VICE–PRESIDENTS, RESPECTIVELY, FOR DELAWARE, GEORGIA, ILLINOIS,
AND DISTRICT OF COLUMBIA.

RUSSIA THE FRIEND OF THE REPUBLIC.

BY JOSEPH SMITH, LOWELL, MASS.

At a time when so many Americans seem to be forgetting the history of their country and are fatuously pursuing the political will-o'-the-wisp called "British friendship"; when a society organized to frustrate the unwisdom of foreign alliances,—the League of American Independence,—is flouted and insulted; when the tendency of the dominant political party in the Republic is towards international folly and its motto appears to be "Away with the Constitution," the incident embodied in the appended letter may perhaps remind sane Americans what the true attitude should be to-day towards the Russian and British empires, respectively. The letter in question is an answer to a request made by me on Mr. Jeremiah Curtin,—the scholarly translator of "Quo Vadis" and other works of Sienkiewicz, and himself the author of a number of remarkable volumes on folklore and kindred subjects,—for a paper on Andrew Curtin, his uncle, the famous war governor of Pennsylvania:

WARSAW, RUSSIAN EMPIRE,
December 28, 1898.

Joseph Smith, Esq.:

DEAR SIR:—I have just received your letter of December 5, and hasten to reply.

The time between this date and the meeting of the American-Irish Historical Society is so short that it would be impossible for me to prepare a paper as you suggest; were I free there would be sufficient time, perhaps, but as I am in the midst of important and urgent investigations I can do no more than write you a few lines.

There are many subjects, of course, which would be of interest to the Society and consequently to America. The time has come when men who are of more than ordinary culture, and interested in the history of America and the British empire, are beginning to understand that the political and social development of these two immense

7

aggregations of mankind cannot be studied in a satisfactory and scientific way without a thorough knowledge of the Celtic race. But, as I understand, the Society is occupied specially at present in showing the part which the Irish have taken in the United States both in winning independence for the republic and afterward in building it up ; the wider aspects of the history and career of the Celtic race may be considered at some later time, should the Society so desire.

Among men of Irish descent who have played an important part in American history, the late Governor Curtin deserves a high place. His father, Roland Curtin, when a young man, was informed by governmental authority that he had twenty-four hours in which to leave Ireland. He went to France, and from France to America. He settled in Pennsylvania, and established the first iron works, if not in the state, in that part of it where he lived.

Without entering into the details of the governor's career and the great part which he took in defending the integrity of the American Union, it is sufficient to state here that it was owing to him that Abraham Lincoln received his first nomination for the presidency. Had it not been for Andrew G. Curtin, Abraham Lincoln would not have been president of the United States. Curtin, then governor of Pennsylvania, received Lincoln on his way to Washington at the boundary of the state; together they planned the manner of the president's further journey, by which he escaped, if not assassination, the possibility of meeting men who had it in mind.

When a separation of the Southern states had become a fact, Governor Curtin invited all the loyal governors to meet in conference at Altoona, Pa., where he made the statement to them, that either the war must be carried on in real and deadly earnest with all the powers of the country placed at the disposal of the president, or be dropped altogether. After due consultation the governors decided to offer all the power of the states to the president, and went to Washington to lay that decision before Lincoln ; all went except Governor Bradford of Maryland. After the Altoona conference and the meeting of the governors with President Lincoln at Washington, the war became that reality which won final success.

Governor Curtin's actions during the succeeding years of the struggle were such that he, Governor Morton of Indiana and Governor Andrew of Massachusetts, were pre-eminently the great war governors, the three governors uppermost in men's minds.

Governor Curtin's untiring work on behalf of the soldiers of his state is well known and universally remembered. It is perhaps not so well known that he founded the first Soldiers' Orphans' Home in the United States, that of Pennsylvania.

Some time after the war he went to St. Petersburg, as Minister Plenipotentiary, where he gained the respect and esteem of Alexander II. At his last interview the Emperor presented him a full length portrait of himself. This portrait, painted in oil, was made expressly for Governor Curtin, and was sent to his home in Pennsylvania by the Russian government.

While at St. Petersburg, Prince Gortschakoff took the governor into the archives of the foreign office, and showed him the correspondence which took place between the Emperor Napoleon III and Alexander II of Russia concerning the recognition of the independence of the Confederate states. The Emperor Napoleon addressed an autograph letter to Alexander II, stating that the government of Her Britannic Majesty and his government were ready to acknowledge the independence of the Confederate States of America, and invited him to join with them. To this the Emperor of Russia answered, also in an autograph letter, that the people of the United States had a government of their own choice, and that they were using their best blood and treasure to defend it, and not only would he not do anything to oppose them, but he would reserve freedom of action to proceed as he deemed necessary under the circumstances. Soon after, the Russian fleets appeared in New York and San Francisco.

Governor Curtin read the two letters of the emperors himself, and gave me the contents, the substance of which I have just given.

Very sincerely yours,

JEREMIAH CURTIN.

The potent action of Russia in our hour of bloody stress, which held the hands of England and Napoleon the Little, speaks louder than the strident clamor of the American ingrates, who, forgetting our debt to the Muscovite, would make us the ally of the Briton, the deadly enemy of our friend and of us. Under the Providence of God, the action of Alexander II saved this republic from being torn asunder, and we were base indeed, if in these days we were to turn from the friend of our hour of need to take the hand red with the blood of a hundred helpless races.

THE "ANGLO–SAXON" SHIBBOLETH CONDEMNED.

BY HON. WILLIAM MCADOO,[1] NEW YORK CITY.

Mr. President and Gentlemen:

I came here to-night simply to excuse myself for not being able, as requested, to read a paper which I had promised your committee on " Immigration to the United States from the Province of Ulster in Ireland."

If I am still honored by your Society, I will be glad to read it at a future meeting, with a view to showing not only the influence of this immigration on the history of the United States, but the fact that these immigrants considered themselves Irish without any qualifying clauses, and were so regarded in America, England and Ireland.

Modern political exigencies are playing sad havoc with ethnology. If an Irishman becomes distinguished at home or abroad, in field, forum, market or shop, he is immediately made an Anglo-Saxon; but if he brings up in the police court he is simply a common Irish Celt. The "Anglo-Saxon" race is claiming everything good in the world, and they are bent upon leaving not much of the world for anybody else.

It is very fashionable now to be an Anglo-Saxon, even if you had an Irish father and a Russian mother. If by some divine miracle and phenomenal transformation, all men and women with Celtic blood in their veins could wake up in the morning with some startling demonstration of the fact, such as green hair and yellow eyes, there would be frightful consternation in the ranks of Anglo-Saxondom, even in the great city of New York, and in some of the back settlements into which the first immigrants from Ireland wandered, and where even their names have been transformed.

If one could run all races other than the " Anglo-Saxon " out of the United States it would not be worth England's while to form an alliance with what remained, and she would treat them in that kindly, patronizing, contemptuous way that she does the ultra-loyal Canadians. It needs no learned historian to show us the splendid record of the Irish in America, nor how enduringly they have stamped their highest and noblest racial impulses on every page of American history. Some of their critics sneeringly point to the apparent fact that they have been almost altogether too conspicuous on the field of military action, and more or less lacking in the more patient and plodding ways of commerce and business. They assert that they have attained more in the intellectual diversions and pleasing arts of speech and hand, or in the mere drudgery of unintelligent labor, rather than in those achievements in agriculture and manufactures, which is said to be a marked characteristic of the heavenly Anglo-Saxon.

This is gross libel on the Irishmen of America. We have here to-night at our board, such a thoroughly representative business Irishman who in vast enterprise, splendid achievement, industry, and dogged perseverance, crowned with the highest success, can give the best Anglo-Saxon in the states or England, in any venture from building railroads to managing them, the sharpest competition of his life; and yet Mr. John D. Crimmins of New York is but one of a splendid army of men of Irish birth or descent who are in the very forefront of the great industrial armies as captains and generals of those tremendous forces which nowhere play so important a part as in the United States, and which nowhere have competition among them more keen, nay, more deadly, nor requiring higher talents and greater courage. Why, in this very metropolis you cannot point to any great field of action—leaving out the learned professions in which the Irish race is most markedly conspicuous—in banking, manufactures, commerce, ship-building, and all kinds of industrial and railroad enterprises, in which Irish names do not appear in the directorates, fill the managers' offices, plan and execute the great battles of modern finance. I say we need not speak of the learned professions, because there the keen wit, the bright, sharp intellectuality, wonderful racial adaptability, breadth and grasp of mind, and love of learning, have given them most commanding influence; the same is true of congress, in legislatures, municipal bodies, and in every court-house of the United States. The same is true of the professions of medicine and teaching, and on the press, where they used to say that Mr. Bennett's pay-roll on the *Herald* read like the roster of the Fenian army. At any rate, there is no newspaper office in New York where they have not conspicuous places.

Politically, I claim for them that impulsively, by reason of their history and experiences, they are the very best of Americans. They oppose entangling alliances because they know better than any one else, by reason of a long, bloody, and painful history, how false are international promises, how hypocritical and treacherous even the great and seraphic Anglo-Saxon can be when he once gets the upper hand. Henry II made with them the first Anglo-Saxon alliance, and Cromwell completed it over the graves of murdered millions; over the ruins of castle, cabin, and church, until its climax was reached when the greatest orator of Ireland said that the instruments of government had been simplified to " the tax gatherer and the hangman."

Is it any wonder, therefore, that the Irish element in the United States should be the first to raise the cry of alarm against the plot to make this great Republic in the very hour of its triumph a mere colonial dependency instead of a regnant and invincible nation? For myself I yield to no man living or dead in the quality of my Americanism. I came to the Republic and have received with unstinted hand the usufruct of its noble freedom, its generous institutions, its magnificent and dazzling opportunities held out to him, however humble, who cultivates the civic virtues, is able, industrious, courageous and honest. I yield to the Republic no double allegiance. I stand for the United States in its vast and tremendous interests here and everywhere against all other countries, fatherlands and motherlands, without stint, without reservation or hesitation.

I am proud of my Irish birth, but above all things I glory in my American citizenship. I glory in the Republic and the splendor of its achievements, and I transmit to my descendants for a thousand years as a priceless heritage, that exhibition of magnificent military courage where American arms, in spite of the axioms of military science, in spite of the handicaps under which they suffered, swept in magnificent fury and heaven-born courage upon the fire-fringed hills of San Juan, brave men dying gladly, to catch a glimpse of the blessed banner of the great Republic; ours and theirs the glory of those ships which thundered at Cervera, that lightened the gloom of barbarian Manila, and in those ranks of the marines at Guantanamo, and the heroes at Santiago.

Who of Irish birth or descent can but read the rosters on sea and shore with a discriminating eye, to find his heart aflame with pride at the splendid and unanswerable percentage of men with the hot blood of the Celt and the high patriotism of the American, and who, next to the flag of our common country, revere the fact that they draw their lineage from the historic island across the sea. Surely they were not all Anglo-Saxons in name or race who went with Hobson in his grand and heroic endeavor, which takes its place as outstripping the classic legends of Greece and Rome. Surely no one will deny that the roster call of the marines at Guantanamo and the army at Santiago fairly teems with representatives of the historic Irish soldier.

The Sixty-ninth New York and Ninth Massachusetts would be far outstripped in numbers by the thousands of units scattered throughout our army and navy, regular and volunteer, for wherever the stars of the Republic light the gloom of the battle-field, or war thunders on the deep, there, his breast bared to her enemies, whoever they be, you find the most loyal and valorous Americans in the sons of the expatriated Irishman. While Anglo-Saxon statesmen may quibble in congress and Anglo-Saxon schoolmen criticise in college, "Like lions leaping at a fold when mad with hunger's pang," you will find in the forefront, disdaining quibble and laughing at criticism, the hot tide of valor and chivalry which, proud to be American, is not ashamed to be called Irish. Out upon the bigots who would do it injustice! Defiance to those who would deride its power or minimize its influence!

It asks no quarter in any field of industry, learning, or strife, and is as great in peace as in war. If its more acknowledged glories are of the more sanguinary fields when Mars sows in blood and night what Minerva reaps in the dews and light of the morning, it is not because of any undue pugnacity, any animal ferocity, but because the Irish Celt, threatened with an extermination more cruel than that of our red Indians, with the schoolhouse closed to his intellect, and the church to his conscience, had to take down the stainless and invincible sword of his fathers and become a universal soldier. In every land, from the Shannon to the Tiber, from the Tiber to the Ganges, from the Ganges to the Potomac, and from the Potomac to San Juan; on every battle-field from Clontarf to Fontenoy, from Fontenoy to Waterloo, from Waterloo to Marye's heights, where the Irish brigade climbed steeps made slippery with their blood; and from Fredericksburg to Santiago and Manila, Irish valor has gleamed a star on the pages of universal history.

A MEETING IN PROVIDENCE, R. I.,

On April 19, 1899, to Observe the Anniversary of the Battle of Lexington, Concord and Cambridge.

The Council of the Society held a meeting at the Narragansett Hotel, Providence, R. I., on Wednesday afternoon, April 19, 1899, in honor of the anniversary of the Battle of Lexington, Concord and Cambridge.

President-General Gargan occupied the chair. A communication was read from the Society of American Authors, suggesting that the organization place itself on record in favor of recognizing December 14, next, as a "Washington Memorial Day" throughout the country.

The date mentioned is the centennial anniversary of the death of the *Pater Patriæ.* The suggestion was adopted, and the secretary was directed to communicate this action to similar organizations interested in the anniversary.

Communications were read from the Maine Genealogical Society, of Portland; the Minnesota Historical Society, of St. Paul; the Pennsylvania Historical Society, of Philadelphia; the Presbyterian Historical Society, of Pennsylvania, and the Pejepscot Historical Society, of Brunswick, Me.

A letter was read from the Navy Department, stating that the torpedo boat *O'Brien* would be launched at Elizabethport, N. J., on or about July 1, this year. It was voted to hold the annual field day of the Society at that time and place, and the secretary was empowered to make all necessary arrangements for the event.

Secretary-General Murray announced that since the last meeting four members of the Society have died, viz.: Hon. Patrick Walsh, Augusta, Ga.; Hon. John H. Sullivan and Col. Patrick T. Hanley, Boston, Mass., and Hon. Eli Thayer, Worcester, Mass.

Resolutions were adopted expressive of the great loss sustained by the Society in the death of those four gentlemen, and of condolence with their respective families.

Hon. John D. Crimmins, of New York, personally subscribed five hundred dollars for the general purposes of the Society.

Stephen J. Richardson, of New York, was introduced by Hon. John D. Crimmins, and explained the plan and scope of a projected "Encyclopædia Hibernica." He asked the Council's endorsement of the enterprise, and the same was gladly accorded, after certain suggestions had been made regarding the work.

The draft was read of a proposed circular to be sent to each member of the Society, inviting financial contributions to assist the organization in its publication work. The Secretary-General was instructed to have copies of the draft made and one submitted to each member of the Council for approval or emendation before the circular is finally issued. After the admission of about forty new members the Council adjourned.

RECEPTION AND BANQUET TO THE COUNCIL.

Soon after the adjournment of the Council meeting just recorded, a reception and banquet was given the members thereof under the auspices of the Rhode Island members of the Society. The event took place in the Narragansett Hotel, Providence.

M. J. Harson, of Providence, presided. The line was formed for the banquet shortly after 8 P. M., and proceeded to the dining-room.

Grace was said by Rev. S. Banks Nelson (Presbyterian), of Woonsocket, R. I., a native of Belfast, Ireland.

Among those present, in addition to Mr. Harson and Rev. Mr. Nelson, were:

Hon. Thomas J. Gargan, Boston, Mass., president-general.
Hon. John D. Crimmins, New York, vice-president-general.
Thomas Hamilton Murray, Woonsocket, R. I., secretary-general.
Hon. John C. Linehan, Concord, N. H., treasurer-general.
Hon. Edwin D. McGuinness, Providence, R. I.

Hon. Charles E. Gorman, Providence, R. I.
Stephen J. Geoghegan, New York City.
James Jeffrey Roche, Boston, Mass.
Joseph Smith, Lowell, Mass.
Rev. Frank L. Phalen (Unitarian), Concord, N. H.
Col. John McManus, Providence, R. I.
Capt. E. O'Meagher Condon, New York City.
William H. Grimes, Pawtucket, R. I.
Thomas F. O'Malley, Somerville, Mass.
Stephen J. Richardson, New York City.
Thomas O'Brien, Pawtucket, R. I.
Michael Fitzgerald, Providence, R. I.
M. E. Hennessy, Boston, Mass.
Edmund Reardon, Cambridge, Mass.
Capt. John F. Murray, Cambridge, Mass.
William J. Feeley, Providence, R. I.
Matthew J. Cummings, Providence, R. I.
P. J. McCarthy, Providence, R. I.
Edmund O'Keefe, New Bedford, Mass.
Samuel C. Hunt, New Bedford, Mass.
D. D. Donovan, Providence, R. I.
T. St. John Gaffney, New York City.
Thomas A. O'Gorman, Providence, R. I.
Joseph Manning, Providence, R. I.

Mr. Harson opened the post-prandial exercises with a spirited address, and concluded by introducing President-General Gargan, who spoke as follows:

PRESIDENT-GENERAL GARGAN'S ADDRESS.

FELLOW-MEMBERS OF THE AMERICAN-IRISH HISTORICAL SOCIETY:

We meet to-day on the anniversary of the Battle of Lexington and Concord to attest anew our patriotism, our love, devotion and allegiance to the Republic of the United States of America,—to recall the lessons taught us by the yeomanry of those two little Massachusetts towns, which unknown in history on April 18, 1775, yet before the setting of the sun on the 19th had won for themselves renown, as imperishable as that won at Marathon or Thermopylæ.

One hundred and twenty-four years ago, in the neighboring state of Massachusetts, the first battle was fought to establish the principle that there should be no taxation without representaton; and that all government should rest on the consent of the governed. I will not trespass upon your time by recalling the events which led up to the American Revolution, nor those seven years of bloody and terrible war. We established a government and framed a Constitution founded on universal suffrage, giving a vote to the good and the vicious, the wise and the ignorant. Thus far we have been a prosperous people, because in our Democracy there have been no inequalities of wealth and condition that we believed would be permanent.

We are a composite nation, comprising people from all the countries of Europe with about one seventh of them of English origin; yet when we hear the foolish speeches and read the foolish articles of the minority in reference to Anglo-Saxonism, and blood being thicker than water, we realize the importance and necessity of the work inaugurated by the American-Irish Historical Society, in recalling and recording the deeds of Irishmen and their descendants in America.

We find on the rolls of the minute-men at the time of the Lexington "alarm," over 150 Irish names, and Col. James Barrett of Concord and Dr. Thomas Welsh, who were prominent in the day's battle, were of Irish descent. We find also the name of Hugh Cargill, who, together with one Bullock, saved the town records of Concord from the ravages of the British soldiery. Cargill died in 1799, and the inscription on his tomb records his birthplace as Ballyshannon, Ireland. He came to America in 1774 in time for the Concord fight. He bequeathed to the town the Stratton farm for the use of the poor.

Many of the men who fought on that as on every other day of battle during the Revolutionary War, claimed Irish birth or Irish ancestry. This Society is now endeavoring to collect records, letters and papers throwing light upon the part borne by the Irish race, that we may have our full share of the glory of our country; also that by critical scrutiny and analysis we may discover the truth, giving credit to all. This is a duty we owe these brave, devoted, self-sacrificing men who perilled so much for this government under which we live, and whose benefits we hope to transmit to our posterity.

We are not unmindful of the dangers threatening us at the end of the century from within and from without. We recognize the fact that if the Republic is to be preserved we must call a halt to this awful headlong rush for wealth, holding up some nobler object of ambition. A great writer has said : " The finest fruit held up to earth by its Creator is the finished man." What our country needs to-day is true men ; men who recognize the truth of Plato's maxim, " Justice is the health of the state."

Where can we find in history better types of true manhood than among the founders of our Republic, many of them of our own race and blood ? This country has passed through four wars, and in our time many are filled with the lust for new conquest. May we not well pause on a day like this and see whither we are drifting ? Shall we seek the friendship and alliance of the great robber nation of the world, whose flag is known where rapine and wrong has been done to weak and feeble races, or shall we not rather adhere to the doctrines laid down by the Father of our Country, and " observe good faith and justice toward all nations ; cultivate peace and harmony with all ? "

ADDRESS OF REV. S. BANKS NELSON.

Rev. S. Banks Nelson, pastor of the First Presbyterian church, Woonsocket, R. I., a native of Belfast, Ireland, said in substance :

FELLOW-COUNTRYMEN AND FELLOW-CITIZENS :

It is a rare pleasure to me thus to address an assembly of this character for the first time in my seven years and a half of residence in the United States, my adopted country. Lexington marked the birth of American Independence and the Republic.

The contiguity of Ireland to England accounts for the comparative ease of conquest owing to the small area of the island, as compared with the huge territory of the United States—absorption of Scotland, almost certain to be followed by absorption of Ireland. The religious oppression under Cromwell and William III, might soon have given way to mutual toleration and freedom of conscience had it not been intensified by economic oppression.

Irishmen who know how the English merchant, manufacturer, landowner, mine-owner, and farmer, were combined by common jealousies to suppress competition in Ireland ; how in cold blood, laws were enacted to hinder the development, and paralyze the energies of Ireland, can never naturally be found strengthening, either at home or abroad, a policy which makes for the aggrandizement of the few by the plunder of the many. The early history of our race developed to a remarkable degree, to a degree unattained, I believe, even in continental or oriental societies, the tribal life and the interdependencies of men in social and family relations.

It is not surprising, therefore, that the political genius of our countrymen has been so splendidly manifested in municipal politics. Nor is it surprising again that through jealousy of the eminent success of Irishmen in local politics, men of other nationalities sneer at us as the world's policemen. The jibe of jealousy is the best compliment of character. We are the world's policemen, and that sarcasm has no sting for us which, wagging its head, says, "Irishmen rule every country but their own," for we make bold to say, that no other race, not even the Jew excepted, against such overwhelming odds, suffering poverty so grinding and so protracted, could have preserved its spirit of patriotism through so many and so terrible baptisms of fire and blood. And, grandest triumph of all, we conserved its manhood, its physical and spiritual energy so full, that, instead of a race crippled by conquest, dwarfed by oppression and inapt through inexperience of self-government, the Irishman to-day, whether in the pulpit or the parliament, in the court-house or congress, on the highway or in the home, as a soldier or a statesman, is *facile princeps*, both in the East and in the West.

It is impossible for Irishmen to think of Lexington without the associated thought of the United Irishmen,

" Who fears to speak of '98 ? "

We remember those noble souls who banded themselves in 1798 for "the purpose of obtaining the repeal of the penal laws against Roman Catholics and for the right of the electoral franchise " and who, after the illustrious Grattan's modest reform bill had been rejected, and the tyranny of coercive laws had changed whips for scorpions, gave their lives for freedom of conscience and civil liberty. As an Irish Protestant I claim in the loftiest pride, kinship with the chivalrous Wolfe Tone, the memorable Simon Butler, the daring Napper Tandy, with James Nelson, the owner and fearless editor of the organ of the United Irishmen in Belfast; with McCracken the Presbyterian minister, who was hanged by the neck in Belfast's High street by the British because of his scholarly influence in the cause of freedom, and last, yet ever first, with the glorious, pious and immortal Robert Emmet,—God haste the day when we may be able to write the epitaph for which he prayed in the hour of his sacred martyrdom.

As a Protestant Irishman, I repudiate the policy, and pity the men with my whole soul, who in ignorant bigotry and misguided zeal—in which they were encouraged by their English masters—persecuted hundreds of their fellow-countrymen whose only offense was that they desired a rational measure of civil and religious liberty, and may the day never dawn when any of my countrymen shall be hounded again with the inhuman cry, "To hell or Connaught."

The skies are brightening. "The blood of our martyrs as the seed of liberty is bearing golden fruit." We have the emancipation of the farmer through Gladstone ; the emancipation of the taxpayers, the county councils through Balfour. What a change as compared with Salisbury's statement in 1884, in debate on Mr. Gladstone's franchise bill when Salisbury was opposing the extension of this franchise to Ireland : We warned you when you gave the ballot to Ireland, and were we wrong?

The Irish Presbyterian clergy are, by poorly informed people, supposed to be of the Orange cult. Not so ! There are seven hundred Presbyterian clergymen in Ireland, and I am certain that not half a dozen of these are in actual or tangible touch with the Orange society.

———

The Rev. Mr. Nelson spoke further for the amalgamation of all classes of Irishmen. He dwelt on the misconception of Irish matters here, as illustrated by the Providence *Journal's* statement recently that the government's scheme of a Catholic University in Ireland had been dropped owing to opposition of Orange bigots. Such opposition would have little weight, he said. The principal opposition arose from the attitude of the Presbyterians of Ireland toward the proposed measure,—an opposition which was in no degree influenced by religious prejudice. " I speak what I know," said he. " It was opposed solely on the ground that non-sectarian education is in their judgment the best policy both for the healing of past dissensions and the development of future citizenship in beloved Ireland."

ADDRESS BY HON. JOHN D. CRIMMINS.

Hon. John D. Crimmins of New York referred to the part Irishmen in Pennsylvania and elsewhere took in the Revolutionary War. He also spoke of men of Irish blood in the business world, saying that with their aggressiveness they should push forward and develop themselves in mercantile life. Mr. Crimmins spoke as a business man against an Anglo-American alliance. He said that if the government wanted to expand its territory he was with it, and we were strong enough to manage alone. Speaking of trusts, Mr. Crimmins said that they were largely experimental, and if the people thought they were injurious to their interests they had it entirely in their own hands to rectify the mistake by voting out of office the party that fostered them.

Capt. E. O'Meagher Condon of New York spoke on the enforced emigration of Irishmen and women to the colonies, under the English penal laws.

Joseph Smith of Lowell, Mass., made an appeal for funds to continue the publication work of the Society.

Hon. John C. Linehan gave some interesting historical information regarding Irish settlers in northern New York.

Addresses were also made by Thomas F. O'Malley of Somerville, Mass., and Rev. Frank L. Phalen of Concord, N. H.

By a vote of the executive council, President-General Gargan sent the following despatch to ex-Congressman Vocke, head of the German-American anti-British alliance movement in this country:

The American-Irish Historical Society, at the thirteenth meeting of its Executive Council, expresses its cordial and hearty support and coöperation in the movement of the German-American citizens of the United States against an alliance with Great Britain.

Secretary-General Murray read a number of interesting letters that had been received.

One was from ex-President Andrews of Brown University:

OFFICE OF SUPERINTENDENT OF SCHOOLS,
SCHILLER BUILDING.

MY DEAR MR. MURRAY :—It is very kind of you to remember
me with an invitation to the banquet on the 19th instant, and you
know that I should certainly attend were I anywhere in New England.

These occasions hitherto have been among the most interesting
which I have ever attended.   Give my kindest regards to Mr. Gargan and to any of the other gentlemen attending who may remember me.   Yours truly,
                                        E. BENJ. ANDREWS.

Chicago, April 13, 1899.

From the town clerk and selectmen of Lexington :

LEXINGTON, MASS., April 11, 1899.

Thomas Hamilton Murray, Esq., Secretary-General American-Irish
Historical Society :

DEAR SIR:—The selectmen of the town of Lexington desire to
express their sincere thanks for the courtesy of an invitation to the
banquet to be held at Providence, April 19, next, but regret that our
official duties preclude our acceptance, as the day is always a busy
one for the official heads of the town.

We take this opportunity of returning the compliment, and trust
that on the one hundred and twenty-fifth anniversary, which occurs
next year, your Society will be represented.   We express the hope
that your banquet will be an enjoyable one, and that the day and
the occasion to be celebrated will furnish the impulse to make the
exercises interesting, instructive and profitable.

Your Society name is typical of history on the one hand; exem-
plification on the other.   The history of that day and the events
which followed it represent a struggle with the same country which
it has been our privilege to subdue, to our immortal honor and the
glory of the world, and it is the same country that again is attempt-
ing the perversion of liberty and justice ; and a parallel is furnished
by the identical principles which animate Ireland to-day, which ani-
mated the men of Lexington, Bunker Hill and Saratoga a century
ago ; and it has been well said, that, while Ireland has not yet
gained the jewel of liberty for herself, yet her sons have given freely

of their bone, their sinew and blood to set that jewel in many a shining crown of freedom in other lands than their own.

Ireland has had her Lexington, and the "winter of discontent" in her Valley Forge is slowly melting and warming into the eternal summer. May her Yorktown be not long delayed!

{ TOWN }   EDWIN S. SPAULDING,
{ SEAL. }   GEORGE W. SAMPSON,
                             CHARLES A. FOWLE,
                                    Selectmen of Lexington.

LEONARD A. SAVILLE,
       Town Clerk.

A similar communication was received from Charles E. Brown, town clerk of Concord, Mass. He was prevented from accepting the invitation owing to a home celebration of the "Concord fight." His communication also bore the seal of the town, with the inscription: "*Quam firma res Concordia.*" Letters were also announced from Thomas B. Lawler of New York city, Ex-Congressman Weadock of Detroit, Mich., and from a large number of others.

8

A MEETING IN NEWPORT, R. I.,

ON THE ANNIVERSARY OF THE BATTLE OF RHODE ISLAND, WHICH
WAS FOUGHT AUGUST 29, 1778.

The Council of the Society held a meeting in Newport, R. I.,
on Tuesday, Aug. 29, 1899. The day was the anniversary of
the battle of Rhode Island, 1778, in which the American forces,
commanded by Gen. John Sullivan, " repulsed the enemy and
maintained the field."

The meeting took place at the Aquidneck House, and was
presided over by Hon. John C. Linehan of Concord, N. H.

It was announced that since the last meeting four members
of the Society had died, namely: Joseph J. Kelley of East
Cambridge, Mass.; William Slatterly of Holyoke, Mass.; the
Rev. George W. Pepper of Cleveland, O., and the Rev. Denis
Scannell of Worcester, Mass. Eulogies were delivered on
these deceased brothers, and minutes adopted expressing regret
at their passing away. Several new members were admitted to
the Society.

A subscription of $100 to the publication fund was announced
from Dr. Thomas Addis Emmet of New York. It was stated
that the torpedo boat *O'Brien* would probably be launched
during September or October, the delay thus far experienced
being due to the non-delivery of steel forgings. A communication was read from the builder of the *O'Brien*, stating that he
would be happy to have the Society participate in the exercises of the launching.

Secretary-General Murray stated that the annual volume of
the Society's proceedings is now in course of preparation, and
that the book would be issued at an early day. It will be
uniform in size with the first volume issued, and will contain
many new features and an increased number of portraits.

It was suggested that the Society erect a bronze tablet in

Charlestown, Mass., to the memory of soldiers of Irish birth or lineage who took part in the battle of Bunker Hill, fighting in behalf of American liberty, and a committee, consisting of President-General Gargan, Dr. J. A. McDonald, the Rev. J. W. McMahon, D. D., the Rev. J. N. Supple, Dr. John Duff and Hon. John R. Murphy, all of Boston, was appointed to consider the matter. To this committee were subsequently added James Jeffrey Roche, editor of *The Pilot;* Thomas B. Fitzpatrick, Dr. W. H. Grainger and Bernard Corr, all of Boston; Joseph Smith of Lowell, Mass., and Hon. John C. Linehan of Concord, N. H.

The Council then discussed Newport from an historical standpoint. Its richness as a field for the Society's work was dwelt upon. Many distinguished men of Irish blood who lived there were recalled,—Dean Berkeley, the famous Kilkenny scholar; the Rev. Marmaduke Brown, at one time pastor of old Trinity church; Capt. Wilkinson, a founder of the Newport Artillery; Commodore Perry, son of an Irish mother, who so splendidly defeated the British on Lake Erie, and his brother, Matthew Perry, to both of whom monuments now stand in Newport.

It was also recalled that at the outbreak of the Revolution a member of the Boston Charitable Irish Society, Colonel Knox, later a general, went to Newport and planned fortifications for the place; that many men of Irish lineage came with our French allies to Newport, including Colonel, the Count Dillon; Lieutenant-Colonel Dillon, his kinsman; McCarty, an officer of the French battleship *Le Conquerant;* Lynch, aide-de-camp to the Chevalier de Chastellux, and many others.

After the transaction of routine business the Council adjourned to meet at Elizabeth, N. J., on the occasion of the launching of the torpedo boat *O'Brien.*

In the evening, after the meeting of the Council, dinner was partaken of at the Aquidneck, there being present some twenty-five gentlemen, including members of the Society and prominent Newport residents who had been invited to attend.

Hon. Charles E. Gorman, of Providence, R. I., presided and grace was said by Rev. Louis J. Deady, of Newport.

In addition to these there were present: Hon. Patrick J. Boyle, mayor of Newport (who is also a member of the Society); Hon. John C. Linehan, Concord, N. H.; Thomas Hamilton Murray, Woonsocket, R. I.; J. Stacy Brown, city solicitor of Newport; Martin Fay, Boston, Mass.; Patrick J. McCarthy, Providence, R. I.; Pardon S. Kaull, chief of police, Newport; Dennis H. Tierney, Waterbury, Conn.; Henry S. Tierney, Waterbury, Conn.; Edmund O'Keefe, New Bedford, Mass.; M. E. Hennessy, Boston, Mass., and the following, all of Newport: Eugene C. O'Neill, Alderman J. E. O'Neill, Rev. W. A. Doran, Rev. Philip Cronan, Rev. Fr. Reddy, Frank F. Nolan, Philip F. Conroy, Patrick Nolan, Dr. McElroy, M. A. McCormack, Alexander O'Hanley, William Sullivan and Michael Driscoll.

The after-dinner exercises included an address of welcome by his Honor, Mayor Boyle; a paper by Thomas Hamilton Murray, on " The Battle of Rhode Island, 1778," and addresses by Hon. Charles E. Gorman, Hon. John C. Linehan, Rev. Louis J. Deady, Dennis H. Tierney, Patrick J. McCarthy, J. Stacy Brown and Edmund O'Keefe.

An original letter written by Gen. John Sullivan in 1778, while in command of the Rhode Island department, was read and exhibited. The letter is the property of George E. Briggs, of New Bedford, Mass., and a vote of thanks was extended Mr. Briggs for his kindness in loaning the letter to the meeting.

Letters of regret at inability to attend the meeting were received from Hon. Elisha Dyer, governor of Rhode Island; Hon. R. Hammett Tilley, state record commissioner of Rhode Island; Hon. John D. Crimmins, New York city; and Joseph Smith, Lowell, Mass.

MR. JOSEPH GEOGHEGAN,
Of Utah.
Residence, SALT LAKE CITY.

COL. P. H. CONEY,
Of Kansas.
Residence, TOPEKA.

MR. M. D. LONG,
Of Nebraska.
Residence, O'NEILL.

MR. HENRY E. REED,
Of Oregon.
Staff of the *Portland Oregonian*.

FOUR STATE VICE-PRESIDENTS.

A MEETING IN BOSTON, MASS.,

HELD AT THE HOTEL BELLEVUE, WEDNESDAY EVENING, NOVEMBER 15, 1899.

A reception and banquet under the auspices of the Society took place at the Hotel Bellevue, Beacon street, Boston, Mass., on Wednesday evening, Nov. 15, 1899. ·

It was a very pleasant occasion, and fully equal in point of interest to previous events of the organization.

The reception lasted from 7 to 8 p. m., and the party then formed in line and marched to the dining hall.

Grace was said by Rev. James J. O'Brien, of Somerville, Mass., a son of the late Mayor O'Brien of Boston. Among those at the table were the following:

From Boston: Hon. Thomas J. Gargan, who presided; Hon. Patrick A. Collins, Judge Burke of the Municipal Court, Thomas B. Fitzpatrick, Edmund Reardon, William Doogue, Joseph P. Flatley, Patrick M. Keating, George F. McKellegett, James Jeffrey Roche, J. E. Reardon, Martin Fay, Bernard Corr, Michael J. Ward, M. A. Toland, James H. Devlin, James H. Devlin, Jr., Peter B. Corbett, N. D. Corbett, Michael McManus, John Shea, George E. Lynch and several others.

From other places there were present: Hon. John C. Linehan, Concord, N. H.; Thomas Hamilton Murray, Woonsocket, R. I.; Eneas Smyth and James B. Hand, Brookline, Mass.; James F. Brennan, Peterborough, N. H.; Joseph Smith, Lowell, Mass.; Dr. M. F. Kelly, Fall River, Mass.; John Hayes, Manchester, N. H.; John T. F. Mac Donnell and John A. Mac Donnell, Holyoke, Mass.; W. J. Kelly, Kittery, Me.; John H. H. McNamee, Cambridge, Mass.; Thomas F. O'Malley, Somerville, Mass., and Timothy Donovan, Lynn, Mass.

William Ludwig, the celebrated Irish baritone, was present, as the guest of Thomas B. Fitzpatrick, and rendered several vocal selections during the evening.

The opening address of the post-prandial exercises was by President-General Gargan. In the course of his remarks he said: "As you are well aware the cost of collecting material and publishing is not small; may I not urge upon every member present to help in the important work in which we are engaged, and if you feel you cannot afford to contribute to our publishing fund, get at least one new member to join our Society. We belong to a race that has contributed to the glory of almost every nation. Here in this republic we are not subjects but citizens, either by birth or adoption, with all that title means. We are part of its life and history, and we will be unfaithful to the history and traditions of our fathers if we do not endeavor to preserve in lasting memorials the story of who they were and what they did in the building of this great Republic."

Mr. Gargan called attention to the fact that on Dec. 14, 1899, occurs the centenary of the death of George Washington, for whom, he said, we still feel an affection and an awful reverence, notwithstanding the imperial policy of the government at Washington, which continues dangling with foreign alliances. Mr. Gargan requested the Society to coöperate with other historical associations in commemorating the event.

The paper of the evening was by Michael E. Hennessy, of the Boston *Daily Globe*, his topic being: "Men of Irish blood who have attained eminence in American journalism." It was an able effort, showing much research.

Joseph Smith, of Lowell, Mass., spoke entertainingly, and then offered the following resolutions, which were adopted:

WHEREAS, The American-Irish Historical Society, a body representing all phases of religious and political opinions among members of the Irish race in this Republic, deems it its duty to reaffirm its faith in the principles of free self-government, and in God's Commandment, " Thou shalt not steal," and

WHEREAS, Freedom and honesty are the basis of all pure self-government, and any injury to them in any part of the world must in the end be an injury to this Republic and its citizens; be it

Resolved, That this Society send greeting and sympathy to the embattled farmers of the South African republics; that we express admiration for the courage, faith, and manhood of a race which has thrown down the gage of battle to a rich and powerful aggressor to maintain its freedom; and that it is our earnest prayer that the God of the weak, the righteous, and the brave may crown their heroic struggles with glorious victory and political independence.

Resolved, That any government which has entered upon a project to plunder and destroy two free republics is unfit to be allied to a nation whose basic principles are thus violated, and such alliance, political or moral, would make this Republic a confederate to the infamies thus perpetrated.

Resolved, That the American-Irish Historical Society is inflexibly opposed to any entangling foreign alliances, and particularly to any alliance between the United States and the government of England, which has so frequently sought by war and intrigue to destroy this Republic, and it pledges itself, through its membership, to strive to curtail the political career of any public official, who formulates, advocates, counsels, aids, or abets any such alliance.

Resolved, That copies of these resolutions be sent to the representatives of the South African republics in this country, and to such other persons as the secretary may deem expedient, connected with the executive and senate of the United States.

Hon. Patrick A. Collins was called upon and greeted as "the next mayor of Boston." He said: " I came here to-night because this is a non-partisan gathering. Its object is the rescuing of the truth of history in this country. It is now not unpopular or unfashionable to be known as a man of Irish lineage or to bear the name of Patrick or Michael. There was a time within our memory when it meant condemnation to servility or obscurity. We have leavened the lump of Puritanism."

After further interesting exercises the festivities were brought to a close.

PAPERS CONTRIBUTED TO THE SOCIETY,

During the Year, for Publication.

THE IRISH PIONEERS OF TEXAS.

BY HON. JOHN C. LINEHAN, CONCORD, N. H.

Philip Nolan can well be styled the original "Texan Ranger." He was one of the first, if not the very first, of the adventurous spirits to explore Texas, and whose daring and persistent bravery finally added the Lone Star state to the American Union. His romantic career and tragic fate, it is said, furnished a name for Edward Everett Hale's "Man Without a Country."

He was of direct Irish origin and a citizen of the United States. He left Natchez, Miss., in the summer of 1797, ostensibly to buy horses, but in reality to reconnoitre and survey the country. A second trip was made in 1800. He was accompanied by thirty armed men. The viceroy of Mexico, looking on his movements with suspicion, issued orders to arrest any foreigners who might enter the Spanish province.

He had been informed that a number of them had gone into Texas, and that Philip Nolan was considered the most dangerous among them; that he was authorized by General Wilkinson to reconnoitre the country, and make maps of it, and that it was of the utmost importance that he be captured and disposed of. In accordance with these instructions an expedition was fitted out to secure him.

It was composed of one hundred men, sixty-eight of whom were regulars, well armed, and possessed of one field piece. It started in pursuit on March 4, 1801. Two weeks later they reached the point where he had entrenched himself on the bank of a river. The Spanish commander thereupon sent a messenger, "Mr. William Barr, an Irishman," who had joined his command as interpreter, to

HON. JOHN J. LINN,

Born in County Antrim, Ireland, 1798; a pioneer
settler of Texas; was a member of the Texan
Congress; author of "Reminiscences of Fifty
Years in Texas."

summon Nolan to surrender. Nolan and his men determined to fight, and at daybreak next morning, began the engagement by firing on the Spaniards. The contest lasted until nine o'clock a. m., when Nolan was struck and killed by a cannon ball. His party then surrendered.

The stream on whose bank he was killed is known as Nolan's Creek, and Nolan county, Texas, was named in his memory. Three of his associates, judging from their names, were of his blood, namely, Michael Moore, William Dandlin and Simon McCoy. John Henry Brown, author of the History of Texas, quotes the following from a Mr. Quintero : " The diary kept by Nolan, and many of his letters which are in my possession, show conclusively that he was not only a gallant and intelligent gentleman, but an accomplished scholar. He was thoroughly acquainted with astronomy and geography. He made the first map of Texas, which he presented to the Baron Carondelet, on returning from his first trip in 1797."

He was followed four years later by Capt. Zebulon Pike. A third invasion was that of the party led by A. W. Magee, a native of Massachusetts, a graduate of West Point, and an ex-officer of the United States Army. This expedition like that of Nolan's ended badly for those engaged. Seventy or eighty of them who were captured by the Spaniards were shot and buried in one grave. They had rendered material aid, however, to the Mexican patriots in their struggle for independence.

In 1822, thirteen years after their death, the governor of Texas, under the new republic of Mexico, collected their bleached bones, and had them interred with military honors. A tablet on an oak tree, near the place of sepulchre, bore the inscription : " Here lie the braves who, imitating the immortal example of Leonidas, sacrificed their fortunes and their lives contending against tyrants." It is not possible to make an estimate of the number in this expedition who were, like Nolan and Magee, of Irish origin, as their names are not given, but that there were many, the record of those who followed proves. From 1813 to 1819 others followed in the steps of Nolan and Magee.

Among them were the parties led by Perry and Young. The latter had served in the United States Army during the war of 1812. He took an active part in the Mexican war of Independence, and lived to see them throw off the Spanish yoke. Perry was not so fortunate. In his last fight with the enemy every man in his command was killed, and preferring death to capture, he took his own life, blowing out his brains. Another expedition left Natchez, the headquarters of the ill-fated Nolan, on the 17th of June, 1819. It numbered three hundred men, and was under the command of Dr. James Long, a native of Tennessee, and surgeon in Carroll's brigade in the war of 1812 and 1815.

After suffering untold hardships, this, like the others preceding it, failed to accomplish its purpose, and the survivors, not prisoners, returned to the state. Later, Long made a second attempt. His party consisted of fifty-two men ; the names of thirty-two are known, among them Lieutenant Eagan from New York, "Dr. Allen, an Irish surgeon, and Capt. John McHenry, an Irishman." Of the latter the historian quoted says :

" It was my fortune in early life to be a neighbor and enjoy the sincere friendship of that true-hearted son of Ireland, Capt. John McHenry. . . . He was a man utterly incapable of falsehood or deception, a true patriot, and a friend to public and private virtue.. . . . He was born in Ireland in 1798, and arrived at New Orleans in 1812. He took part in Long's expedition, and, returning in 1822 with one hundred and fifty others in the sloop-of-war *Eureka,* he participated in an expedition organized in aid of the Revolutionists in South America. A year or so later he entered the trade between New Orleans and the Texas coast, as owner and commander of a schooner. In 1826 he settled permanently on the Lavaca river, where he reared a family and lived until his death, passing through the Revolutionary and Indian wars as a brave man and an honorable citizen. He died honored by those who had known him for half a century."

Long's expedition met the same fate as those preceding it. He and his men were captured. Eagan died in prison, and Long, who was taken to the City of Mexico, was shot dead by a soldier, said to be an assassin hired for the purpose. The time had, however, arrived when largely to the enterprise, tact and bravery of the descendants of the men who had established the United States government, Texas was thrown open to all who desired to create new homes on its broad expanse. The leader in this new and successful colonization enterprise came from far-off New England.

His name, now a household word in Texas, was Moses Austin. He was born in Connecticut. Early in life he went to Philadelphia, later to Virginia, and still later to Missouri, or what is now known as Missouri. While here his adventurous nature was attracted toward Texas by the reports of Nolan, Magee and their successors. His ventures heretofore had been failures, and he became interested in the founding of a colony in the territory coveted by all who had seen or heard of it. With this object in view, and desirous of securing permission from the proper authorities, he made a journey to San Antonio de Bexar in December, 1820.

His residence in Missouri, then under the dominion of Spain, familiarized him with the language and customs of its people. His mission was successful. He returned to his home, but like Moses, he was not destined to see the promised land, for he died shortly afterwards, transmitting to his son, Stephen F. Austin, the duty of executing his plans.

His application for his grant of land for a colony had been approved by the Spanish power, about eight months before its fall, and the fact that this concession had been made, while the memories of the invasions of Nolan, Magee and Long were still fresh, proves that Austin was a man of tact and resources. His daughter had married James Bryan, so that here in the beginning, the Saxon and the Gael intermixed. Three sons, the product of this union, William J., Moses A., and Hon. Guy M. Bryan, have been among its most honored citizens.

Not only was Austin's application for land for a colony granted, but a special commisioner was sent to the United States with instructions to conduct the first band of immigrants into the country. Stephen F. Austin returned with the commissioner to secure a transfer of the grant made to his father, and was accompanied by fourteen persons, all of whom became settlers. Of these were Erwin, Barre, Beard, Belew and Dr. James Hewitson. The latter was born in Ireland, the others bear Irish names.

The overthrow of the Spanish power and the establishment of the Mexican government, a year later, did not affect the concessions made to Austin. They were confirmed by the new government, and the grantee's powers to colonize were increased. Others, as well as he, were granted similar privileges. Each head of a family was to receive four thousand four hundred and twenty-eight acres of land, and one thousand seventy-six acres were assigned to each single man.

It will not be amiss to write that during the period mentioned, namely, the struggle for Mexican independence, General Count

O'Donoju was in command of the Royal forces, and that his failure to bring about a reconciliation between the Revolutionists and his government occasioned his death, which occurred in the city of Mexico, July 5, 1821. Among the original three hundred colonists led by Austin into Texas were the following : Martin Allen, John and Edward R. Bradley, James Beard, Charles Breen, William Barrett, James Cummins, John Cummins, William Cummins, Morris Callahan, David Fitzgerald, Isaiah Flanagan, David Fenton, Charles Garrett, C. S. Corbett, Daniel Gilliland, John W. Moore, Michael Goulderich, William Holland, Francis Holland, Samuel Kennedy, John Kelly, Alfred Cannon, James Kerr, James Lynch, Nathaniel Lynch, Robert James, William Millican, William McWilliams, David McCormick, James McCoy, James McNair, John McNeil, Luke Moore, Daniel, John G. and Geo. W. McNiel, Arthur McCormick, John McFarland, John McClosky, Thomas McKenny, Stirling and Pleasant D. McNeil, Frederick Rankin, Elijah Rourk, Patrick Reels and John McCormick.

Among others to whom grants of land were made were "James Power and James Hewitson, 'Irishmen,' for two hundred families on Arransas Bay." This colony was known as "Refugio," and the grant was made on June 11, 1828. Another was to "John McMullen, and Patrick McGloin, 'Irishmen,' dated August 17, 1828, for two hundred families on the Nieces river." This colony was known as "San Patricio."

Both were composed mainly of natives of Ireland, with a sprinkling of Americans of their own blood and of mixed origin. The members of these two colonies took an active part in the movements which ended in the establishment of the Texan republic, and the ultimate annexation of Texas to the American Union. This tribute is paid them by John Henry Brown in his history of Texas, in connection with what he has written of the other colonies :

" The colony of DeLeon had increased considerably by the incoming of a good class of Mexicans, and quite a number of Americans, including several Irishmen and their families from the United States, the younger members being natives of that country, and among whom were the veteran John McHenry, a settler since 1826 ; John Linn with his sons, John J., Charles, Henry and Edward Linn, and two daughters. Subsequently, the wives of Major Kerr and John A. Moody, Mrs. Margaret Wright, Joseph Wright and others.

"From 1829 to 1834 the colonies of Power and Hewitson, with headquarters at the Mission of Refugio, and McMullen and McGloin, of which San Patricio was the capital, received valuable additions in a worthy, sober, industrial class of people, chiefly from Ireland, a few of Irish extraction born in the United States, and others who were Americans.

"They were more exposed to Mexican oppression than the colonists further East, and equally so to hostile Indians. Twenty-six of these colonists signed the Goliad Declaration of Independence, Dec. 20, 1835. Four of them signed the regular declaration of Texan independence, March 2, 1836, and fourteen of them fell in the slaughter of Fannin's men, March 27, 1836. In the foot-note below is given a partial list of these bold and open-hearted pioneers in reclaiming the southwestern portion of our territory."

Those mentioned in the foot-note are as follows: Signers of the Goliad Declaration of Independence—Morgan Bryan, John Dunn, Spirce Dooley, James Elder, E. B. W. Fitzgerald, Peter Hynes, Timothy Hart, Thomas Hansom, J. B. Kirkpatrick, Michael Kelly, Walter Lambert, Charles Malone, Edward McDonald, Hugh McMinn, Thomas O'Connor, C. J. O'Conner, Patrick O'Leary, Michael O'Donnell, James O'Connor, John Pollan, William Quinn, Dr. Alexander Lynch, Edward Quirk, John Shelly, Edward and James St. John and John W. Welsh.

Those butchered with Fannin's men were—Matthew Byrne, Daniel Buckley, Matthew Eddy, John Fagan, John Gleason, John James, John Kelly, John McGloin, Dennis McGowen, Dennis Mahoney, Patrick Nevin, Thomas Quirk, Edward Ryan and Capt. Ira Westover.

Signers of the regular Declaration of Independence—Edward Conrad, James Power, David Thomas and John Turner.

Others of the Irish colonies of Refugio and San Patricio who had distinguished themselves otherwise in the cause of Texan independence were—Lewis Ayers, Elkanah Brush, John Bowan, Michael Cahill, John Coughlan, Robert Lawrence, John Carlisle, Festus Doyle, William Donahue, Benjamin Dale, Patrick Downey and his sons Francis, Thomas, Patrick, Jr., John and James Downey; Patrick Fitzsimmons, Nicholas Fagan, William Gamble, John Hefferman, Robert Hern, William Hewes, Dr. James Hewitson, James Hewitson, Jr., John Hynes, John Hart and his sons Patrick, John and Luke Hart; Thomas Hennessy, Timothy Hoyt, Charles Kelly, John Keating, John

Malone, Thomas Mullen, Patrick, Edward and James McGloin, Malcolm McAuley, John McMullen, Martin O'Toole, Daniel Driscoll, James O'Connor, Daniel and John O'Doyle, Edward Parry, James and Martin Power, Patrick and John Quinn, Michael Kelly, William Redmond, William St. John, Peter, John and Thomas Scott and John Toole.   The entire number of names given is one hundred and two.

The historian adds: " Yet in a time of political frenzy in 1855, it was charged that these colonists were not true to Texas in the Revolution of 1835-'36.   It was the privilege of the author of this work to crush the infamous slander by presenting the preceding facts, and many others attesting their fidelity in suffering, heroism, and in death, till the republic became the state of Texas in 1846." The malignant slanders were repeated a few years ago when the patriotism and loyalty of the Irish in the Union army were assailed by the legitimate successors of the Know Nothings of 1855—the A. P. A.'s of 1895.

The entire number of signers of the Goliad Declaration of Independence, which was adopted more than two months before the signing of the general Declaration of Independence, was ninety-one. Of this number, twenty-seven, whose names have been given, were of the Irish colonies of Refugio and San Patricio.   In addition to these, the following names, Irish in appearance, from the other colonies, were also appended to the Declaration : George W. Welsh, John Shelly, Robert McClure, Andrew Devereau, George W. Cash,— making thirty-two in all, or over a fraction of one third of the whole number of signers.

Among those who went into Texas with DeWitt's colony in 1828 were Maj. James Kerr, Arthur and Squire Burns, George Blair, Matthew Caldwell, John Daly, John Duncan, John Fennell, Michael Gillan, Daniel, John, Joseph, Jesse, John, Jr. and Samuel McBay, Stephen Morrison, George Monoghan, B. D. McClure, John A. Neill and James B. Patrick.

"Among the early most worthy settlers at the extreme northwestern corner of Texas, on the Red river, was Collin McKinney." He was the oldest man who signed the Texan Declaration of Independence, being seventy when he affixed his name to it.   Capt. Thomas William Ward went to Texas, in 1835.   He was a native of Ireland and at the outbreak of hostilities in Texas was a member of the " New Orleans Grays."   He commanded an artillery company at the capture of San Antonio, where he lost a leg.

He lived in Texas until his death in 1872, honored and respected by his fellow-citizens. He had held honorable positions in the gift of both state and nation. Elijah Rourk went from North Carolina to Texas in 1821. He was one of the pioneers of the state. While in company with David McCormick and two others, on his way to San Antonio to market a drove of hogs, he was killed by Indians, Dec. 25, 1829. Rourk's son, who was with him, and McCormick made their escape. The former died as late as 1892. He had served in the War for Independence, and in himself was a living reminder of the sufferings of the early colonists of Texas.

William M. Logan went to Texas in 1826, one of a family which has given eminent men to the nation for over a century. With him were several of the Moore family. In an Indian fight reported by the celebrated James Bowie, Dec. 10, 1831, he mentions for bravery the names of ten persons; three of them were Matthew Doyle, Daniel Buchanan, wounded, and Thomas McCaslin, who was killed.

In an encounter with the enemy at Anahuac in 1832, the following were mentioned: Thomas H. Brennan, James S. McGahey and Edward Miles.

"The good Father Muldoon" has mention in an account of the battle of Velasco, June 26, 1832. He "was an Irish priest, resident of Mexico, and held in high esteem by the colonists." He is also spoken of in the prison journal of Stephen Austin. Santa Anna gave him permission to visit Austin while the latter was in prison. He is also mentioned in the Quarterly of the Texas Historical Society of January, 1899, and a toast given by him at a banquet held in Anahuac is printed therein. It showed his sympathies for the colonies, although not one of the colonists, and was as follows:

> "May plow and harrow, spade and tack,
> Remain the arms of Anahuac,
> So that her rich and boundless plains
> May yearly yield all sorts of grains.
> May all religious discords fall
> And friendship be the creed of all.
> With tolerance your pastor views
> All sects of Christians, Turks, and Jews.
> I now demand three rousing cheers,
> Great Austin's health, and pioneers."

Previous to the battle of Velasco, Father Muldoon was allowed to visit the Mexican commander, and authorized to adjust the affairs in conflict. His mission was a failure, the enemy deeming itself strong enough to secure its end, a mistaken idea ; after a contest in which two thirds of the Mexicans were killed or wounded, the survivors surrendered to the Americans.

Among those who are named as participating in the engagement were John G. Stirling, Pinkney McNeal, George B. McKinistry and Andrew Scott. Among the delegates to the first convention held in Texas, in October, 1832, were William D. Lacy, George W. McKinistry, James Kerr, Hugh McGuffin, Joseph, Samuel and James Looney, John Connell, Jacob Garrett, George Butler, John M. Bradley and James Morgan.

A second convention, held on April 1, 1833, had among its members George Butler, John M. Bradley, Jesse Grimes, Jacob Garrett, Sam Houston, James Kerr, John H. Moore, James Morgan, William McFarland and B. D. McClure.

Mention is made of William Donoho in connection with the massacre of the survivors of the Grant colony by the Indians. He was a merchant in Santa Fé.—" One of those great hearted, sympathetic men who honor humanity." His children are credited with being " the first American natives of the ancient town of Santa Fé." He was from Missouri. He is credited with being the medium through whom three English ladies were released after being captured by the Indians, survivors of an English colony in Texas, and whose sufferings while in possession of the Indians were terrible. He was born in Kentucky. He died in Clarksville, Texas, in 1845, "lamented as a true son of Kentucky." He is spoken of in the highest terms in Brown's History of Texas and the Texas Scrap Book.

Daniel McCoy has mention in an account of a fight with the Indians at San Marcos in the spring of 1835, and with him were Matthew Caldwell and B. D. McClure. In another fight with the Indians near the Brazos, at Washington, in July, 1835, a detachment of three companies was commanded by Col. John H. Moore. The adjutant was Joseph C. Neill, and others in command were Capt. Robert M. Coleman and Capt. Coheen.

Among those in attendance at the " Navidad and Lavaca meeting on July 17, 1835," were William Millican and Major James Kerr, " the veteran John McHenry who had fought for liberty in South America," and was with Long and suffered imprisonment with Millan and Austin ; Patrick Usher, Coleman, Loony, McNutt, and Scott. Among those who made a reputation in Texas in those early days were three brothers, Patrick C., William H. and Spencer H. Jack. They were the sons of Capt. Patrick Jack of North Carolina.

Captain Jack was the messenger selected by the Mecklenburg Convention, held in May, 1775, to convey the Declaration of Independence adopted by it to the Continental Congress in session at Philadelphia.

In a movement to prevent the taking away by the Mexicans of a four-pounder left with the people of Gonzales for protection against the Indians, the following participated: John H. Moore, Matthew Caldwell, James Kerr, John J. Linn, and representatives of the McClure and McCoy families. Mrs. Margaret Linn took an important part in the affair, and this tribute is paid her by the writer quoted: "Pause a moment, reader, to reflect that this note was written to a young bride, not yet a mother, educated, refined and accomplished, as many were whose graces gave tone to society in that period of danger and excitement."

Mrs. Linn's duty was to forward an important despatch to a point where aid could be procured. These were exciting times in Texas. The storm which was to end at San Jacinto was brewing, and the settlers were constantly on the alert, in order to be prepared for it. A party of forty men captured the Mexican fort, Lipantitlan, twelve miles from San Patricio. Major James Kerr, John J. Linn and James Power distinguished themselves in this affair. No doubt there were many of their kindred with them whose names were not given. It was a gallant and daring enterprise, and occurred on the 5th of November, 1835.

It prevented the three men named from attending the consultation which took place at San Felipe on the third of the same month, but "it caused the release of several Irish prisoners held by the Mexicans."

Some time after this event, for reasons which he deemed sufficient, Stephen F. Austin removed the commander of a company, many of which had aided in the capture of this fort. The company adopted a resolution against a change, every man but the captain, Dimmitt, signing it, sixty-seven in all. Among them were: James O'Connor, George McKnight, James Duncan, Edward Quirk, Spirse Dooly, Robert McClure, Thomas O'Connor, Thomas Brien, Michael Riley, Andrew Devereau, J. B. Dale, Michael O'Donnell, Chas. Malone, Thomas M. Blake, J. L. McKenzie, Morgan Brien, Martin Lawlor, William Cumming, Patrick O'Beary, William Quinn,

9

John Bowan, Jeremiah Day, Patrick Quinn, John Dunn, Thomas Todd and James Fagan.

A company, known as the New Orleans Grays, arrived at Brazoria to aid the Texan cause. They numbered sixty-two. Among the members were Chas. W. Connor, John Connell, Michael Cronican, Geo. H. Gill, William Harper, " of Ireland ; " Nicholas Herron, Francis Leonard, Dennis Mahoney, M. B. McIver, John D. McLeod, John D. McNeill, James Nowland, Christopher O'Brien, Richard Ross, Thomas William Ward, Allen O'Kenney,—sixteen in all. Of these, Gill, Harper, Kenney and Mahoney were butchered with Fannin.

Among the signers of resolutions declaring for independence at Columbia, Dec. 25, 1835, were John Sweeney and P. R. Splane. Among those massacred with Fannin, and not mentioned thus far, were George McKnight, James Fagan, John Donoho, James McDonald, Robert Owens, R. R. Rainey, Lieut. John Grace (brother of subsequent Bishop Grace of Minnesota), James Logan, John O'Moore, John S. Scully, James McCoy, Moses Butler, J. M. Powers, Michael Carroll, Dominick Gallagher, Martin Moran, Patrick Osborne, J. B. Murphy, J. H. Moore, John McGowan, Cornelius Rooney, Edward Fitzsimmons, John O'Donnell, —— Glennan, George W. Coghlan, Lieut. J. B. Manomey, James Kelley, William McMurray, Z. O'Neill, Arthur G. Foley, D. Moore, Alfred Dorsey, J.W. Duncan, John Kelly, W. E. and James Vaughn and William Quinn.

S. Tucker Foley and James Foley, brothers of Frank G. Foley, were killed by the Indians. Among the few who escaped the Fannin butchery were Capt. James H. Callahan, Peter Griffin, J. McSherry, Nicholas Waters, W. Welsh, A. M. Boyle, Capt. Wm. Sherlock, William Brennan, J. H. Neely, N. J. Devenny, Bennett Butler and William Murphy.

During General Houston's march he encamped at the ranch of a Mrs. McCurley. The historian writes that the condition of affairs just before the battle of Jacinto was such that the hopes and fears of the whole American population west of the Trinity gathered around General Houston.

Many of those who inhabited the western portion were without means of escape. Among the number were many of the Irish families of Refugio and San Patricio, still weeping and wailing for their sons and brothers who had been massacred with Fannin. The wife, sister and first-born child of John J. Linn were of the number.

The battle of San Jacinto occurred on April 21, 1836. Among those who participated of known Irish origin, or bearing Irish names, were the following,—Gen. Sam Houston, Col. Robert M. Coleman, Surgeon J. P. T. Fitzhugh, Lieut.-Col. J. C. Neill, John M. Wade, Willis Collins, J. Neil, E. Nixon, Jacob Duncan, W. B. Sweeney, Lieut. Robert McClusky, Daniel O'Driscoll, and Cassidy, Flynn, Farley, Montgomery, O'Niel, Sullivan, Moore, Hogan, Callahan, Capt. Richard Roman, McStea, McAllister, Morgan, McNeill, Donan, Gill, Adjutant Nicholas Lynch, Griffin, Hayes, Welsh, Magill, Cunningham, Herron, Conley, Dempsey, Blahey, Connell, McClelland, Bryan, Duncan, Maher, O'Conner, Connor, McNeill, Malone, McLaughlin, Hagan, McCrabb, Sennatt, O'Connor, Ryan, John, Lewis and Stephen T. Foley; Waters, Rainey, Cannon, Gentry, Dunn, Adjutant B. McNelly, Kincannon, Mitchell, McCoy, McLinn, Logan; Patrick Carnell, McManus, McFadden, Orr, Cornelius Devoy, Duffy, Cole, Lieut. David Murphy, Bradley, Boyd, Barr, Sweeney, Gallaher, McGay, McCormick, Hayes, Kenyon, Brennan, Corry, Capt. Thomas McIntire, Gill, Boyle, Campbell, McCorley, Madden, Montgomery, John and Andrew Ferrall, McMillan, O'Bamion, Capt. Bryan, Irvine, Clarke, McGary, Maxwell, McGowan, Hughes and Hannan.

When Santa Anna was captured and brought before General Houston a youth named Bryan, nineteen years old, acted as interpreter. Among those butchered by the Indians pending the siege of the Alamo, was the Dougherty family, but two members escaping. Of another party attacked about the same time, five of the males were killed. Five persons more, three of whom were females, were taken away by the Indians. One of the latter was rescued in 1860, after being a captive nearly twenty-five years.

Her recovery was made by Capt. Lawrence Sullivan Ross, commanding a company of Texas Rangers, later a general in the Confederate army, and still later governor of Texas. The counties of Refugio and San Patricio had been almost depopulated by the ravages of Mexicans and Indians. In consequence, the scattered exiles from these localities wherever they might have been, were allowed to vote for representatives and senators to represent their county in the first congress of the Texan republic.

This congress met on the third of October, 1836. Sam Houston had been chosen president, receiving 5,119 votes of a total of 6,640. The two Irish colonies were represented in congress as follows : Refugio, Elkanah Brush ; San Patricio, John Geraghty.   The colony of Victoria had quite a sprinkling of Irish settlers, among them the family of the McLinns.   It was represented by Richard Roman.   It is not at all unlikely that this may originally have been the name Ronan, a common Irish name.   Sabine sent John Boyd.   Collin McKinney represented Red River, and Jesse Grimes, Washington.   Among the judges appointed by this congress were W. H. McIntire, Massillion Farley, Patrick Usher, Bartlett Mc-Clure, Geo. B. McKinstry, John Dunn, John Turner (the two latter were for Refugio and San Patricio), William McFarland and John McHenry.

Stephen F. Austin died in December, 1836.   "Among the touching episodes connected with the death of General Austin was the presence with him in the hour of death of perhaps his oldest friend, Major James Kerr, of Lavaca, who had served with him in the territorial legislature of Missouri, twenty years before, and who had ever been his warm and confidential friend in Texas."   What this friendship meant to Austin none but the readers of Texan history, or those who took part in the stirring events of the period, can determine.

Among the commanders in the new Texan navy was Capt. J. D. Boyland, and among the members of the second congress were Patrick J. Jack, James Power, John Boyd, John J. Linn, Collin McKinney, Thomas H. Brennan and John Dunn.   In the third congress were Holland Coffee, James Kerr, Richard Roman, Benjamin Odlum, John J. Linn and Anthony Butler, the latter afterwards United States minister to Mexico.

Austin, the capital of Texas, was laid out and building begun in 1839.   Before November of that year, it was said to contain fifteen hundred souls, and this was written of it : "Certainly in no settlement where defence against savages depended upon the members of every household, was there ever more enlightenment and refinement."

Among the prominent residents at this period were Martin Carroll Wing, Col. Hugh McLoud, A. C. McFarland, William H. Murrah, James Burke, H. Mulholland, John D. McLoud and Richard F. Brennan.   Among the killed and wounded in an affair with the Indians at San Antonio in March, 1840, were a Mr. Casey and Private Kelley.   In an engagement brought about by an Indian raid on Victoria and Linnville, in August, 1840, the following took part: John H. Moore, Capt. Matthew Caldwell, Capt. Thomas William Ward, Capt. Andrew Neill and W. H. Magill.

One of the three commissioners accompanying the expedition to New Mexico, under command of Gen. Hugh McLoud, in June, 1841, was Dr. Richard F. Brannan, "as gallant a gentleman as was ever born on the soil of Kentucky," and accompanying him was a Mr. Fitzgerald. This expedition, partly owing to the treachery of one of its officers, was obliged to surrender to the Mexicans. Many were taken captives to the City of Mexico, and were treated in the most inhuman manner by those having them in charge. One of them, John McAllister, being unable to march, was shot dead by the brutal commander, who cut off his ears as trophies.

Among other officers in the Texan navy, were Captains Brennan and McKinney, Lieutenant Gallaher and Doctor Quinn. James Morgan and William Bryan were appointed commissioners by President Houston to take possession of vessels of the Texan navy on the Mississippi, in 1843. During Houston's second term, James Reilly was minister to the United States, and Captain Thomas William Ward was commissioner of the land office.

William Bryan represented Texas as a local agent in New Orleans in 1835. It was through his influence largely that the services of the New Orleans Grays were secured. M. A. Bryan was secretary of legation at Washington under the presidency of Lamar, 1838 to 1841. James Reilly was one of four commissioners to effect a foreign loan under the same administration, and two of the United States ministers to Texas during the same period were William H. Murphy and George H. Flood, both of whom died in Galveston.

In the movement to repel the attack of Vasquez on San Antonio, in 1842, the following took a prominent part: Capt. John C. Hayes, Cols. Matthew Caldwell and John H. Moore, Capt. James H. Callahan, John R. Cunningham, John Twohig, James Dunn, Capt. Andrew Neill, James P. Kincannon, Stewart Foley, Maj. James Kerr, Matthew Talbott, John J. Linn, David Murphy, John Sweeney and M. A. Bryan. The name of Capt. William M. Ryan appears as the commander of a company for the invasion of Mexico about the same period. Among others were Capt. S. McNeill, Capt. John C. Hayes, Maj. David Murphree, John Sweeney, Edward Linn, Lieut. M. A. Bryan, Jr., and Adjutant Thomas A. Murray.

Among the "doomed seventeen" Texans shot by the Mexicans after their surrender at the Battle of Mier were P. Mahoney, Henry Whaling, J. L. Cash, W. N. Cowan and Martin Farrell Wing. Among those shot in the City of Mexico was Capt. Ewen Cameron, a

"Highlander" native of Scotland. He had been the loved and trusted leader of his band of Rangers for seven years. Among the others killed or butchered, connected with this expedition, were James Urie, W. J. McIllrea, Dr. Richard F. Brennan, A. Fitzgerald, Patrick Lyons, L. L. Cash, Patrick Mahan, William Rowen and James Neely. Among those who died in prison were W. B. C. Bryan, John Irvin, Mr. McDade, John Owen and Patrick Usher. Among the prisoners who survived were Nathan Mullin, Jerry Lehan, Thomas A. Murray, Patrick Doherty, John Fitzgerald, John Morgan, Major McQueen, John Canty, —— Donnell, John Brennan, Thomas Burke, Frank Hughes, Edward and Richard Queen, John Lacy, Patrick and S. G. Lyon, P. M. Maxwell, William Moore, G. McFall, John McGinley, Charles McLaughlin, —— McMath, James McMicken, John McMullin, James B. and H. Neely, Francis Kelly, A. J. Rourk, William M. Ryan, Daniel C. Sullivan, John Twohig, Andrew Neill and Francis McCoy.

In January, 1842, Henri De Castro received authority from President Houston to settle a colony west of the Medina, and before his labors were completed, he had introduced over five thousand emigrants from the Rhenish provinces of France. Castro and his colony are spoken of in the highest terms by all Texan writers. They received a cordial welcome from the Texans, many of whom visited them in person. These new immigrants, added to the others preceding them, furnished the new republic with a most composite population. In the convention of 1845, which voted for annexation to the United States, among others were: Philip M. Cuney, John Caldwell, A. S. Cunningham, Spearman Holland, H. L. Kinney, Andrew McGowan, John T. McNeill, Francis Moore, James Scott and James Power.

Sam Houston was chosen one of the two first United States senators to represent the new state. Among those whom the historian of Texas writes should be held in grateful remembrance for what they have done for Texas are: Sam Houston, David Crockett, Patrick C. Jack, Thomas William Ward, Robert C. Wallace, Henry W. Karnes, John Forbes, James Power, John McMullen, Patrick McGloin, Francis Moore, Thomas McKinney, Holland McKinney, Jesse Grimes and John H. Moore.

The outbreak of the Mexican War, which followed annexation, furnished opportunity to settle old scores, and here Irish names galore appear, battling in a contest which was to extend still farther the boundaries of the United States. Their history, however, more properly belongs to the nation than the state. Many of those mentioned heretofore, surviving the contests with the Indians and the Mexicans, participated in the Mexican War, and with them many of their kindred of Irish origin,—men like General William S. Harney, the immortal Phil Kearney, who fell at Chantilly; Commodore Kearney, Maj. Andrew McReynolds, a native of historic Dungannon, and a schoolmate of Gen. James Shields, and who, like Shields, lived to take part in the Civil War, being a major-general in the Union army; and many others.

Among the signers of the Texan secession ordinance were : Lewis F. Casey, Lewis W., Thomas and Burns C. Moore, Thomas Mc-Craw, T. C. Neal, Thomas J. Devine, Edward Dougherty, John N. Fall, John H. Feeney, John Ireland, W. C. Kelly, J. R. Hayes, W. N. Neyland, D. M. Pendergast, John H. Reagan, W. T. Scott and J. S. Lester. John H. Reagan became postmaster-general of the Southern Confederacy, and T. J. Devine took a prominent part in public affairs during the Civil War.

Among the Texans who distinguished themselves in that war in the Confederate army were : Col. James Bowland, Maj. Joseph A. Carroll, Gen. Lawrence Sullivan Ross; Colonels : Hugh McLoud, James E. McCord, James Duff, John C. Burke, James Reilly, Harry McNeill, W. H. Griffin, F. I. Malone; Majors: John Ireland and Thomas Flynn, and Gen. John D. McAdoo.

James W. Flannigan was the first lieutenant-governor of Texas elected under the reconstruction period, November, 1869. Later, James W. Flannigan was elected United States senator. Webster Flannigan was president of the state senate in 1871, and Guy M. Bryan speaker of the house in 1874.

John H. Reagan was chosen United States senator in 1887. Among the representatives chosen since the Civil War to congress were : John C. Conner, W. P. McLean, W. H. Martin, L. W. Moore and Silas Hare.

S. B. Donley was one of the judges of the supreme court in 1867, and associated later with him was John D. McAdoo. On the reorganization of the supreme court in 1874, George F. Moore, Thomas J. Devine, and, later, John Ireland were appointed judges of the supreme court. John Ireland was elected governor in 1882, serving two terms. He was succeeded by Gen. Lawrence Sullivan Ross, who also served the same number of years.

Father Timon was the first priest to say mass in the new towns of Galveston, Houston and Austin, in 1838. He did not remain in Texas. A year later Fathers Joseph Hayden and Edward A. Clarke came from Bardstown, Kentucky, to minister to the Catholics, who were numerous in Lavaca county, and many of whom came from Missouri, Pennsylvania and Kentucky.

Father Hayden also attended to the spiritual wants of the Catholics in Refugio and San Patricio, and the other settlements in the coast country. He died less than two years after his arrival. Father Clarke labored in Texas for eighteen years, dying in Houston. Rev. John Murray Odin was ordained bishop of Galveston in 1847. In 1893 there were three Catholic bishops, namely: Gallagher of Galveston, Nerez of San Antonio, and Brennan of Dallas. Rev. Daniel Carl, Rev. A. Rourk and Rev. Andrew McGowan were Methodist clergymen laboring in Texas in 1837.

Dr. Francis Moore was one of the proprietors of the *Telegraph and Texas Register* in 1837; Martin Carroll Wing was assistant editor of the *Texas Sentinel* in 1840; and Michael Cronican was one of the proprietors of the *National Register.* B. F. Neill was one of the founders of the *Galveston News* in 1842, and John D. Logan of the *Texan Advocate.* Robert Loughery in 1848 established the *Texas Republican.*

Among the counties named in honor of persons of Irish origin are: Callahan, Coleman, Collin, Cochran, Crockett, Donley, Foley, Grimes, Hayes, Karnes, Kinney, Linn, McLennand, McMullen, Montgomery, Moore, Martin, Mitchell, Nolan, Terry, and the two Irish colonies are remembered in two counties named San Patricio and Refugio.

Sam Houston, in a speech made in 1855, during the Know-Nothing period, is quoted by the *New Hampshire Patriot* of June 30, 1855, as saying: "Every drop of blood in my body comes from an Irish source." It is also stated in the Quarterly of the Texas Historical Association for January, 1899, that when he first went to Texas he was baptized a Catholic, his godmother being Mrs. Eva Catherine Rosine Sterne, wife of Capt. Adolphus Sterne, and mother of Mrs. W. A. Ryan of Houston, Texas.

The Quarterly of the same association for October, 1898, contains an article on Rutersville college. It was founded in 1838 by the Methodist denomination, and the first teacher was Rev. D. N. V. Sullivan. The trustees and honorary trustees, or among them, were:

Joseph, William, A. W., Lewis N., Quincy S. and Clarke D. Nail, E. L. and John C. Moore, Daniel Barrett, Jordan Sweeney and Mr. Sweeney, Martha Reagan, Miss Reagan and Elvira Nail. An article in the same Quarterly, written by A. M. Kenny, states that the first school in Austin's colony was opened in 1835, and was taught by an Irishman named Cahill. Another, in 1836, had for a teacher a Miss McHenry, and a third was taught by a Mr. Dyas, "an old Irish gentleman."

The Texas Historical Association is but two or three years old. One of its founders is Hon. John H. Reagan, ex-postmaster-general of the late Southern Confederacy. Its only life-member in January, 1899, was D. M. O'Connor of Victoria county. Associated with him as honorary life-members were Guy M. and Joel Bryan and John H. Reagan. The Texas *Scrap-Book* states that the father of David Crockett was an Irishman, and his mother a native of Maryland. He was born in Tennessee.

Most of the material for this paper was compiled from Ramsay's History of Tennessee, Pickett's History of Alabama, and Brown's History of Texas.

The latter can well be considered one of the fairest historical works, so far as nationality and creed are concerned, of any published since Ramsay's History of the United States. It is about the only work relating to the early history of a state in which the Irish, as a race, have had due credit given. The term " Scotch-Irish " is not found in either volume of the work.

No attempt has been made in this paper to give a history of the stirring events which brought about the separation of Texas from the Mexican republic. The only object was to place on record in proper form the names of those whose character denotes the origin of those who bore them, and at the same time to endeavor to arrange them, partially, in the shape of a narrative, in order, if possible, to make it interesting to the reader.

The part taken by the Irish in Texas is pleasant reading for those of that element. Three Texas members of the American-Irish Historical Society, all bearing distinguished Irish names, are : Gen. A. G. Malloy, Capt. Moses Dillon and Mr. Charles Mehan, of El Paso, Texas, and to them this paper is respectfully dedicated.

NOTE.—Since writing this paper on Texas I have received a communication from the Rev. T. K. Crowley, of Dennison, Texas. He writes that having seen mention of what I was preparing, he took the liberty of sending me a book entitled

"Reminiscences of Fifty Years in Texas," published in 1883 and written by Hon. John J. Linn, who is one of the Irish-American pioneers mentioned in this paper. Mr. Linn was born in the county of Antrim, Ireland, in the year 1798. His father was identified with the United Irishmen Association, and being one of those fortunate enough to escape death or imprisonment, came to this country with his family early in the nineteenth century. They were Catholics, true adherents of the old faith, and this fact evokes the thought that had the Linns been Presbyterians instead of Catholics, and had they immigrated to New Hampshire instead of to Texas, their descendants would, undoubtedly, in our day, have styled them Scotch-Irish, and as is the custom, claimed they were of pure Saxon blood.

Father Crowley wrote that he knew Mr. Linn very well, and that he served Mass for him in the cathedral in Galveston when he was eighty years of age. He was truly one of the original pioneers of the Lone Star state, going there as early as 1829. This is but a little over a quarter of a century after the death of the ill-fated Philip Nolan.

The very fact that the mention of this paper in the press brought this communication from Father Crowley, is proof that the leaven is working, and many facts now hidden will, in time, through the labors of the Society, be brought to light.

J. C. L.

MR. JAMES CONNOLLY,
Of California.
Residence, CORONADO.

REV. JOHN J. McCOY, P. R.,
CHICOPEE, MASS.

COL. JAMES MORAN,
PROVIDENCE, R. I.

MR. HUGH McCAFFREY,
PHILADELPHIA.

STATE VICE–PRESIDENT FOR CALIFORNIA, AND THREE OTHER MEMBERS
OF THE SOCIETY.

EARLY IRISH SETTLERS IN KENTUCKY.

BY EDWARD FITZPATRICK,[1] LOUISVILLE, KY.

Kentucky was admitted to the Union as a state June 1, 1792, but long before that time Irishmen had invaded the " Dark and Bloody Ground." Indeed, when Daniel Boone took time to write a little history for future generations, on one occasion, by carving in the bark of a tree with his jack-knife : " Here D. Boone Cilled a Bar," it is not improbable that an Irishman was within speaking distance.

Simon Kenton, the companion of Boone, and who came to Kentucky in 1771, was of Irish parentage. His father was born in County Donegal. Another Irish companion was Michael Stoner. Kenton's life was even more romantic than Boone's. While yet a minor he fled from his state because he believed he had killed a rival for the hand of a fair Virginia damsel, and, coming to the wilds of Kentucky, assumed the name of Simon Butler. To recount his many deeds of personal bravery and privation would fill a volume. Indeed, it was asserted by many that he was the greatest Indian fighter the country ever produced.

In 1782, hearing that the man he had struck down with his fist was still alive, he resumed his name, and in 1795 served as major under Gen. Anthony Wayne. He founded Kenton's Station and Maysville, and planted the first corn raised in the state north of Kentucky river. Michael Stoner, one of his companions, and Thomas Kennedy, another Irishman, built a cabin and made some improvements on Stoner's fork of Licking river, in Bourbon county, in 1774. Future generations are indebted to men of Irish blood for many of the early settlements of this state, made under so much difficulty, and it would be impossible to fully treat the subject in one paper or in a dozen, so romantic are many of the characters.

Kentucky was only a colony or county of Virginia up to 1791, and the latter state exercised full control over its lands until Gen. George Rogers Clark disputed this right shortly before the state

[1] Of the staff of the Louisville *Daily Times.*

was admitted to the Union. The records show that with the sur-
veying parties sent out by the state of Virginia to this territory
were many men bearing Irish names, not " Scotch-Irish," but plain
Irish.

Col. George Croghan, an Irishman, writing in his journal June 1,
1765, says : "We arrived within a mile of the falls of the Ohio
(Louisville) where we encamped after coming 50 miles this day."
This was even before Boone's time. Colonel Croghan was a connection by marriage of Gen. George Rogers Clark, who reduced the
British possessions in the entire Northwest and made it first possible for the United States, instead of England, to acquire this territory. If General Clark was not an Irishman himself, his records
show that he had many Irishmen with him as soldiers. His sister
married William Croghan.

The first survey made of Louisville was in 1773 by Capt. Thomas
Bullitt ; his associates were John Fitzpatrick, James, George and
Robert McAfee. Dr. John Connolly owned two thousand acres
of land in Louisville in 1773. Col. John Campbell, a native of Ireland and a resident of Louisville about this time, was afterward a
member of the first state constitutional convention, held in Danville
in 1797.

Colonel Campbell was an Irish Presbyterian and proud that he
was Irish. He never mentioned once in any of his letters or
speeches that he was "Scotch-Irish," though he made many
speeches and wrote many letters. He was speaker of the Kentucky
house of representatives and afterward a member of congress. He
was often a delegate to the Presbyterian Synods in Kentucky and
was always spoken of as an Irishman, without any prefix, though he
was born in the province of Ulster. Colonel Campbell was a
pioneer of whom the Irish might well feel proud. He was an
intense patriot, and being a large landowner, sent for many of his
countrymen to come to Louisville, and this was another cause for
swelling the early Irish immigration to Kentucky.

William H. English spent much money and five years of his life
writing a history of the " Conquest of the Northwest Territory," by
George Rogers Clark and his associates. While Mr. English may
perhaps be forgotten by future generations as the man who was the
running mate of Gen. Winfield S. Hancock on the Democratic presi-
dential ticket of 1880, he will ever be remembered by reason of the
publication of this most accurate and valuable history. He, during

twenty years, collected while a congressman and at other times, the names of nearly all the soldiers who were with General Clark in his fights with the British and Indians, beginning in 1780, several years before Kentucky was a state. He devotes seven hundred pages to the deeds of Clark and his men, and they deserve all of it. It would take a good deal of space to give the Irish names in this roll of Clark's soldiers.

With General Clark came to Louisville, in 1778, John Haggin and John Montgomery, and both were captains in his command. They landed at Corn Island, in the Ohio river, at the head of the falls, opposite where Louisville now stands. In 1782 there lived in Louisville, with their families : John MacManus, Hugh Cochran, John Doyle, John Caghey, John Cunningham, Michael Humble, John Handley, Andrew Hines, Thomas McCarty, Thomas Purcell, James Sullivan, James Brown and John McCarland, and most of these came with Clark. That was a pretty good Irish settlement for those days when a man who went out to plough corn was obliged to take his rifle along to defend himself against hostile Indians.

No one will venture to say that Matthew Lyon, born in County Wicklow, in 1746, was a " Scotch-Irishman," though I have heard lately that some of his descendants are now claiming that rather peculiar distinction. Matthew Lyon brought the first printing office across the mountains to Kentucky, and it did not come in a railroad train either. It was fetched in a jolt wagon and a good deal of the type was "pied" before it ever got here. From this type and press the first newspaper ever printed in Louisville was issued. Matthew Lyon's father was executed in Ireland for alleged treason in 1765. The boy, aged thirteen years, was bound by himself to the captain of the vessel which brought him across the ocean, to work for twelve months to pay for his passage.

A Connecticut farmer gave the captain two bulls for Matthew Lyon's services, and he worked out his time faithfully with that farmer. Ever afterward his great oath was " By the bulls that bought me." Lyon county, Ky., is named for him, and his remains lie buried at Eddyville, which town he founded. Matthew Lyon, though once sold for two bulls, took no mean part in the making of history for his country, not only in Kentucky, but also in Vermont, where he went after working out his time with the Connecticut farmer. He belonged to the Green Mountain Boys, was a colonel in the Revolutionary War, and afterwards a member of congress

from the Granite state as well as from Kentucky.   In 1798 he was
prosecuted under the Alien and Sedition laws and fined one thousand dollars and confined in jail for four months.   While in jail he
was elected to congress, and by his vote broke the deadlock which
elected Jefferson president.

Coming to Kentucky soon afterward, he was a pioneer in the
wilderness where Lyon county is now situate, and his neighbors
sent him to the legislature at Frankfort.   He afterwards served in
congress from Kentucky for eight years (1803–'11).   He was in
1813 appointed to an Indian agency in Arkansas, and was elected
to congress from that state.   So Matthew Lyon, a plain Irishman,
claiming no Scotch prefix, has the record of being elected to congress from three states.   His son, Chittendon Lyon, was a member
of congress in 1827, and his descendants still live in the state.

Many of the old families in Louisville are of Irish descent, but it
would take too much space to mention even a fair portion of them.
In 1784 Patrick Joyes settled in Louisville, and his family grew,
leaving many descendants, one of them being the present county
attorney of Jefferson county.   The original Joyes was a man of
education, speaking French, Spanish and other tongues fluently, so
that at least one Irishman was of polished intellect in the early settlement of the city.

William H. English, being a millionaire, could afford to spend a
great deal of time and money in collecting information about the
Northwest territory and Kentucky.   On one of his visits to Louisville he told me that had it not been for the Irish in Clark's
command the latter would never have whipped the British and Indians.   The Irish, fresh from persecutions in the old country, were
very bitter against the English, and were of great help to Clark.   Mr.
English had a great deal of information on this subject which has
never been published.   Of course, in his history he makes no reference to nationalities except where it was absolutely necessary, it
being his purpose to simply give credit to Clark and his soldiers
for their wonderful work.

Dr. Thomas Dunn English, writing of a trip he made through the
mountains of Kentucky, on one occasion tells of an incident which
shows that many people of Irish descent in this state are ignorant
of the fact.   He was riding along one day in a wagon when his companion, a lanky native boy of the mountains, saw a rabbit run across
the road.   " Stop a minute, Dock," said the boy, "till I heave a

dornick at that rabbit." Dr. English coming to inquire, found that the mountains of Kentucky had been settled long ago by Irish and that "dornick" was one of the many Irish words which survived.

Even before Clark came to Louisville, Simon Kenton records that, in 1775, he located in the Upper and Lower Blue Licks, where there was an abundance of game, and he considered it a paradise. One day, to his great astonishment, there came out of the woods toward his cabin, two men who gave their names as Fitzpatrick and Hendricks. They had been living in the vicinity for sometime. Fitzpatrick said he wanted to return to Virginia, and Kenton escorted him to the Ohio river, bidding him good-by near where the town of Maysville now stands. While Kenton was taking Fitzpatrick to the river, Indians entered the cabin and killed Hendricks. Michael Stoner, another Irishman, who was Boone's companion in 1774, told Kenton that there were a number of settlers in the interior who were not from Virginia.

In 1775 Hugh Shannon, Patrick Jordan, John Lee and others settled at what is now known as Lexington. It is recorded that Patrick Jordan found a spring down the fork on which they camped. Joseph Lindsey afterward paid Jordan two guineas to allow him to locate near the spring, and the first clearing was made there. This is now the garden spot of the Blue Grass region of Kentucky, where all the fine fast horses and the pretty women and good whiskey come from. In 1775 the first roasting ears were gathered from this clearing. John Haggin located there soon afterward, having come down the Ohio and up the Licking river to the settlement.

There were probably other Irish people eating roasting ears in the Blue Grass region one year before the Declaration of Independence was read in Philadelphia, but their names have not been preserved. Certain it is that the people living in this settlement, first peopled by the Shannons and the Jordans, as soon as they heard of the Revolutionary battle of Lexington, Mass., named their settlement after that battle. They were certainly not English sympathizers to do this.

In 1775 Ben. Logan settled where the town of Stanford is. Both his father and mother were born in Ireland. Logan was a companion of Boone. He planted the first corn in what is now known as Lincoln county, was a colonel in the militia, and was one of the most daring of the early pioneers.

Daniel Boone, in 1775, found in Powell's Valley, Richard Hogan, Hugh McGarry, Thomas Denton, and their families. These located afterwards at Harrodstown. Mrs. McGarry and Mrs. Hogan were the first white women to go up Salt river, which historic stream is now so frequently mentioned in connection with the defeated candidates after elections. The Hogans and the McGarrys have frequently "gone up Salt river" since, figuratively speaking, but the Indians were not waiting for them on the banks with a tomahawk as they were for Mrs. Hogan and Mrs. McGarry in 1775.

People of Irish birth or extraction were pioneers in the educational line in this commonwealth, even before the Declaration of Independence. Bishop Spalding, in his notes on Kentucky, says that Mrs. William Coomes, an excellent Catholic lady, taught school in Harrodsburg in 1775. This was before a church or a court was opened in Kentucky. Smith, the historian, though not a Catholic, agrees with Bishop Spalding, and says that "in the year 1775 Dr. Hart and William Coomes settled Drennon Spring in Henry county, but afterward moved to Harrod's Station. Dr. Hart practised medicine, and Mrs. William Coomes opened a school for children." "Thus," he observes, "the first physician and the first school teacher in Kentucky were both Catholics." Whether they were Irish or not they got the credit as being of that race, as did all the Presbyterian Irish in the early history of the state get the reputation of being Scotch.

Joseph Doniphan taught school in Booneboro in 1779, and the children of Daniel Boone were his pupils. Nothing is known of his early history, but it has been asserted that his proper name was Donavon, and was corrupted into Doniphan or Doniphant.

A writer with the leisure and means could strike a rich field in looking up the names of the Irish connected with the early settlement of the state, and it is no exaggeration to say that seventy-five per cent. were of that nationality.

REV. RICHARD HENEBRY, Ph. D.,

Professor of Keltic Languages and Literature,
Catholic University, WASHINGTON, D. C.

HON. EDWIN D. McGUINNESS,

Ex-Secretary of State, Rhode Island; ex-Mayor
of PROVIDENCE.

COL. JAMES ARMSTRONG,

CHARLESTON, S. C.

COL. WILLIAM H. DONOVAN,

LAWRENCE, MASS.

FOUR MEMBERS OF THE SOCIETY.

THE IRISH PIONEERS AND FOUNDERS OF PETER-
BOROUGH, NEW HAMPSHIRE.[1]

BY JAMES F. BRENNAN, OF PETERBOROUGH.

MR. TOASTMASTER, LADIES AND GENTLEMEN :

My memory leads me back over a comparatively brief part of the
time covered by the recollections of the gray haired men and women
who are here present.   I was born in this beautiful village ; my first
hallowed recollections cluster here ; its territory is familiar to me ; I
know its people and something of its history, and wherever I go my
mind reverts with pride to this good old town.

It is with great pleasure that I accept the honor of responding
to this toast, and in what I have to say shall not refer to the comparatively modern generation of Irishmen—Murphy, Brennan, Hamill, Noone, and scores of others—and their descendants, who have
helped to build up this town, and whose history should be left for a
résumé of fifty years hence, but to those early settlers who came
across the ocean, and their descendants ; men who risked all, even
life itself, to make this spot a fit place for the abode of man.

They were composed in a very small part of Scotchmen, Englishmen and other nationalities, but the essential part of the pioneers of
our town, in fact nearly all of them, were Irishmen, for I assume that
where men were born in Ireland, as they were, where many of their
fathers, perhaps, also, some of their grandfathers were born, they
were men who can unqualifiedly be called Irishmen.   Adopt any
other standard and a large part of the inhabitants of Ireland at the
time they emigrated would not be considered Irishmen, and probably
few persons in this town to-day would be considered Americans.

The Scotchmen who came to Ireland, and from whom some of the
pioneers of this town trace their ancestry, landed on that Emerald
Isle, as our town history records it, in 1610, more than a century and
a quarter before their descendants came to this country in 1736.

---

[1] This article comprises an address delivered by Mr. Brennan on the occasion of the 150th
anniversary of Peterborough.   Mr. Brennan is our Society's state vice-president for New
Hampshire.

These immigrant descendants were indeed Irishmen to the manor
born, with all the traits, impulses and characteristics of that people,
having, as the Rev. Dr. Morison said in his centennial address, the
"comic humor and pathos of the Irish," and to their severe character
and habits "another comforter came in, of Irish parentage ; the long
countenance became short, the broad Irish humor began to rise," etc.
Need I ask the indulgence of my hearers if I occupy a part of the
time allotted me in naming some of these men who were the
founders of this town and the inaugurators of civilization in this
section ?

Samuel Gordon and wife (Eleanor Mitchell) were born in the
County Tyrone, Ireland, as were also his father and mother ; they
are all buried in the old cemetery on the hill. By marriage the blood
intermixed with Holden, Kimball, Barnes, Pierce, Cochran, Dickey,
White, Brooks and Hurd.

William Alld was born in Ireland in 1723, and was one of the
early settlers. The blood mixed by marriage with Swan, Metcalf,
Worcester, Way and Whitten.

John McKean was born in Ballymony, Ireland, in 1714, and was
the ancestor of all the McKeans in this section. His son James
lived and died on the David Blanchard place.

John Ferguson was born in Ireland in 1704, and came to this
country with the Smiths, Wilsons and Littles. The blood infused
into Morison, Stuart, Duncan, Miller, Moore, Evans and Whiting.

George Duncan was born in Ireland and was the ancestor of all of
that name in this section. Shortly after immigrating he married Mary
Bell of Ballymony, and their progeny married into the Taggart, Todd,
Black, McClellan, Moore, Wallace, Wells and Cummings families.

John Swan came from Ireland, and the family mixed by marriage
with Parker, Stuart, Gilchrest, Morse, Caldwell, Alld, Sawyer, Graham, Chamberlain, Nay, Hoyt, Steele, Hannaford, Moore, Mitchell,
Cutter and White.

Joseph Turner and wife immigrated from Ireland with their sons
Thomas, Joseph and William, who were all born there. The blood
by marriage went into Wellman, Sanders, Shedd, Converse, Nichols,
Goodhue, Nutting, Taggart, Davis and Preston.

John Moore immigrated from Ireland in 1718, and is the ancestor
of all of the same name here. The blood mixed by marriage with
Jewett, Priest, Taggart, Woodward, Smith, Gregg, Dinsmore, Wood,
Steele, Turner, Holmes, Burnham, Jordan and Phelps.

Andrew Todd was born in Ireland in 1697, and married a daughter of John Moore. Their progeny married with Morison, Miller, Taggart and Brown.

John Smiley, after his marriage, immigrated from Ireland. The blood by marriage went into Miller, Hovey, Parker, McCoy, Wilson and Leonard.

Abial Sawyer was born in Ireland in 1721, where also his wife was born in 1726. From them all of the name about here trace their origin, intermixing by marriage with Gregg, Bailey, Scott, Farnsworth, Howard and Nichols.

Matthew and James Templeton came from Ireland, and their blood intermixed by marriage with Holmes, Miller, Robbe, Wilder and McCoy.

William Robbe, both of his wives, and seven children were all born in Ireland, three generations of the family having lived there. From them all of the name in town trace their origin. They mixed by marriage with Taggart, Whittemore, Farnsworth, Mussey, White, Redding, Chapman, Gowing, Livingston, Morrison, Moore, Follansbee and Swallow.

Thomas Steele was born in Ireland in 1694, and came here in 1718. The blood mixed by marriage with Gregg, Mitchell, Wilson, Smith, Ramsey, Swan, Senter, Willey and Rice. With another branch of the Steeles which emigrated from Ireland was the father of the late John H. Steele, governor of our state in 1844–'45.

William Wilson immigrated from County Tyrone, Ireland, in 1737, with his wife, daughter and son Robert, who was born in that county, and commanded a party of men organized to go to Lexington, armed, as our town history says, with guns, pitchforks and shillelahs. The blood by marriage went into Swan, Steele, Johnson, Hunter, Lee, Gibbon, Scott, Jackson, Sherwood, Fisk and Taintor.

Thomas Davidson immigrated from Ireland with his brother John Davidson and Matthew Wright. By marriage the blood went into Patrick, Hoar, Dodge, Clark, Cutter and Nichols.

Thomas Cunningham was a native of Ireland. The blood mixed by marriage with Robbe, McKean, Treadwell, Hale, Goodhue, Jackson, Caldwell, Porter and Bishop.

John Wallace came to Londonderry from County Antrim, Ireland, in 1719, and was the ancestor of the name here. The blood is mixed with Mitchell, Noone and Spline.

James Gregg emigrated from Ireland to Londonderry in 1718,

and was the ancestor of all of the name in this section. The family intermixed with Steele, Gibbs, Hutchins, Nelson, Macy and Wright.

William McNee, born in Ireland in 1711, was one of the settlers of the town. Before he came to this country he married Mary E. Brownley, by whom he had all his children. His descendants have now reached the eighth generation, but unfortunately the name is entirely lost. The first and second generations retained the name, but the third changed it to Nay. They intermixed with Cunningham, Taggart, Millikin, Swan, Upton, Weston, Davidson, Turner, Miller, Gilbert, Frost, Buss, Wood, Felt, Cross, Porter, Jaquith, Vose, Adams, Young, Balch, Perkins and Hapgood.

Nathaniel Holmes (the ancestor of our able orator[1] here to-day and of all of the name in this section) was born in Coleraine, Ireland, as was also his father. Thus we have three generations of this family which lived in Ireland. He was an early settler and by marriage the blood mixed with Whittemore, Adams, Clement, Swasey, Leach, Kimball, Dickey, Hall, Griffin, Gregg, Miller, Aiken, Bruce, Sewall, Smith, Newton and Livingston.

There were two distinct families of Millers in town, remotely related; the ancestors of both, however, came from Ireland. Back to these people our president of this day[2] and all of the name hereabouts trace their ancestry. They intermarried with Patterson, Burns, Campbell, Vickery, Johnson, Mead, Shipman, Templeton, McFarland, White, Duncan, Davis, Ropes, Wilkins, Phelps, McCoy, Thompson, Cunningham, Taggart, Gowing, Clark, Gregg, Holt, Sanderson, Wilder and Scott.

All the Whites in town, including the marshal of this day,[3] are descendants of Patrick White, who was born in Ireland in 1710. By marriage they intermixed with Stuart, Shearer, Gregg, Upton, Cram, Stearns, Carley, Parker, Grant, Dennis, Goodwin, Farmer, Perry, Swan, Pierce, Fisk, Washburn, Whittemore, Shattuck, Leighton, Burns, Alld, Grimes, Loring, Holmes, Mitchell, Scott, Cunningham, Lakin, Spafford, Longley, Kyes and Tenney.

Samuel Morison and wife emigrated from Ireland, leaving their parents, but taking with them eight children, who were all born there. From them descended all that family in this section who spell their name with one r, including our poet of to-day,[4] and the

---

[1] Judge Nathaniel Holmes, Cambridge, Mass.
[2] Hon. John R. Miller.
[3] Gen. Daniel M. White.
[4] Prof. Nathaniel H. Morison, Provost of Peabody Institute, Baltimore, Md.

venerable gentleman[1] whom we are proud to have with us here, who delivered the oration at our centennial fifty years ago. By marriage their blood went into the following named families : Steele, Mack, Knight, Johnson, Bassett, Williams, Mitchell, Smith, Moore, Todd, Wallace, Hale, Graham, Felt, Wilcox, Holmes, Buxton and Wells.

James Smith, the progenitor of all the Smiths in this section, was from Ireland. His son Robert was born in Moneymore, Ireland, and with his four children, John, Sarah, Mary and William, all born near Lough Neagh, came to this country in 1736. Thus we find that three generations of this family were from Ireland. Dr. Smith, the historian of our town, was a descendant of this family. By marriage the blood went into Bell, McNee, Morison, White, Annan, Dunshee, Fletcher, Smiley, Burns, McCrillis, Emery, Findley, Pierce, Russell, Barker, Fifield, Cavender, Walker, Gordon, Fox, Foster, Reynolds, Kilbourne, Jones, Leonard, Blanchard, Lewis, Cheney and Dearborn.

William Scott immigrated in 1736 from Coleraine, Ireland, where all his children were born, among them William, who settled here the same year. This man and his father were Irish, as was also Alexander Scott, progenitor of another branch which settled here and immigrated at the same time. From these families sprang every person of the name in town, among them our efficient toast-master,[2] and by marriage the blood has mingled with Cochran, Robbe, Wills, Maxfield, Cummings, Ramsey, Whitney, Lincoln, Loomis, Gray, Bullard, Jewett, Fuller, Bowers, Orr, Allyn, Blanchard, Clark and Ramsdell.

This is only a partial list of the Irishmen who were the founders and builders of Peterborough—which may be completed at some future time. It could be extended considerably, but sufficient names are here given to show the nationality of the men to whom this town owes its existence. All the brief facts here given are taken from the history of this town and that of Londonderry, N. H.

Thus we see that there are comparatively few persons in town to-day, with the exception of recent comers, who have not coursing in their veins the blood of those sturdy Irishmen who made this town what it is, whose bodies have long since returned to clay in the old cemetery on the hill, and whose history is the history of the

[1] Rev. John H. Morison, D. D.
[2] Col. Charles Scott.

town itself.   Long may their memory be cherished!   Long may the pride which exists in such ancestry be retained!   They were brave, honest, manly men, who broke down the barriers that civilization might enter.   Their lot was a life of hardship; it is ours to enjoy the fruits of their work.

Not only the privations of this cold, uninviting country were theirs to suffer, but intolerance and bigotry met them at the threshold of the country to which they were about to bring a blessing. Rev. Dr. Morison, in his centennial address, said that when the Smiths, Wilsons, Littles and others arrived, "It was noised about that a pack of Irishmen had landed." They were denied even lodgings.   Mr. Winship of Lexington, who extended a welcome to them, however, said, "If this house reached from here to Charlestown, and I could find such Irish as these, I would have it filled up with Irish, and none but Irish."

If there is a town or city in this broad land owing a greater debt of gratitude to that green isle over the sea than does this town, I know it not.   If there is a place which should extend more earnest and loving sympathy to Ireland in her struggles, I know not where it is.   It was there that your forefathers and mine were born; there where their infant feet were directed; there where they were educated in those grand principles of honesty, sturdy manhood and bravery well fitting them to become the pioneers of any country, and fortunate it was for that land toward which they turned their faces.

Here they built their log cabins and shrines to worship God, and reared families of from eight to sixteen children, for they were people among whom large families were popular, and the more modern aversion to a large number of children had not taken possession of those God-fearing men and women.   Happy it was that the duty of populating this country was theirs, and not that of the present generation, whose disposition to do this might be doubted. Dr. Smith writes in our town history: "Of the large and influential families of Todd, Templeton, Swan, Alld, Stuart, Cunningham, Mitchell, Ritchie, Ferguson and many more, not a single individual of their family remains in town; and of the large families of Steele, Robbe, Smith, Morison, Moore and Holmes, their numbers are greatly lessened, and they are growing less every year."

In reviewing the character of these men, we should not, as a first essential, go into an inquiry of how they worshipped God; or what were their religious or political beliefs ; whether Protestant or Catholic, Whig or Tory. We only ask were they honest men, holding fast to those principles which they believed right ? The answer to this will not bring the blush of shame upon our cheek, nor the consciousness of regret that their blood is part and parcel of our bodies. If we follow in their footsteps in our dealings with men ; if we are as honest and courageous as they ; if we do an equal share to make the world better and more attractive to future generations, we can, when the toil of this life is over, rest in the secure belief of duty well done.

SKETCH OF AN EARLY IRISH SETTLEMENT IN RHODE ISLAND.

BY THOMAS HAMILTON MURRAY, WOONSOCKET, R. I.

Among the old-time, honored names in Rhode Island is that of Dorrance. It has figured prominently for a long period. About 1715–1720, George Dorrance and his two sons—George and James —came from Ireland to the colony and settled in what is now the town of Foster. They bought a large tract of land which subsequently became known as the Dorrance Purchase.

This tract was at that time supposed by some to be within the jurisdiction of Connecticut. When, however, the boundary between Rhode Island and Connecticut was finally settled, the Dorrance Purchase was decided to be a part of Rhode Island. The controversy had lasted sixty-five years and was not definitely adjusted until 1728.

The territory thus aquired by Rhode Island was commonly known as Head Lots and included, as has been stated, the great Dorrance property. Later, it was comprised in the town of Scituate, R. I., and when, in 1781, Foster was set apart from Scituate, the Dorrance Purchase was comprised in the boundaries of the new town thus created.

Soon after their arrival from the old country, the Dorrances, with true Irish enterprise, erected a sawmill at a stream on their estate. This stream was called Quandock brook. Here they sawed lumber for building purposes for themselves, and also for their neighbors. Subsequently, a grist mill was added, and the locality became widely known as the Dorrance Mills.

The elder George Dorrance from Ireland, was born in 1675. He died at his home on the Purchase in 1754, at the age of seventy-nine years, and was buried on the " Plains," near Oneco, Conn.

His son, Captain George, also from Ireland, settled on the northern part of the Purchase, on the road going west by " Tyler's store " into Connecticut. This was later named the Brooklyn road. Captain George obtained his military title for valuable services rendered. He passed away in 1793, and was buried with his father. He left two sons, George and Alexander, and some say a third, named John.

James Dorrance, the other son of the elder George from Ireland, located in the central portion of the Dorrance Purchase and built a substantial dwelling. It fronted south and comprised two stories. In the centre of the house was a huge stone chimney, measuring 10x18 feet. In each room was a large, old-fashioned fireplace. In the great east room downstairs was one ten feet wide and six feet high, constructed on the same plan as many in Ireland. There was a large oven in the back. Those were the days of the spinning-wheel, and of blazing logs whose flame mounted up the great chimney and shed light over the family group after nightfall.

They were a sturdy race—the Dorrances—and worthy representatives of Irish pluck, energy and progressiveness. This James was one of the sons who came from Ireland. He died in 1779, while our Revolution was still in progress, at the venerable age of ninety-six years, a good instance of Irish longevity. He was buried with his father and brother, and was sincerely mourned by all the country roundabout. He left two sons, James and Michael Dorrance.

The third George Dorrance, or grandson of the first George, the immigrant, had extensive military experience, and was known as Major Dorrance. He erected a house near the old homestead. It was two stories high in front and one in the rear, with a "lean-to" roof. Like the other house just mentioned, it had an enormous stone chimney. Major Dorrance died in 1827 or 1828, aged seventy-seven years. He left considerable property, but no children.

The most eminent member of this famous Dorrance family was John, who was born about 1747. He entered Rhode Island college, now Brown university, and was graduated in 1774. On that occasion he delivered an oration on "The Necessity and Advantages of Cultivating our Own Language." He also participated in a syllogistic dispute in Latin, taking the affirmative on the question: "Should the Dictates of Conscience Always be Obeyed?"

He was twice married. His first wife was Polly Whitman, daughter of Jacob Whitman of Providence, who owned the "Turk's Head" property. His second wife was Mrs. Amy Clark, widow of Dr. John Clark and daughter of Commodore Esek Hopkins. John Dorrance had previously removed from Foster to Providence and lived at the corner of Westminster and Exchange streets, where the National

Exchange bank was afterwards located. He studied law and in 1794 was elected judge of the Court of Common Pleas for Providence county. This eminent position he also filled by annual election until 1801. He was then defeated. The defeat was owing to the bitter opposition of Gov. Arthur Fenner, which arose over a lawsuit between the two.

Judge Dorrance was likewise a member of the General Assembly for several terms. In 1789 he was an assistant (senator) to Gov. John Collins, and, with George Sears, was appointed by the Assembly a committee to audit the accounts of "the late intendants of trade for the ports of Newport and Providence." In 1790 his name appears as a member of the Providence Society for the Abolition of Slavery. The *Rhode Island American*, Jan. 8, 1811, notes his election as a director of the Exchange bank of Providence. In 1792 or 1794 he was a candidate for congress and received a flattering vote.

Speaking of Judge Dorrance, Dr. Pardon Bowen declared that "he possessed an adequate law knowledge and was a man of the strictest integrity." The judge died June 29, 1813. That excellent authority, the *Providence Gazette*, in its issue of July 3, the same year, had a notice of his death, and after stating that "the Honourable John Dorrance" had departed this life, it went on to say: "Judge Dorrance was descended from Irish parentage, but was himself born in Foster, in this state. He received a degree from Rhode Island college, and afterwards became a tutor and since a member of the corporation of that institution."

Continuing, it states that he was of unblemished integrity and undeviating patriotism; that for many years he was a member of the state legislature from Providence, "both in the senate and as a representative." It likewise chronicled the fact that for the last sixteen years of his life, the citizens of the town (Providence), manifested their confidence in him by making and continuing him president of the town council.

The obituary notice referred to thus concludes: "His intimate knowledge of the science of jurisprudence made him the adviser of all who were in distress. His life was marked by an honesty that neither power nor wealth could swerve from its duty."

Judge Dorrance's death was deeply regretted throughout the state. He left a widow and "a large train of relatives." The deceased was prominent all through the Revolution, and by his patriotic activity rendered incalculable service to the cause of liberty.

There was also a Samuel in the Dorrance family at an early period. His name is found in the records in 1734. At the period of the Revolution, the records, 1775, show that George Dorrance, probably a grandson of the senior Irish immigrant, was ensign in the lieutenant-colonel's company of the regiment of Providence. In 1780, a George Dorrance was appointed lieutenant of the second company of Scituate. In 1781, George Dorrance, Jr., was captain in a Scituate company. The same year Capt. George Dorrance had a company in a regiment raised by act of the General Assembly. In 1782, George Dorrance, Jr., was commissioned major of the Third regiment of militia in the county of Providence. There is not much doubt but that in all the operations throughout Rhode Island during the Revolution, these and other members of the Dorrance family took an active part.

Alexander, another grandson of the senior Dorrance from Ireland, settled in the northerly section of the Dorrance Purchase on the road running through the centre of Head Lots and at right angles with the Brooklyn road. He died in 1840 leaving two sons, Palmer and Frink. Palmer Dorrance was born at the old homestead in Foster in 1804. He embarked in business at an early age, went to New York, and engaged in the rubber trade with Erastus Corning, his brother-in-law.

In 1831 he located in Providence and engaged in the boot and shoe business on Weybosset street, nearly opposite the present post-office. In 1833 he returned to Foster, his native town, and was in business there until 1839, when he removed to the northerly part of Foster, bought the Colonel Hopkins property and conducted a tavern and store for several years. In 1847 he removed to Apponaug, R. I., and was in the hotel business there, and at Natick and Button-woods, until 1854. At the time of his death, 1873, he was engaged again in Providence.

The second James Dorrance, grandson of the first George from Ireland, was born in 1762, and resided on the homestead in Foster until his death, at the age of seventy-one years. He had a son, Abram, who passed away in 1859, leaving no heirs. He used to say there was " stone enough in the old chimney to wall in the farm."

Michael Dorrance, a son of the first James, who immigrated with his father from Ireland, was a native of Foster, and erected a substantial dwelling on the southerly part of the Purchase. He left two sons, George and James. The former became a man of much prominence, and was commissioned as captain in 1834. Michael' the father, passed from earth in 1874, being then seventy-three years of age. Michael's father-in-law, Mr. Placet, was town treasurer of Foster from 1810 to 1828, and later represented the town in the General Assembly. For many years he was cashier of the Mount Vernon National bank, and was also in charge of the Mount Vernon post-office. He died at Foster in 1849.

In the preparation of this article, I have received much material from Casey B. Tyler, who is well acquainted with the history of the Dorrances, and is likewise excellently posted on that of many other prominent Rhode Island families. Mr. Tyler also sent me the following interesting facts relating to the subject of this sketch :

"I have had in my possession," he says, "a pane of glass which Susanna [Dorrance] Wells presented me many years ago, which she said came from the old country [Ireland], and was originally set in a lead sash and brought from Ireland by her great-great-grandfather, George Dorrance, and used in the same old house for many years, until replaced by a wood sash and a 6x8 glass. This old pane of glass is yellowish and coarse and in diamond shape, and measures four inches on each side. She also said that she kept a part of the sash for a long time, but the boys used it up making shot and bullets to hunt with. This Susanna Dorrance was born in 1799, and married Jeremiah Wells, son of Benjamin Wells at Foster, and lived to a good old age, a very intelligent and highly-esteemed woman.

"Maj. George Dorrance, who lived in the other old house, and who died in 1827, aged seventy-seven years, without children, had many articles which came from Ireland with his ancestors. They were sold at auction in 1833 by Palmer Dorrance, one of the heirs-at-law. Among the rest was an old-fashioned solid mahogany double-bureau, which was purchased by John Tyler of 'Tyler's store,' who had the old brass trimmings taken off, and had it made into two nice bureaus with more fashionable trimmings.

"One of these bureaus was later owned by his granddaughter, Matilda Rathbun, in Mossup Valley, and highly prized. The other came into possession of his grandson, Albert Tyler, near the Centreville, R. I., depot. These two bureaus were altered by Israel Lyon in 1833, while he carried on the carriage business in the basement of the house in Foster, where his brother, Hon. Sheldon P. Lyon, lived and died.

"An old-fashioned silver tankard, holding two quarts, with a cover like a Brittania teapot cover, was sold at the same time, and it was a well-known fact that Major Dorrance, when first born, was very small, and was put into that tankard, and the cover shut down, although he was a man afterwards six feet two inches in height. John Tyler always regretted not buying the tankard."

The Dorrance mills remained in the Dorrance family down to 1808. During the next few years the mills changed hands several times. In 1813 they were sold to Peleg Place, whose daughters married Dorrances. Mr. Place occupied the mill property until 1824, the balance of the estate, or most of it, still remaining in the Dorrance family.

In 1824 Mr. Place sold the mills to Stephen Potter, who put up another building, introduced "water looms," and made cotton cloth for several years.

George Dorrance and Phebe (Place) Dorrance left several sons. One of them was named Thomas G., and another Albert L. The latter became an influential farmer on the homestead inherited from his grandfather. He died, leaving a widow and two daughters.

The Dorrance name is still found in Rhode Island, and Dorrance street, a leading thoroughfare in Providence, helps perpetuate it. Bearers of the name, descendants of the immigrants, are likewise found, some of them in Providence. The old dam at Dorrance mills was long since demolished. The original dwellings have long been ruins, the great chimneys being the last to go, but the history and the memories of the Dorrance Purchase still form one of the charms of that section of the state.

AN EARLY IRISHMAN OF WATERBURY, CONN.

BY MARTIN SCULLY,[1] OF WATERBURY.

A good deal of research has been indulged in during the past ten or fifteen years, with a view to ascertaining for a certainty the name of the Irishman who first visited the territorial limits of Waterbury, Conn.

So far the question seems to be an open one, the preference having been ascribed to various persons by different writers. Half a dozen or more of the old Irish settlers of the town who came here over half a century ago and who have resided here continuously since, tell conflicting stories in relation to this subject, and as they were the only source from which much information on this matter could be obtained, the question has never been fully decided, each naming a different person as being the first to lead the way for his countrymen into this section of the state.

I recently conceived the idea of making some investigation on this point from sources other than those which have heretofore been brought into use, with the result that I have succeeded in obtaining information in relation to this issue, which will be of interest to future historians, of the first Irish residents of this town, and cannot but help settle the much disputed question on this point.

As nearly as data can at present be collected, the first known Irishman to see this part of the country was Joseph Rourke, a soldier who served in one of the companies attached to a regiment in command of General Putnam in the Revolutionary War. He was with Putnam through most of his campaigns and took such a liking to that dashing soldier that he refused to serve under the command of any other captain. It was this fascination which led him to follow Putnam to his home in Brooklyn, this state, and he was seriously wounded in the retreat of the Revolutionary troops from Horseneck to Stamford, Conn., in 1779.

[1] Staff of the *Waterbury Daily Democrat*.

During his service in the Revolutionary army Rourke met and formed the acquaintance of a son of Gideon Hotchkiss, the great-great-grandfather of Judge George H. Cowell of this city, and in 1784 he accompanied young Hotchkiss to the family residence, then situated about three miles southeast of Prospect Centre. Remaining here for about twelve or thirteen years, he learned of the intended uprising in his native country, which culminated in the rebellion of 1798, and left on the old stage line for Derby, Conn., thence by way of the Sound for New York, with a view of reaching the scene of the conflict in time to render what service he could to the cause of the Irish patriot party. Whether he reached the scene of operations and met the fate of many of his countrymen who had dared throw down the gauge of battle to the enemies of Ireland will never be known, but sufficient information has been obtained to satisfy me that the story of his visit to these parts is founded on fact.

Judge Cowell can tell many reminiscences of the man's characteristics which he often heard related by his maternal grandmother. "There is nothing strange about this," said Judge Cowell, when asked about the matter; "everybody knows that the Irish people had been fleeing to all parts of the world to shun the persecution to which they were subjected at home for centuries prior to that time, and it is the most reasonable thing in the world to believe that some of them should show up in these parts. It is a well-established fact that there were a large number of Irishmen in the Revolutionary War, not only in the rank and file, but as captains and generals. Were not several of the signers of the Declaration of Independence Irishmen?

"Joseph Rourke was not the only one of his race who came along here after the close of the Revolutionary War, but he is the only one I have a good recollection of hearing talked of when I was a boy. What made the old people remember him so well was the fact that in addition to being a brave soldier he was an excellent shoemaker and earned his living during his stay here by going among the farmers, repairing and making new footwear, and the handsomest footwear ever worn in this state by the forefathers of many of the old American families of this section was put up by Joseph Rourke.

"He was in the place," continued the judge, "for a good many years, and made a practice of leaving every year a couple of months before the winter season, telling his friends that he wanted to reach New York in time to attend divine service on Christmas day. In those days Christmas was not the great religious festival in New England that it is to-day, and the people were practically ignorant of the real meaning of the tenets of the Catholic faith. Rourke never tried to deny his religion, and it was a common thing for the farmers for miles around to gather at the house where he was making a pair of boots and hear him tell of the inhuman cruelties perpetrated on his countrymen on account of their faith, and in my opinion he was the first man that told the old settlers of this town the Catholic meaning of the word 'Mass.' After an absence of a few months he was sure to return and remain until the following Christmas, when he was off again. Finally he expressed a determination to revisit the scenes of his early boyhood and use his genius in defence of his native country, and that was the last the townspeople ever heard of him."

HON. FRANKLIN M. DANAHER,
ALBANY, N. Y.

MR. THOMAS F. O'MALLEY,
SOMERVILLE, MASS.

MR. JAMES P. BREE,
NEW HAVEN, CONN.

MR. THOMAS J. LYNCH,
AUGUSTA, ME.

FOUR MEMBERS OF THE SOCIETY.

SOME IRISH SETTLERS IN VIRGINIA.

BY HON. JOSEPH T. LAWLESS,[1] RICHMOND, VIRGINIA.

Perhaps the most distinguished man of Irish birth who identified himself completely with Virginia, was Gen. Andrew Lewis, who was born in Ireland about 1720, and came to Virginia with his parents in 1732. John Lewis, the father, was the first white man who fixed his home in the mountains of West Augusta.

Andrew Lewis served as a major in the regiment commanded by Washington in the Ohio campaign of 1754 and 1755. He served with valor in the French and Indian wars, and was highly regarded by Washington, at whose suggestion he was appointed a brigadier-general in the Continental army. Four of his brothers served in the Revolutionary War, one of them, Col. Charles Lewis, being killed at Point Pleasant. No better evidence of the value which Virginia placed on the services of this Irishman could be wished than the fact that she has deemed his effigy worthy to stand for all time beside the immortal group of Henry, Mason, Marshall, Nelson and Jefferson, which surrounds the heroic equestrian statue of Washington in the Capitol Square at Richmond. This celebrated work of Crawford's is pronounced by the critics to be one of the finest in the world.

Descendants of John Lewis, the father of Gen. Andrew Lewis, are numerous in the state at this day. Some of them have been very distinguished men: John F. Lewis, who died recently, was lieutenant-governor of Virginia, and a senator of the United States. Lunsford L. Lewis, his half-brother, was president of the supreme court of appeals of Virginia for twelve years, retiring from that office a few years ago. Dr. Lewis Wheat is a well-known practising physician of Richmond. Judge John Lewis Cochran, whose mother was a great-granddaughter of John Lewis, father of Gen. Andrew Lewis, and whose great-grandfather, with his wife, *née* Susanna Donnelly, came to America about 1742, was a gallant soldier in the Confederate army, and a distinguished lawyer and judge.   James C. Cochran, brother to the foregoing, was a colonel of Confederate militia in the late war.   Henry King Cochran served as a surgeon in the Confederate service throughout the war. William Lynn Cochran was a major in the Confederate service, and a lawyer by profession.   Howard Peyton Cochran was a captain in the same service.   It is claimed that there were one hundred and five of the Lewis family in the service of the Confederate states.

Another Irishman who came to Virginia and left his impress was John Daly Burk, of Petersburg, Va.   He was born in Ireland, and educated at Trinity college, Dublin.   Because of his political opinions and affiliations he was compelled to leave the country (1797) while yet a student at college.   He first tried his fortune in Boston, and afterwards in New York.   But he received no encouragement.   His love for Ireland and his ardent democracy made against his success at the North, and he finally came to Virginia. Here he became the friend of Jefferson and John Randolph, both of whom encouraged the brilliant young refugee.

He was a lawyer, poet, dramatist and historian, and was undoubtedly one of the most accomplished men in the state during his day. His history of Virginia in four volumes was the first comprehensive history of the state written, and is regarded as one of the best ever compiled.   He also wrote " A History of the Late War in Ireland," with an account of the United Irish Association, from the first meeting in Belfast, to the landing of the French at Killala (8 vols., 1779, Philadelphia).   Before he completed the fourth volume of the history of Virginia he was killed in a duel with a French gentleman at Campbell's Bridge, Chesterfield county, Virginia, on the 11th of April, 1808.

The Preston family in Virginia is a distinguished one.   Its propositus John Preston was born in Ireland, and came to Virginia in 1735.   He married Elizabeth Patton before coming to America. She was a sister of Col. James Patton, also of Irish birth.   The latter was killed in Virginia by the Indians in 1753, leaving two daughters, from whom descended John Floyd and John B. Floyd, governors of Virginia; Hon. James D. Breckinridge of Louisville, Ky., and Col. Wm. P. Anderson of the United States army.

John Preston left one son, William, and four daughters, from whom are descended some of the most distinguished men in American history. Dr. R. A. Brock in his "Virginia and Virginians" says, "Scarce another American family has numbered as many prominent and honored representatives as that of the yeoman-founded Preston, with its collateral lines and alliances." In support of this claim he continues: "It has furnished the National government a vice-president [Hon. John Cabell Breckinridge], has been represented in several of the executive departments and in both branches of congress. It has given Virginia five governors—McDowell, Campbell, Preston and the two Floyds—and to Kentucky, Missouri and California, one each, in Governors Jacobs, B. Gratz Brown and Miller ; Thomas Hart Benton, John J. Crittenden, William C. and William Ballard Preston, leading moulders of public sentiment ; the Breckinridges, Dr. Robert J. and William L., distinguished theologians of Kentucky ; Professors Holmes, Venable and Cabell, of the University of Virginia, besides other distinguished educators."

Nor is their battleroll less glorious. It is claimed that more than a thousand of this family and its connections served in the contending armies during the late Civil War. Among the leaders were Generals Wade Hampton, Albert Sydney Johnston, Joseph E. Johnston, John B. Floyd, John C. Breckinridge and John S. and William Preston. When it is stated that besides the names enumerated, the family is connected with those of Baldwin, Blair, Bowyer, Brown, Buchanan, Bruce, Cabell, Carrington, Christian, Cocke, Flournoy, Gamble, Garland, Gilmer, Gibson, Grattan, Hart, Henry, Hughes, Howard, Lee, Lewis, Madison, Marshall, Mason, Massie, Mayo, Parker, Payne, Peyton, Pleasants, Pope, Radford, Read, Redd, Rives, Seddon, Sheffey, Taylor, Thompson, Trigg, Venable, Watkins, Ward, Watts, Winston, Wickliff, among many others, as well-esteemed, some idea may be formed of its mental characteristics and social influence.

Judge Peter Lyons was born in Ireland, and came to Virginia in his early life. He was made a judge of the general court in 1779, becoming also a judge of the first court of appeals. He served as such until his death, July 30, 1809. As a jurist he ranked high. Among his colleagues on the bench were Chancellor Wythe, Edmund Pendleton, St. George Tucker and Spencer Roane. His descendants for several generations were eminent in the professions, and some of them are still living in Virginia. James Lyons, Jr., who was a colonel on the staff of Governor O'Ferrall, is the oldest male descendant in the direct line. He married a daughter of William Wirt Henry, grandson of Patrick Henry, and by her has several children living.

Another judge of the supreme court of appeals was William C. Burks, of whose ancestors little is known except that they were Irish. He died recently, mourned by the profession which he had so signally adorned by the profundity of his juridical learning and the simplicity and spotlessness of his life. His opinions are as highly regarded as those of any man who sat upon the bench of that court within a half century. He was of weak frame and never enjoyed good health—"a creaking door," was the expression he commonly used to indicate himself—and never held public office other than that mentioned. Yet his capacity for labor was truly remarkable. He was one of the early presidents of the Virginia Bar Association, which he was largely instrumental in organizing; and until the time of his death was one of the editors of the *Virginia Law Register*, the organ of the profession in this state.

Perhaps the ablest Irish lawyer in the state was Thomas J. Michie, whose reputation extended throughout Virginia as a brilliant wit as well as able jurist. Among the judges of the present supreme court of appeals of Virginia is John W. Riely, who was a major in the Confederate service, and whose ancestors were Irish. The speaker of the House of Delegates, session of 1897–8, was John F. Ryan. A late governor of Virginia was Philip W. McKinney, of Irish descent. His successor was Charles T. O'Ferrall, a man of Irish descent. Among the state officers of Irish descent may be mentioned P. H. O'Bannon, public printer; John Bell Bigger, clerk of the House of Delegates; Major B. W. Lynn, superintendent of the penitentiary, and the writer (Secretary of State Lawless), both of whose parents were born in Galway, and came to America after the "black famine."

Gen. William Mahone was a descendant of an Irish progenitor who settled in Virginia in colonial days. Judge Anthony Kiely is of Irish lineage, and you know his history. After his appointment as minister to Austria by Mr. Cleveland, and the indication on the part of Francis Joseph that he was at Vienna *persona non grata*, Mr. Kiely was made one of the judges of the international court at Cairo, Egypt, and became its president.

Dr. Hunter McGuire, who was medical director of Stonewall Jackson's corps and the intimate friend of that great soldier, is of Irish lineage. His great-grandfather, Ed. McGuire, left Ordfest, County Kerry, in 1756, and settled in Winchester, Va.

The Dooleys, Pattersons, Glennans, Kevills, Barrys, O'Connors, Fitzgeralds, Keans, Rheas, Kendricks, Kellys, McChesneys, Goolricks, Wards, Higgins, Doyles, Lawlers, Rafters, Ferriters, McKenneys, McCrackens, Youngs, Coles, Macgills, O'Bannons, Irvings, Irwins, Nolans, O'Sullivans, Sullivans, Walshs, O'Neills, Kanes, Murphys, Ryans and a hundred others, came largely during the present century. Perhaps most of these families left Ireland in the great exodus which followed the famine of 1846-'47. Certainly Virginia received about that time the greatest number of immigrants who, unfortunately for themselves and for their race, have preferred for the most part to lead urban lives. But they and their progeny have not failed to leave the impress of their character upon the people among whom their lot was cast.

And it is not too much to say that in the years to come, when, in the expiring hours of the twentieth century, some chronicler pauses to consider the virtues and deeds of Virginians, he will dwell in loving admiration upon the talents and traits of those of Irish blood, who have already made bricks without straw, and won the confidence and esteem of their neighbors.

They are a people whose genius under the ægis of the Constitution enjoys here that freedom of thought and liberty of action which have been denied their fathers for eight hundred years—who love the Republic and its institutions next only to their God, and who read their own happiness and the fulfilment of all their earthly hopes in the increasing and enduring glory thereof.

Capt. Page McCarty, of Richmond, Va., writes: " I learned something of Irish-Americans from the papers of my father, governor of Florida at one time, and member of congress in 1839. The 'Scotch-Irish' appear to have established a theory of pre-emption or monopoly, and of that I learned but little. O'Brien, of General Washington's staff, was from Alexandria, Va. Colonels McClanahan and Andrew Wagoner and Maj. Richard McCarty, of the Revolution, were descendants of a small group of Irishmen who named the little town of Kinsale on the Potomac about 1662. Daniel McCarty, speaker of the Virginia House of Burgesses 1715, was of this set of people, and grandson of McCarty, of Clenclare, though

I see that some of his kin are trying to Scotch-Irish him also.   The main immigration of Irish was through Philadelphia and Charleston, S. C., and they penetrated to the mountains with the most adventuresome pioneers and met in the valley that extends from the Peaks of Otter to the headwaters of the Tennessee river."

MR. BERNARD CORR,
BOSTON, MASS.

MR. EDMUND REARDON,
CAMBRIDGE, MASS.

HON. PAUL H. KENDRICKEN,
BOSTON, MASS.

POLICE CAPT. JOHN F. MURRAY,
CAMBRIDGE, MASS.

FOUR MEMBERS OF THE SOCIETY.

THE WHISTLERS—A FAMILY ILLUSTRIOUS IN WAR AND PEACE.

BY JOSEPH SMITH, LOWELL, MASS.

The following sketch of the Whistler family appeared originally in the *Illustrated American* of May 25, 1895, and is reproduced with some few slight emendations, because it is germane to the work of the American-Irish Historical Society. It was the intention of the writer to make a brief sketch of the famous artist, whose birthplace was at that time the subject of much amusing discussion, but he found the antecedents of the artist such interesting personalities and their history so romantic, that he amplified his first sketch into a brief story of the family.

Major Whistler's connection with the beginnings of Lowell, Mass., led the writer further afield and gave him material that may at some future time be added to the literature of the society. It is sufficient to say here that this splendid seat of American industry—Lowell— was conceived, founded, cradled and fostered by the grandson of an Irishman and the husband of that grandson's sister, Patrick Tracy Jackson and Francis E. Lowell, from the latter of whom it received its name.

The French savant, Guèrinsen, may or may not have been scientifically correct when he wrote, " Genius is a disease of the nerves ; " but certainly the eccentricities of genius point too frequently to neurotic degenerations, to aberrations from the normal, and to symptoms that are " conceived in spleen and born in madness." Modern instances of this truism are on every hand. There is that in James Abbot McNeill Whistler, for instance, which marks him distinctly as standing among the eccentrics of genius ; and which, in his splenetic vagaries, shows him to be hovering on the borderland of madness.

While his affectations in art, his " harmonies," " symphonies " and "arrangements" in blue and gold, and gray and green, and so on *ad nauseam*, might seem to set him down among the Barnums of art, with the poseurs of the æsthetic, Whistler's work shows him to be a man of undoubted genius, a most uncomfortable and irritating genius perhaps, but still a genius whose brilliancy is flawed by his aggressive ego-mania. When we have discounted all the theatrical "isms" in which he frames his art, we are compelled to recognize the fact that he is an artist whose work will live. No ordinary man, no merely artistic charlatan, could make the impression on the age that Whistler has done. Whistler is a writer of deliciously clever and disagreeable things; he has a literary quality whose acidity has etched his personality on this decade; he is a brilliant talker, overflowing with quirk and bon mot, satire and repartee, alert and resourceful in the battle of wits, and he is easily the central figure at the social functions he honors, outshining all other lights, out-roaring other lions, a meteor among the stars.

While English in his remote racial root, his forbears lived long enough in Ulster to extract from the soil and atmosphere of Ireland that Celtic wit and pugnacity, that brilliance and originality so characteristic of the man. The transplantation of his immediate ancestors to American soil added to the mental celerity and nervous alertness of his fiber, giving to his personality that Gallic flavor which the English-speaking races acquire under our skies in sloughing off the heavy heritage of insularity of the land of fogs.

Great talents are seldom transmitted from one generation to another, yet certain characteristics which are physiological rather than psychological, may mark the branches of a common family tree. Whistler owes his intellectual qualities to his racial fiber, to his mixture of blood and the changing environments of his ancestors; they are in fact highly developed racial characteristics, while his artistic instincts—raised in him to the plane of genius—are a family inheritance. His wit, humor and mental dynamics he owes to his Irish fathers; his merciless mockery, his acidulous aggressiveness, his satirical sardonism, are the Calvinism of his Scottish strain run to seed and sprouting in the soil of Bohemia: a sparkling champagne, which has been spoiled with vinegar.

The son of a great father, standing in the glare of a great light, has his own brilliance minimized and is deprived of that natural light and shade so necessary to his artistic proportion. If he be great himself, his contemporaries will institute comparisons that are ever odious, unless their greatness be in different directions. On the other hand, when the son is great his glory only adds to the aureole of the great father.

Whistler's father was a famous man in his day; but time has done for the father what it has yet to do for the son—it has stilled the voices of contemporary panegyric and detraction, it has estimated his true worth, measured and ascertained his proportion and given him a definite historical verdict.

A glance at Whistler's antecedents will be of interest to all, for they have added to the glory of the Republic and given it as loyal service as any one family in its history.

The Whistler family is remotely of English origin, and it was Ralph, son of Hugh Whistler of Goring, in Oxfordshire, who founded its Irish branch, removing to Ulster as a tenant of one of those predacious London guilds which exchanged its guineas for the broad acres which that thrifty monarch, James Stuart, had despoiled from the O'Neills and O'Donnells of Ulster.

The first Whistler on American soil was John, a scion of this Ulster settler of the Plantation. While little that is definite is known of this branch, the internal evidence forces us to conclude that it was one of some social and political importance, for it was on terms of intimacy with the landed proprietors of the province. The character of this John indicates that whatever the religious and political opinions of the Irish Whistlers may have been, they had grown on the soil to be Irish of the Irish. John Whistler was a high-strung, bold, brave, devil-may-care blade, who loved adventure and excitement and had the Irishman's love of a fight and a soldier's life. While yet a mere boy he ran off from home, enlisted in King George's army and was hustled off in a transport to America to aid in the work of subduing the rebellious colonies.

He reached Canada in season to march with the luckless Burgoyne and to come to grief and captivity with his superior at Saratoga. He fell in love with his captors and the country, and doubtless registered a vow that he would make his home in America at some future period. In time he was exchanged and sent back to England. He was poor, yet, with that amusing contempt of poverty so characteristic of the Irish gentleman, he aggravated his troubles by falling rapturously in love with the pretty daughter of his father's friend, Sir Edward Bishop. The maid was as ardent and foolish as her lover, but the father looked askance at the suit of the young soldier of fortune.   The lovers solved the problem for themselves in Irish fashion by running away, marrying and taking ship for the rebellious colonies before the elders woke up.   The young couple landed at Baltimore with full hearts and empty pockets and settled down at Hagerstown to begin the battle of life.

It is certain that fortune continued as unkind and capricious under American skies as she had been under Irish ones, and we next hear of the young husband bidding adieu to his young wife and child, and marching with a musket on his shoulder, as a soldier of the United States, into the wilderness of the West, under General St. Clair.

Fighting and soldiering in those days were done in rough and ready fashion under conditions that called for courage and endurance, when pluck and dash and personal prowess were the prime essentials of a soldier; and in such a school an Irish daredevil like Whistler easily made his mark.   In that disastrous battle on the Miami in 1791, where the forces of St. Clair were surprised and routed by the vengeful tribesmen under Blue Jacket and the renegade, Simon Girty, young Whistler was wounded, but his gallant conduct in the battle and on the retreat earned him his shoulder-straps, and gave him a position that his birth, breeding and education enabled him to fill with honor to himself and credit to the republic.   It gave him an assured position in the calling he loved best, and for which his talents and taste fitted him.

As the years rolled by, he served in many a hard-fought campaign against the enemies of his adopted country, earning promotion and fighting the soldiers of King George with as much enthusiasm as in other days he had served that fat-witted monarch.   His devoted wife followed his fortune, traveling in the military train, and living at lonely frontier forts with as much content as she would had fortune strewn their paths with brighter flowers.   This heroic woman had much to do in forming the character of the children born to their marriage, and her brave and gentle personality made a lasting impression on them.   The Whistlers were good fighting stock, and when his sturdy boys were old enough, the fighting old major placed a sword in their hands and gave them to the land he loved, and true, loyal soldiers they were in every emergency.   When age, disease and wounds stiffened the old warrior, and rendered him unfit for active service in the field, the government appointed him store-keeper at the military post at Newport, Ky., and later transferred him to Jefferson Barracks, near St. Louis, Mo., where he died in 1829, at the age of seventy-three.

The splendid old soldier had served the land of his adoption bravely, faithfully and loyally, and, dying, he bequeathed to his sons an unsullied reputation, and to the republic children who never failed her in the hour of need.

William Whistler, the major's first-born, first saw the light of day in 1780 at Hagerstown, Md., and grew up with drums for his music and swords for his toys, and became a lieutenant in the army in 1801. He fought against Indians and British on the frontier with gallantry, and was badly wounded at the battle of Maguaga, Mich., in the year 1812. He passed through the various grades, fought in nearly every war the army was engaged in, and was retired with the rank of colonel of the Fourth United States infantry in 1861. Next to Gen. Winfield Scott, William Whistler was then the oldest soldier in the American army. William's son, Joseph Nelson Garland Whistler, was, like his father, a soldier. He was graduated from the West Point Military Academy in 1846, served with distinction in the Mexican War and the Rebellion, and was colonel of the Fifteenth United States infantry, when he was placed on the retired list in 1886.

George Washington Whistler, the father of the artist and writer of "the gentle art of making enemies," was the second son of Maj. John Whistler. He was born on the ragged edge of civilization, in the shabby frontier post of Fort Wayne, in the territory of Indiana, on May 19, 1800. He traveled up and down the rough trails of the Western wilderness with his father's regiment, receiving what education he could from his mother until he was sent, while yet a boy, to West Point. He had a well-developed talent for draughtsmanship, and was a man of refined and artistic tastes ; he was a charming companion, and withal a handsome, soldierly gentleman. One of the brightest men ever turned out of West Point, he was graduated high in his class, and commissioned as a second lieutenant in the United States artillery corps ; but his engineering talents were utilized by the government in topographical surveys while in the service, except for the brief period when he was an assistant professor at the academy. One of the burning questions of those days of the early twenties was the frontier between the republic and the British dominions, our government claiming much that is still a fishing and hunting-ground in the province of New Brunswick ; John

Bull, with unerring instinct, seeking to push his lines south to include the country that has blossomed into the commonwealths of Iowa, Minnesota and the Dakotas.

From 1822 to 1826 the young lieutenant was engaged in tracing and defining the boundary in the terrible wilderness that stretches from Lake Superior west to the Lake of the Woods, enduring cold, hunger and incredible hardships, and laying the seeds of disease that was to cut him off in the prime of manhood and the zenith of his success. When he came back to civilization from these arduous duties, he found the country agog with railroad excitement, caused by the work of the Stephensons in England. American capitalists were eager to build railroads, but they realized that the radically different conditions of the two countries necessitated essentially different systems of construction and operation.

Needing the best engineering skill in the country, they applied to the government, and Whistler was, with others, detailed to survey the routes, report on systems and supervise construction of the roads. He was engaged in this responsible work for years, but, knowing that such talents as his—and he was recognized as one of the ablest engineers in the country—found but slender rewards in the service of the republic, and were better appreciated in civil life, he resigned his commission in December, 1833. His services were secured at once by the railroads, and he was sent with Jonathan Knight, William Gibbs McNeill and Ross Winans to England to examine the system there, and returning he occupied himself with the affairs of the Baltimore & Ohio and Boston & Albany railroads.

It is not too much to say that, practically, George Washington Whistler laid down the lines upon which the American railroad system was built, and along which it has grown to be the most splendid and advanced in the world, the most potent agency in the progress and civilization of the republic.

In 1834 Whistler became the engineer of the proprietors of the Locks and Canals of Lowell, Mass., the corporation whose wisdom and shrewdness have been instrumental in changing the fields and pastures along the slopes of the Merrimack into the foremost and most prosperous manufacturing city devoted to textile industries on this continent. Besides looking keenly after their strictly local interests, he spent months in the corporation's machine shops, drawing plans, evolving inventions and improvements and supervising the construction and remodeling of a Stephenson locomotive, in order to adapt it to the needs and peculiar requirements of American railroads. Those most familiar with railroads and their history in this country are best equipped to appreciate the work done in that little machine shop by Whistler and to understand its value.

Whistler lived in Lowell from 1834 to 1837, in a modest house on Worthen street, and there his famous son, James Abbot McNeill Whistler, was born, probably in 1834. The parish records of the old Episcopal church of St. Anne state " James Abbot Whistler, son of George W. and Anna M. Whistler," was baptized there Nov. 9, 1834, by him who was long and reverently known to the people of Lowell as Father Edson. This is the artist who is alleged to have been born in Baltimore and Stonington, and who himself rather oddly claims Moscow in Russia as his birthplace; but this is the record, given under the signature of the present rector, the Rev. A. St. John Chambre of Lowell.

In 1837, Mr. Whistler left Lowell for Stonington, Conn., where he took charge of the affairs of the Stonington railroad, and three years later he removed to Springfield, Mass., to take up the duties of chief engineer of the Boston & Albany road. His reputation had grown apace with his work and achievements and it was now thoroughly established as that of a wise, prudent, skilful engineer, masterful and resourceful in all emergencies. He had been engaged on the most difficult and puzzling engineering problems of the day and had successfully overcome them. His fame was commensurate with his success; he was patient, industrious, ingenious, bold, sagacious, tenacious and incorruptibly honest; he had the confidence, trust and affection of those with whom he labored, and his manly, scholarly, soldierly and tactful personality brought him a wide and well-earned esteem.

It was at this time that the Emperor Nicholas of Russia sent a commission of officers to the United States to study the American railroad system, with a view of introducing it into the empire if better adapted to its needs than the English system, which they had already investigated. Colonels Menlikoff and Krofft not only reported emphatically in favor of the American system, but spoke in terms of highest admiration of the impression made on them by the ability and courtesy of Whistler. The emperor made up his mind that Whistler was the one man to introduce the railroad system into Russia, and he made a flattering offer for his services, among many other inducements being that of an annual salary of $12,000. Major

Whistler accepted the offer of the emperor and sailed for St. Petersburg in 1842, in company with Major Boultattz of the Russian Engineer Corps, who had been sent to escort him to Russia.

An extraordinary task lay before Whistler in Russia, and one that might have made an ordinary man hesitate. The route had to be surveyed for the contemplated road between Moscow and St. Petersburg, the road-bed had to be constructed, the tracks laid, bridges, stations and engine-houses designed and built, gauges considered and decided upon, machine shops constructed, mechanics trained, locomotives and rolling-stock planned and built, and, in fact, every detail of the immense undertaking had to be deliberated over, thought out and carried to completion under this one man's supervision. It was an herculean task that his marvelous executive capacity was to meet and conquer.

The jealousies of officials, suspicious of a foreigner and imperial favorite, the impediments thrown in his way by a corrupt officialdom, the delays of the bureaus, the greed of contractors, the importunities of inventors and the solicitations of a horde of corrupt harpies that gather round such an enterprise, had to be reckoned with; and these he did with consummate skill and tact, taxing the resources of his urbane but firm diplomacy and exhausting the vitality of his physical being. He overcame all obstacles, he earned the respect, admiration and affection of his Russian associates, he smoothed the friction of bureaus and officials, he made the fortune of his American associate, Winans, and others, he obtained the sincere regard and respect of the autocrat of the empire and was content to remain a poor man and an honest man. His monument was the finest and best-equipped railroad on the continent of Europe. The Emperor Nicholas, anxious to show his admiration and esteem for the American, urged him in vain to accept a high commission in the Russian army, but he refused everything, contenting himself with the decoration of the Order of St. Anne.

But Whistler's work was nearly done; he had worked too hard and too faithfully. Beside his railroad work he planned many important improvements in the fortifications at Cronstadt, which balked the British under Napier a few years later; he made useful and needed changes in the naval school and docks at St. Petersburg, and planned many other public works. In November, 1848, he had an attack of Asiatic cholera, which precipitated upon his already exhausted system a complication of diseases, and he lingered along until April, 1849, when he died in the Russian capital in his 49th year.

Posthumous honors were paid the distinguished dead by the emperor; Whistler's family were treated with great kindness and consideration by the government, and it was ordered that no changes of any nature would be permitted in completing the great railroad enterprise he had created.

Major Whistler's first wife was Mary, daughter of Dr. Foster Smith of the United States army, who fell in love with him as a cadet at the academy where her father was stationed. The son by this marriage, George William Whistler, followed in his father's footsteps and became a famous railroad engineer. His second wife was Anna Matilda McNeill, a daughter of Dr. C. D. McNeill of Wilmington, N. C., and a sister of William Gibbs McNeill, his friend and associate. She was the mother of the artist, James Abbot McNeill Whistler.

Major Whistler's body was carried to America and deposited in St. Paul's church, Boston, but it was subsequently buried at Stonington, the place of all places that this wanderer loved best and which he called home. A beautiful monument stands in Twilight Dell, in Greenwood cemetery, erected to his memory by the Society of American Engineers, which bears upon it this inscription :

"In memory of George Washington Whistler, Civil Engineer. Born at Fort Wayne, Indiana, May, 1800. Died at St. Petersburg, Russia, April, 1849. Educated at the U. S. Military Academy. He retired from the army in 1833 and became associated with William Gibbs McNeill. They were, in their time, acknowledged to be at the head of their profession in this country. He was distinguished for theoretical and practical ability, coupled with sound judgment and great integrity. In 1842 he was invited to Russia by the Emperor Nicholas, and died there while constructing the St. Petersburg & Moscow Railroad. This cenotaph is a memorial of the esteem and affection of his friends and companions."

It can well be said that Whistler, the artist, has come honestly and honorably by his brilliant gifts, and it can be stated with equal emphasis that the Genesis of a Genius is seldom as great and worthy.

DAVID HAMILTON, A SOLDIER OF THE AMERICAN REVOLUTION.

BY DANIEL M. O'DRISCOLL, CHARLESTON, S. C.

David Hamilton was born in Cork, Ireland, in November, 1749. He came to Charleston, S. C., when quite young. He was well educated, a man of property, and about 1774 wedded Elizabeth Reynolds. She was a daughter of Rev. James Reynolds, an Irish Presbyterian clergyman of James Island, S. C., and of his wife, Mary Ball, a native of that island. James Island was then as now the site of many large plantations.

After a siege of many months, General Lincoln, who with a small number of troops had gallantly defended the city of Charleston, surrendered May 19, 1780. The British had thought that on account of the scattered population and the number of slaves, it would be easier to subjugate the inhabitants of the Southern states than those of the Northern and Middle, whose hardy population inured to labor, especially among the mountains of Vermont and New Hampshire, had successfully resisted all efforts to overcome them. But in this they were mistaken, for although Savannah and Charleston, the chief cities of Georgia and South Carolina, were now in the hands of the enemy, still from every brush and bracken, Marion and Sumter and their scouts would spring at unexpected moments and unlooked for times.

Among those who were taken prisoners at Charleston was David Hamilton, the subject of this sketch. There is a tradition in the family that he held the rank of lieutenant.[1] This point, however, cannot be substantiated now, as the family papers and Bibles, which were in the possession of his daughter, Mrs. Sullivan of Hampton county, S. C., were lost or destroyed during the Civil War.

When the city of Charleston was surrendered to the British commander, David Hamilton, being a member of a regiment taken

---

[1] A Lieut. David Hamilton is mentioned in the Revolutionary records of Massachusetts; also at the national capital in the official records of that period.

under arms, became a prisoner of war. He was offered with others a parole if he would promise not to take up arms again against the mother country. This he declined to avail himself of, and Ramsay's History of the Revolution in South Carolina records his name as among the prisoners confined on board the prison ship *Torbay* in Charleston harbor in May, 1781.

This vessel conveyed these prisoners to Philadelphia where they remained until the treaty of peace was signed at Paris in 1783. Family records tell that during his detention, receiving permission to go about the city, his wife Elizabeth, at his solicitation, joined him there. The voyage in those days was a long and tedious one, but David Hamilton having vessels of his own, Mrs. Hamilton and her two children were able to perform the journey in one of them.

During her sojourn there a third daughter, Grizelle Agnes Hamilton, was born, who became in womanhood the wife of Capt. Joseph Taylor, U. S. N. After the Revolutionary War, David Hamilton, on his return to Charleston, became the partner in business of his brother-in-law, Christopher Fitz Simons, who, also an Irishman of wealth and culture, is the ancestor of the "Sir Rupert" of South Carolina, Wade Hampton, the third, the brave cavalry leader of the Southern army in Virginia. They carried on an extensive shipping, shipbuilding and wharfage business, Hamilton owning the ships and Fitz Simons the wharves. David Hamilton owned one hundred black men, slaves, with their families.

Mr. Fitz Simons was still wealthier, having $700,000, as his will still on record shows, and when his daughter, Anne Fitz Simons, became the wife of Wade Hampton the second, it was as no dowerless bride, she receiving $100,000 as her portion. The father of Colonel Hampton was the richest planter in the South, claiming to own 3,000 slaves. Christopher Fitz Simons dying a few years before David Hamilton, his will records that he leaves to David Hamilton £50 as a souvenir, according to the old English custom, and that he desired the business to continue under the firm name of Hamilton & Co.

David Hamilton died in Charleston, Nov. 29, 1794, and is buried in St. Philip's churchyard, the Colonial Episcopal church of that city. In these sacred precincts also rest the ashes of many of his descendants. David Hamilton left five daughters and three sons: Elizabeth, who became Mrs. Pritchard; Anne, Mrs. Harvey; Catherine, Mrs. Pritchard; Grizelle Agnes, Mrs. Taylor; Mary, Mrs. Sul-

12

livan ; of his three sons, David, John and William, David and William died unmarried. His married son, John, left a son and two daughters, from one of whom (Mary), Mrs. Nesbit, springs the family of the same name, wealthy planters of Georgetown, S. C. Of David Hamilton's daughters, Mrs. Pritchard's descendants attained distinction both in peace and war.

William Pritchard, her grandson, whose name is carved on the white marble tablet which stands in the vestibule of St. Philip's Episcopal church, was a member of the historic Washington Light Infantry of Charleston, and died of country fever during the Civil War. Mrs. Harvey's daughter, Anne, married Commandant Knight, U. S. N. Commandant Knight died while in service on the coast of Africa, of African fever. His remains still rest there. Mrs. Taylor's grandson, William Joseph Magill, commanded a regiment of Georgia regulars during the Civil War. He was a graduate of the Military Academy of South Carolina, a man of fine physique and pleasing address. Colonel Magill lost an arm at the battle of Sharpsburg, and died some few years ago in Florida where he had settled after the war.

Another grandson of Mrs. Taylor, Dr. James Ervin Godfrey, was educated in Paris and became a surgeon in the Confederate army, with the rank of major. He married in Madison, Ga., where he still resides, as do also many of his descendants. The youngest daughter, Mary, married Timothy Sullivan (O'Sullivan), a native of County Cork, Ireland, a merchant whose name is mentioned as a broker on Vendue Range, Charleston, more than eighty years ago. Mrs. Sullivan's eldest daughter married Patrick Cantwell (also an Irishman), an officer of the customs in Charleston. Mr. Cantwell was a first cousin of Lieut. Stephen Cassin, one of the heroes of the battle of Lake Champlain, and also a nephew of Commodore John Cassin, U. S. N., who was commander of the naval forces at Norfolk during the War of 1812, and at Charleston from 1821-'22, where he died the latter year. His remains lie in St. Mary's churchyard. Mr. Cantwell's eldest daughter, Mary, married Daniel O'Driscoll, of the O'Driscolls of Baltimore, born at Cork, Ireland. Of their two sons, one is a graduate of the College of Charleston, and has entered the profession of teaching; the other, a student at the Military Academy of South Carolina.

Among the surviving descendants of David Hamilton are the Godfreys of Georgia, the Magills of Florida, the Harveys, Stroheckers, Pritchards, Knoxes, Poppenheims, Milers, O'Driscolls, Langleys, Cantwells, Nesbits and Morrisons of South Carolina, and a family of Prestons in Alabama. A granddaughter, Mary Pritchard, married Dr. Barnard of New Haven, Conn., and her descendants still reside in that city.

THE IRISH CHAPTER IN THE HISTORY OF BROWN UNIVERSITY.[1]

BY THOMAS HAMILTON MURRAY, WOONSOCKET, R. I.

The founding of Brown University marks a pivotal era in the educational history of Rhode Island. It is not the beginning of that history any more than it is the ultimate conclusion thereof. For, before the founding came the pioneers of education, the skirmish line, clearing the underbrush, paving the way, opening the battle for the cause of knowledge.

In the van, then, were the private teachers who received pupils into their homes or taught them at their own firesides. Many of these teachers in early Rhode Island history were talented Irishmen. Indeed, Irish schoolmasters were numerous throughout all the colonies. In reading the lives of the men of the Revolution, we are astonished at the number receiving their education from these Irish teachers.

Of the Irish masters who taught in Rhode Island at an early period may be mentioned Brown, MacSparran, Crocker, Knox, Kelly, Jackson, Phelan, Reilly and others.

Rev. Dr. MacSparran was a leading Irish preacher and teacher whose educational influence without doubt helped pave the way and render desirable the founding of a Rhode Island college. His arrival in these parts dates from about 1718, when he located in Bristol. Later, and for a period of nearly forty years, he was pastor of St. Paul's church in Narragansett. Dr. MacSparran always had a warm affection for his native land, and loved to speak and read the Irish language. During his long period of service in Narragansett he received many pupils at his home, imparting a knowledge of the Greek and Latin classics and various other branches. Writing in 1752, he says: "Mr. Thomas Clap, president of Yale college, was my scholar when I came first to these parts, and on all occasions gratefully acknowledges his receiving the first rudiments of his

[1]Brown University is located in Providence, R. I.

learning from me, who, by the way, have not but a modicum to boast of myself." MacSparran died in 1757.

Rev. Marmaduke Brown, an Irishman, while rector of Trinity church, Newport, opened a school for the instruction of negro children. In 1763 he had provided for teaching thirty pupils, fifteen of each sex. He likewise contributed in many other ways toward creating and perpetuating an educational spirit in the community. This Irishman, Brown, is mentioned in the charter of the university as a member of the first board of Fellows. He also appears as a member of the board in 1770. His wife was an Irish woman of sterling worth and fine intellect. His father, Rev. Arthur Brown, a native of Drogheda, in Ireland, came to Rhode Island about 1729, and was pastor of King's church in Providence. Marmaduke Brown had a son, Arthur, who became senior Fellow of Trinity college, Dublin, and member of the Irish parliament. It is not known,—at least I do not know,—that these Irish Browns of Newport and Providence were related to the family from whence the university derives its name.

Stephen Jackson of Kilkenny was another Irish teacher. Some of his descendants have been identified with Brown university. Stephen came to this country in 1724. He was a resident of Providence in 1745 and is mentioned as a "schoolmaster." In 1762 he was living on Benefit street. One of his sons married Susan Waterman. A grandson of this Kilkenny teacher was town clerk of Providence for many years, another was cashier of the Exchange bank, a third was president of the Washington Insurance company, while a great-grandson of the Irish immigrant became governor of Rhode Island and was always a warm friend of the university.

Another Irish teacher who must have settled here before Rhode Island college was instituted, and who thus helped create the educational atmosphere which so eventuated, was "Old Master" Kelly. He lived and labored at Tower Hill, in South Kingstown, R. I., and vicinity. In the Narragansett Historical Register (Vol. 1) it is stated that "Master Kelly was an Irishman and noted for his love of a good joke, a good dinner and his courtesy of manner." When Commodore O. H. Perry was a boy Kelly was his teacher, having already taught three generations of the youth of that neighborhood. Anecdote and reminiscence of Kelly are still numerous among the old families of that part of the state. "It is recorded of the worthy pedagogue, that during the whole of his long servitude at Tower Hill, he had never once been known to lose his temper, but

ever preserved a blessed equanimity, to be envied by all of his arduous and important calling."

Cole's History of Washington and Kent Counties, R. I., states that
"Before 1800, Masters Knox and Crocker, natives of Ireland, taught
school at Bowen's hill [in Coventry] and the neighborhood." The
name Knox is found in Coventry in 1766. Perhaps the schoolmaster was there as early as that period or about the time of the founding of Rhode Island college.

Terence Reilly was a schoolmaster in Providence at the period of
the Revolution and, it may be, for some years previous thereto. I
am told that representatives of old Providence families still have in
their possession receipts for tuition fees paid Master Reilly by their
grandfathers or great-grandfathers.

John Phelan was one other old time schoolmaster in Providence.
His quarters in 1792 were on the west side of the "Great Bridge,"
where he conducted a day and evening school. But Reilly and
Phelan came after the establishment of Brown and so had no bearing on that fact. I merely mention them here in order that their
names may be perpetuated for future treatment.

It is a remarkable fact that one of the earliest suggestions of
which we have record, for the establishment of a college in Rhode
Island, came from an Irishman—the peerless and immortal Berkeley. No name in the intellectual life of the colony and the state is
more cherished than his. He was a native of Kilkenny and one of
the most illustrious Irishmen of his day. Born in 1648, he entered
the ecclesiastical calling, and in 1724 was made dean of Derry. For
many years he had entertained a plan for christianizing and civiliz-
ing the American Indian. His central idea was to establish a college in Bermuda, where missionaries were to be educated for work
among the red men.

He was promised funds with which to carry out this project.
Relying upon these assurances, he resigned his deanery, and in "a
hired ship of 250 tons" arrived at Newport, R. I., in 1729. His
object was, according to numerous authorities, to here await the
arrival of the expected funds, when he would proceed to Bermuda.
It is now also believed that while in Rhode Island he intended to
influence well-to-do people here in behalf of his plans.

Soon after his arrival in Newport his great merit was recognized
and he was quickly conceded the intellectual leadership of the colony. Berkeley often visited the Updikes and other noted families in

Narragansett. It was during one of these visits he declared that if the promised funds for his college ever arrived he would build the institution on Barber's Height, North Kingstown, R. I., instead of in Bermuda.

Alluding to this intention, Mr. William E. Foster, public librarian of Providence, declares of Berkeley that by " thus anticipating by over a third of a century the actual establishment of a college in Rhode Island, his plans unquestionably had an important bearing on the steps leading to it."

The direct cause, however, that led to the establishment of Brown was the action taken in 1762 by the Philadelphia Baptist association and which resulted as aforesaid. The details for the inauguration of the institution were entrusted largely to Rev. Morgan Edwards of Philadelphia, and Rev. Samuel Jones of Lower Dublin, Penn. The institution was incorporated in 1764, its first location being Warren, R. I., a town named in honor of an Irishman, Sir Peter Warren. In 1770 it was removed to Providence, and in 1804 the name was changed from Rhode Island college to Brown University.

Dr. Guild in his production on " The First Commencement of Rhode Island College " declares : " It is a singular and well-known fact, and it may perhaps be stated in this connection, that the first funds of the college were obtained from Ireland, in guineas and half guineas, from Mary Murphy, Susanna Pilson, Joseph Fowke and other members of Protestant churches and societies in Cork, Waterford, Belfast, Ballymony, Coleraine, Londonderry and Dublin." " This," Dr. Guild continues, " may be accounted for when we learn that Mr. Edwards's first settlement in the ministry, before coming to this country, was in Cork, where he married his wife [Mary Nunn]. The original subscription book, with genuine signatures, is one of the most interesting documents on file in connection with the history of the university."

Morgan Edwards's journey to Ireland and England was made in 1767. His Irish subscription list, mentioned by Dr. Guild, is still preserved in the university archives. It bears the following heading, written by Edwards himself :

"A list of persons in Ireland who have contributed towards endowing the college in Rhode Island government. Published, according to promise, partly for the honor of the benefactors, and partly to satisfy them and the college of the fidelity of their humble servant, by whom the money has been collected. The sums are put down in English currency, because better known in America."

Let us accompany him on his Irish visit. I am inclined to believe that not all his contributors were Protestants. Doubtless there were also generous, large-hearted Roman Catholics who aided him. In Cork he found over fifty subscribers. They included Mary Murphy, Matthew O. Dwyer, Francis McCarthy, Humphrey Crowley and Samuel Neale. In Waterford he found many friends. In Dublin his contributors included Mrs. Luke Kelly, Rachel Connor, John Reilly, William Gowan, James Martin and sixty or seventy others. Samuel McCormick was one of the many who aided him in Antrim. James Brennan and several others helped him in Westmeath. And so it was elsewhere throughout the country—a cordial greeting and a generous reception. The sums contributed were remitted to the college, from Cork, Newry, Belfast and Derry. Before leaving Ireland, he designated certain agents in Dublin to whom additional contributions intended for him could be sent.

In concluding his Irish tour he thus wrote: "Mr. Edwards begs the excuse of those gentlemen on whom he has not been able to wait a second time to receive their subscriptions; and desires they will be pleased to pay the same to Mr. Abram Wilkinson of Park street, or Mr. John Pym Joshua of Ushers Quay, Dublin, who will soon be authorized by the college to solicit, receive and remit money for its use. Mr. Edwards has also heard, since he left Ireland, of several who expressed a willingness to become benefactors to said college. He thanks them for their good will; and entreats them to deposit their gifts, whether money or books, with the above mentioned merchants in Dublin. This list may be had of the Rev. W. Boulton, in Golden Lane, Dublin."

From the foregoing it would appear that Irish friends of Rhode Island college gave books as well as money to the institution. Writing from abroad in 1768 to President Manning at Warren, Edwards says:

"My Dear Friend: I long to hear from you. Your last was of October 12, 1767. . . . Mr. Miles informed me that he had sold one of my Irish bills . . . for £138 12s 4d, which gained for the college upward of £13. I have not had any account of the sale of the other bill for the same country. I want much to know how you intend to put the money out. . . . You must also observe that in England, as in Ireland, I solicit for money towards endowing the college, and, therefore, take care that you all attend to the design of the donors. Inclosed you have a list of all the sums I received in Ireland, which list was distributed in the several places where I have been. The design was to let every one of them see that I gave credit for what I received."

Irish generosity was likewise early displayed in this country toward the young institution. In 1769-'70, Rev. Hezekiah Smith solicited funds in South Carolina and Georgia. He says in his diary of the tour: "Thursday, March 1 [1770], went to Malachi Murfee's." The list of those who subscribed in aid of the college on this Southern trip includes Edward Dempsey, Charles Reilly, Patrick Hinds, James Welsh, Hugh Dillon, John Boyd, Matthew Roach and Capt. John Canty. Their names deserve to be perpetuated.

Rev. and Mrs. Edwards, to whom reference has just been made, had several children. Some of the latter were perhaps born in Ireland. One of the sons, William, was graduated from Brown in 1776, under President Manning. At the commencement in 1770, six years previously, this incident occurred as narrated in the *Providence Gazette:*

"The business of the day being concluded, and before the assembly broke up, a piece from Homer was pronounced by Master Billy Edwards, one of the Grammar school boys, not nine years of age."

Joshua, another son of Mr. and Mrs. Edwards, was hale and hearty in 1849, at over 80 years of age, and presented his father's Irish and English subscription lists to the university. I think it may be justly claimed that if Brown is now prosperous, vigorous and progressive, she is largely indebted for it to the assistance rendered in the formative period by Morgan Edwards and his Irish wife.

We have already seen how Marmaduke Brown, an Irishman, was a member of the university's first board of Fellows. We now come to another man of Irish blood who was a graduate of the institution and subsequently a member of its governing body. I refer to John Dorrance. The immigrant Dorrances arrived from Ireland about 1715–1720. They settled in what is now the town of Foster, this state. The immigrants included George and his two sons, George and James. John Dorrance, the alumnus of Brown, was born about 1747. He entered Rhode Island college, and in 1774 was gradu-

ated therefrom.   For the last sixteen years of his life, the citizens
of the town (Providence) manifested their confidence in him by
making and continuing him president of the town council.

Thus as head of the town he enjoyed a period of duty nearly as
long as the late Mayor Doyle, head of the city.   Dorrance was
elected sixteen times and Doyle, I believe, eighteen.

The study of Ireland and the Irish people has for a long period
received attention from many students of Brown.   Thus at the
graduation exercises in 1824 Ezra Wilkinson's oration was entitled
a "Defence of the Irish Character."   At the exercise in 1848,
Samuel B. Vernon took as the subject of his oration "The Mission
of St. Patrick to Ireland."

Joseph Moriarty graduated in the class of 1830, at which time he
delivered an essay on the "Character of Roger Williams."   Mark
D. Shea graduated in 1865.   James G. Dougherty was also of that
class.

Pleasant memories cluster around the walls and halls of old
Brown.   The university is rich in reminiscence and association.
In 1799 the institution conferred the degree of LL. D. upon Hon.
James Sullivan, a son of the Limerick schoolmaster.   James was a
brother of Gen. John Sullivan, and with the latter participated in
the siege of Newport and in the battle on the island of Rhode
Island.   He became governor of Massachusetts.   James Sullivan
was, no doubt, intimately acquainted with leading Rhode Island
people and was in all probability a frequent visitor here.   Brown
honored herself in honoring him.

In 1844, over fifty years ago, the degree of D. D. was conferred
by Brown upon John Sharp Maginnis.   His parents—John and
Jane Maginnis—were from Ireland.   In May, 1827, John was
licensed to preach as a Baptist.   He was a student of Brown, but
his health being poor, his studies were interrupted.   In the winter
of 1837-'38, he became pastor of the Pine Street church in Providence.   Delicate health obliged him to resign, however, and he
later became professor of philosophy in Rochester University.
Brown recognized his ability and showed her appreciation of his
talents by making him a doctor of divinity, as stated.

In 1860, Brown again conferred eminent honor upon a gentleman
of Irish lineage.   I allude to John Meredith Read, the great jurist,
a descendant of one of the Irish signers of the Declaration of Independence.   Brown gave him the degree of LL. D.   Dr. Read was

chief justice of Pennsylvania. His son, John Meredith Read, Jr., was a graduate of Brown, and received the degree of A. M. During his residence in Providence this latter gentleman became captain of the National Cadets, or Tigers, and also served on the staff of Governor Hoppin.

Early in the present century, when Brown had a medical department, there were several students of the latter whose names are indicative of Irish extraction, though one or two may be of Scotch blood. Among these were John Mackie (A. B. 1800), believed to have graduated in medicine about 1813; Andrew Mackie (A. B. 1814), medicine 1817; John McGore (A. B. 1811), medicine 1816; and Joseph Mulliken (A. B. Dartmouth, 1802), medicine, Brown 1817.

At the centennial of the university in 1864, General Burnside, always a warm friend of Brown, was among the speakers, as he indeed was at various other times. It is not generally known, perhaps, that maternally Burnside was of Irish descent. Yet such is the fact. Ambrose E. Burnside, whose portrait occupies an honored place on the walls of the university, was a son of Edghill and Pamelia (Brown) Burnside. Pamelia Brown, the general's mother, was the daughter of John Brown, an Irish immigrant, who had located in South Carolina. Ben: Perley Poore's " Life of General Burnside " refers to Pamelia, his mother, as " having the fair skin and brown hair of her Celtic ancestors, with large, expressive hazel eyes." She was born in the Laurens district, S. C.

It is generally claimed that Burnside, in the male line, was of direct Scottish descent. I do not dispute this, although Burnsides are numerous in Ireland, and have been so for nearly three hundred years. The Irish Burnsides have been allied with prominent families in Cavan, Donegal and other parts of the country. The name is mentioned in O'Hart's Irish Pedigrees. Betsy Burnside, an Irish woman, was a resident of Lincoln, R. I., some years ago, being then ninety-five years of age. We read that at Fredericksburg, as Meagher's shattered lines were retiring from their heroic efforts, Burnside saluted Meagher as the latter passed and silently grasped his hand. It was a meeting of two valiant commanders, the one of Irish birth, the other of maternal Irish descent, a fit subject for the greatest painter that ever lived. Fitting it was that an Irish sculptor was selected to produce the equestrian statue of Burnside which stands in Providence.

But Burnside is not the only personage of Irish lineage whom Brown has honored by permanently displaying his portrait on her walls. There is another—Commodore Perry, the hero of Lake Erie. Perry of Irish lineage? Yes, on his mother's side. Who was his mother? Sarah Alexander, a native of Newry, Ireland. During our Revolution some American prisoners of war were confined by the British at Newry, Sarah's native place. Among them was Christopher R. Perry. The American prisoners naturally elicited much commiseration from the Irish, who were in hearty sympathy with the Revolution.

Miss Alexander became acquainted with Mr. Perry during his imprisonment. This acquaintance in after years ripened into love and marriage. Commodore Oliver H. Perry was their son. Shortly after their marriage they came to Rhode Island and settled in South Kingstown. They were described as "a young and uncommonly handsome couple," and their advent was celebrated by feasting and sociality.

None gave a heartier welcome to Mr. Perry and his fair young Irish bride than the former's maternal grandfather, the venerable Oliver Hazard. As Mrs. Perry, Sarah Alexander became one of the most noted women in Rhode Island history. She had five sons —all distinguished—and three daughters. Speaking of Mrs. Perry, Mackenzie, a biographer of Commodore Perry, states that her friends in the old country "had been involved in the Irish rebellion. She, herself, had felt a lively interest in the cause of liberty, and had listened with deep interest to every account she had heard [in Ireland] of battles and skirmishes in the neighborhood. She took a pleasure in recounting to her son the achievements of her countrymen, and always insisted that they [the Irish] were the bravest people in the world." These narrations fired the mind of young Perry and created a desire in him to pursue the profession of arms. His mother, "to great strength of character added high intellectual powers and rare social grace, training her children with extraordinary care to high ideals of life and duty." It was also said of her that she fitted Perry "to command others by teaching him early to obey," and when he was old enough to attend school she consigned him to the care of Old Master Kelly, the Irish teacher whom I have already noticed. For years after the Lake Erie triumph it was spoken of in Rhode Island as "Mrs. Perry's victory," in allusion to the manner in which Oliver had been reared.

The university also possesses a portrait of Andrew Jackson. The latter visited Rhode Island while president of the United States, and may have been a guest in Providence and likewise have visited Brown. Jackson was of Irish descent. In an address to the Charitable Irish Society of Boston, in 1833, he said : " I am glad to see assembled on this occasion so many of the countrymen of my father. I am proud," he continued, " to be descended from that race which has so much to recommend it to the good wishes of the world." The portrait of Jackson in possession of the university was, I understand, to be seen a few years since in Rhode Island hall. Possibly it is still there.

In 1850—quite half a century ago—a committee was appointed to raise a fund of $125,000 for the university. President Wayland was then at the head of the institution. Among the subscribers to this fund was Matthew Watson, who contributed $500. Watson was, I believe, a descendant of a sturdy Irish immigrant, who settled in Barrington, R. I., in 1722. This immigrant's name was also Matthew Watson, and nearly every generation of the family since that day has had a Matthew in it. Bicknell, in his "Sketches of Barrington," tells us that Matthew the settler became a brickmaker and in time wedded Miss Read, the daughter of his employer. Her father opposed the match and represented to her the "folly" of throwing herself away, as he expressed it, on "a little poor Irishman." His arguments were of no avail, however, and she and Matthew were married at Barrington in 1732. The marriage was a happy one. The "little poor Irishman" subsequently purchased the farm of his father-in-law and conducted the brickmaking business on an extensive scale. He erected a commodious brick house, which became known to the country round about as "the great Watson mansion." Matthew, the immigrant, at one time held the position of judge of the court of common pleas for Bristol county. He is estimated to have accumulated in his brickmaking industry a fortune of $80,000. Some of his descendants are still living on the homestead. Matthew Watson, the benefactor to Brown in 1850, is believed, as I have stated, to be a descendant of this old Barrington settler.

The part taken by students and alumni of Brown University in the Civil War has been alike honorable and eminent. A memorial volume has been published on the subject. Of the graduates in 1856, Thomas Ewing, Jr., became one of the most distinguished.

He came of a prominent Ohio family and on his mother's side was of Irish descent. He was made colonel of the Eleventh Kansas Volunteers, 1862 ; brigadier-general of United States Volunteers, 1863, and brevet major-general United States Volunteers in 1865. Later he became chief justice of Kansas.

John C. Sullivan of the class of 1867 served in the Fourth Massachusetts Volunteers, entering the regiment in 1862. He became a student of Brown University after leaving the army.

In 1861, when the literary society of Brown was arranging its annual reunion, the question of a poem, of course, came up. It was finally decided that Fitz James O'Brien, a brilliant young Irishman, should be invited to officiate as poet of the occasion. O'Brien was a native of Limerick, Ireland, and born in 1828. His father was a lawyer and his mother a woman of uncommon beauty. Fitz James was educated in Dublin. He came to this country in 1852 with letters of introduction to prominent Americans. He quickly gained entrance to literary and fashionable society, where his talents soon made him a great favorite. He wielded a prolific pen. Among his contributions were: "The Ballad of Sir Brown," "The Gory Gnome," "The Wonderful Adventures of Mr. Papplewick" and "The Demon of the Gibbet." Among his poems, in addition to those mentioned, were: "Down in the Glen at Idlewild," "The Zouaves," "Helen Lee," "The Countersign," "Sir Brasil's Falcon," "The Song of the Locomotive," and "The Prisoner of War." His stories include "The Diamond Lens," "The Golden Ingot," "The Dragon Fang" and "The Pot of Tulips."

O'Brien enlisted in the Seventh New York regiment and marched with it to the defence of Washington. At the expiration of his term of service he returned to New York and started in, personally, to raise a regiment to be known as the McClellan Rifles. It was while thus engaged that he received the invitation to attend the exercises at Brown. After considering the matter, he replied, expressing regret at being unable to accept. Said he :

"A regiment of rifles which I am now engaged in raising demands all my time. If you can put me on the track of one hundred good men, you will please me better than if you crowned me with bays. If there is a spare population up your way, I would take a recruiting trip thither, and present my regrets in person."

So he did not come and the assemblage at Brown was denied the sunshine of his presence. O'Brien died of a wound received in battle and was given a soldier's burial in Greenwood. Nowhere was his death more deeply felt than among his friends in Providence.

I have already alluded to James G. Dougherty of the class of 1865. In 1862 he enlisted in the Tenth Rhode Island Volunteers, and saw service in Virginia. The close of the war was enthusiastically celebrated at Brown. Dougherty was chairman of the committee of arrangements and introduced President Sears to the great gathering assembled on that occasion. Mayor Doyle of Providence was also among the speakers. There was music, an illumination and unbounded enthusiasm.

The university has long numbered among her brightest students young men of Irish lineage. From the days of long ago down to the present, graduates of Irish descent have gone forth and won honorable distinction in life. The dear old *alma mater* has proudly watched their career and rejoiced in the credit reflected by their success. Americans they are, Americans they have been, by birth, by association, by education, in sympathy, in allegiance, in patriotism. Not that they love the land of their ancestors less, but that of their nativity more. Of Brown's alumni may be mentioned in this connection :

McGuinness, twice secretary of state of Rhode Island, and twice mayor of Providence.

Whitney, later ordained to the Roman Catholic priesthood.

Harson, the prominent merchant, the vigorous writer, a founder of the fraternity Phi Kappa Sigma.

Sheahan, clerk of the house of representatives ; member of the bar.

Monaghan, United States consul to Mannheim and Chemnitz.

Brennan, a lawyer of note ; judge-advocate-general on the staff of Governor Davis.

And so on, through a long and imposing list,—Murphy, Quinn, Holland, O'Connor, Kiley, McDonald, Gillrain, McGinn, Smith, Corcoran, Fitzgerald, Magill, Sexton, Cunningham, O'Neil, Hamill, O'Donnell, Mahoney, Hoye, Feeley, Cavanaugh and the rest.

The late George J. West, the eminent lawyer, the able legislator, the earnest friend of public education, was also a graduate of Brown. He was born in Ireland.

Nor should we forget that other graduate, Hon. Augustus S. Miller, who became speaker of the Rhode Island house of representatives. He himself has told me of his paternal Irish ancestry.

Sarah E. Doyle, on whom the university recently conferred a degree, likewise should not be overlooked. Eminent honor has she reflected on her Irish father.

And so I conclude. I have endeavored in this paper to show that in the history of Brown there is an Irish chapter and one of which we may be proud; one, too, of which the university may be proud. I have by no means exhausted the subject, which is capable of much additional development.

HON. C. T. DRISCOLL,
Mayor of NEW HAVEN, CONN.

HON. JEREMIAH CROWLEY,
Mayor of LOWELL, MASS.

REV. JAMES H. O'DONNELL,
WATERTOWN, CONN.

MR. CORNELIUS HORIGAN,
BIDDEFORD, ME.

FOUR MEMBERS OF THE SOCIETY.

BRIGADIER-GENERAL THOMAS W. SWEENY, U. S. A. —A BIOGRAPHICAL SKETCH—1820-1892.

BY WILLIAM MONTGOMERY SWEENY, ASTORIA, L. I., N. Y.

Thomas William Sweeny, popularly known as "Fighting Tom" Sweeny, was born in Cork, Ireland, Dec. 25, 1820. He immigrated to the United States in 1832, and died at Astoria, L. I., N. Y., April 10, 1892.

He was the youngest son of William Sweeny of Dunmanway, in the county of Cork, of whom it is said that he "was a true Celt, gifted with uncommon force of character, and not less remarkable for his courage, daring, and manly spirit than for that nice sense of honor that ever distinguishes 'the noblest work of God, an honest man.'" He died in 1827 and was buried at Macroom, Cork, where numerous generations of the family are interred.

The branch of the family from which Gen. Thomas William Sweeny, the subject of this sketch, was descended, has been located in the county of Cork since the thirteenth century, having migrated thither from Donegal, in the north of Ireland. Of the parent stock, Dr. McDermott states that "it was itself a branch of the O'Neills which settled in Donegal and founded three great families, namely: MacSweeny of Fanad, who had extensive territories west of Lough Swilly, and whose castle was at Rathmullen; MacSweeny of Banagh, who had a castle at Rathain, and MacSweeny na D'Tuatha, signifying MacSweeny of the Territories. According to O'Brien and other authorities he was called MacSweeny na D'Tuagh, signifying Mac-Sweeny of the Battle Axes, a title said to have been derived from their having been standard bearers and chiefs of gallowglasses to the O'Donnells. It is from the latter MacSweeny that the subject of our sketch was descended.

Dr. Smith, in his History of the County of Cork, states that "the MacSweenys had the parish of Kilmurry, in the territory of Muskery, county of Cork, and their chief castle at Cloghda, near Macroom, and had also Castlemore, in the parish of Moviddy." He

13

likewise mentions that "they were anciently famous for Irish hospitality," and relates "that one of the family erected a large stone
near the castle of Cloghda, inviting all passengers to repair to the
house of Edmund MacSweeny for entertainment." John O'Mahony,
the distinguished Irish scholar, author of the standard translation of
Keating's History of Ireland, says: "The MacSweenys were
standard bearers and marshals of the O'Donnells. They were
famous throughout Ireland as leaders of those heavy-armed soldiers
called gallowglasses. A branch of the family settled in the county
of Cork in the thirteenth century, as commanders of those soldiers
under the McCarthys of Desmond."

On the passage to the United States, with his mother and brother
William, in 1832, Thomas W. Sweeny, the subject of this sketch,
was swept overboard from the ship *Augusta*, by a huge wave, and
narrowly escaped drowning, being rescued by three members of the
crew who put off in a boat. He had been in the water thirty-five
minutes.

After finishing his education in the schools of New York city,
young Sweeny was apprenticed to the printing business in the well
known firm of Gould, Banks & Company (now, 1899, Banks &
Brother), at that time the leading law book publishers of the United
States, "where his many good qualities made him a general favorite."

He early evinced a taste for military training, and in 1837, while
a mere youth, attached himself to a military and literary association
of young men known as the "Paul Jones Parading Club," commanded
by Capt. Joseph Hinken. Afterwards they placed themselves under
the command of Capt. W. W. Tompkins, and adopted the name
of "Tompkins' Cadets." They then consolidated with the "Scott
Cadets," commanded by Capt. Charles Baxter, and in 1842 or 1843,
they were again strengthened by a portion of the seceders from the
"Tompkins' Blues," whereupon, for the purpose of identification,
they adopted the name "Independent Tompkins' Blues."

At the breaking out of the Mexican War, in 1846, Sweeny was
one of the first to volunteer, and he was elected second lieutenant
in Company A of the First New York Volunteers, commanded by
Col. Ward B. Burnett. On Christmas day, 1846, Messrs. Gould,
Banks & Company, uniting with a large number of individuals in
their employ, took the occasion—which was also his birthday—to
present Lieutenant Sweeny "a handsome pair of revolving pistols as
a token of esteem and regard."

On Jan. 8, 1847, Sweeny's regiment, to the number of about 800 men, sailed from New York for the seat of war. At Lobos Island, near Vera Cruz, where the troops landed, Lieutenant Sweeny was placed in command of a detachment to prepare the ground for encampment. This was his first command, and was "executed with dispatch and to the full satisfaction of his superior officer." Speaking of his subsequent movements an eye witness says: "After the bombardment of Vera Cruz, his regiment with the others, was marched into the interior. It was at Cerro Gordo, April 18, 1847, that Lieutenant Sweeny first practically smelt powder. Company A and one other were detached to support Capt. Francis Taylor's battery in taking the first height. They cut a road through the chaparral for the artillery, to the left of the enemy's position, in order to turn it. After reaching the base of the hill, and winding around it, they halted for orders. They were here exposed to a raking fire of grape and canister from the Mexican batteries."

At Contreras, Aug. 19, 1847, where the New York regiment stood the whole night in a gully up to their knees in mud, the men were greatly encouraged by the bearing of Lieutenant Sweeny.

At Churubusco, Aug. 20, 1847, while leading his men into action, Sweeny was struck in the groin by a spent ball. It passed through three pieces of clothing and produced a painful, though not dangerous, wound. Although advised to retire, he refused so long as he was able to stand. In a few minutes he was again wounded, receiving a musket ball in the right arm, but nevertheless he continued to lead and animate his men until he sank from exhaustion and loss of blood and had to be carried to the rear.

The wound in his arm proved to be so serious that amputation was found to be necessary in order to save his life. General Shields, who was present at the operation, was affected even to tears at the fortitude displayed by Sweeny, who, notwithstanding the fact that no anæsthetics were used, showed not the slightest signs of flinching under the terrible ordeal.

On his return to New York city, in 1848, Lieutenant Sweeny was received with much honor; he was brevetted captain by the governor of the state, and was presented a silver medal by the city government. He was also given a " grand reception ball " at Castle Garden, which was described as the "largest and most brilliant ball of the season." Among the invited guests were ex-President Martin Van Buren, Major-Gen. John A. Quitman, U. S. A., Hon. Simon

Cameron of Pennsylvania, Hon. William B. Maclay, M. C., representatives of the city and state governments and other people of note.

On recommendation of General Scott, Sweeny was appointed by the president a second lieutenant in the Second United States Infantry, March 3, 1848, and from March to July, 1848, he was stationed at Fort Columbus, Governor's Island, New York harbor. During August and September, 1848, Lieutenant Sweeny was at Jefferson Barracks, Missouri, and in October, 1848, he was stationed at Fort Hamilton, New York harbor, on recruiting service.

Nov. 8, 1848, his regiment, under command of Brevet Maj.-Gen. Bennett Riley, who had been appointed military governor of California, sailed from New York for California *via* Cape Horn. At Rio Janerio, where they stopped several days, they were entertained at a ball aboard the United States steamship *Brandywine*. They reached Monterey, Cal., April 6, 1849, and soon established regimental headquarters at San Diego.

On June 11, 1851, Sweeny was promoted to be first lieutenant in the Second Infantry. In 1852 he engaged in the Yuma Indian War, and commanded an expedition of twenty-seven men, who penetrated into the Cocopa country in May, and after a sharp engagement, captured one hundred and twenty-five armed warriors and marched them into Camp Yuma, where a treaty was entered into which broke up the confederation of the River tribes. While engaged on this duty, Sweeny received a severe arrow wound in the neck.

In 1854 he was ordered to Fort Pierre, in what was then northern Nebraska, where he served as aid to Gen. William S. Harney, participating in the campaign against the Sioux in 1855-'56, and was present at the "Great Treaty" made with the Sioux nation at Fort Pierre, at which many famous chiefs were present. In 1858 Sweeny was ordered to New York city on recruiting service, and was stationed there when the Rebellion broke out.

Jan. 19, 1861, he was promoted to captain, and soon after was ordered by General Scott to proceed to St. Louis, Mo., and assume command of the United States arsenal there. It contained at this time sixty thousand stand of arms, several field batteries, a number of heavy guns, a million and a half of ball cartridges, over forty tons of powder and a large quantity of other munitions of war. Captain Sweeny had only forty unassigned recruits under him to defend this vast property, while in the city were over three thousand Confederate minute-men, armed and drilled, to be ready at a moment's notice. Learning of a threatened attack, Sweeny let it be known that he would blow up the arsenal sooner than allow it to be captured, and he meant what he said. So they did not make the attempt.

Sweeny was brigadier-general of Missouri Infantry, May 20 to Aug. 14, 1861; made colonel of Fifty-second Illinois Infantry, Jan. 21, 1862; was brigadier-general of volunteers, Nov. 29, 1862, to Aug. 24, 1865; commissioned major in the Sixteenth United States Infantry, Oct. 20, 1863, and was retired with the full rank of brigadier-general, United States army, May 11, 1870.

In June, 1861, General Sweeny took command of the Southwest expedition, and proceeded to Springfield, Mo., where he assumed command of all the United States forces in that part of the state, including Siegel's and Saloman's regiments, which had left St. Louis with two 4-gun batteries. July 20, General Sweeny took command of a flying column of twelve hundred men, moved on a depot of Confederate supplies at Forsyth, Mo., and captured the same. He led the Second Kansas regiment at the battle of Wilson's Creek, Aug. 10, 1861, General Lyon leading the First Iowa. Sweeny was severely wounded, but after the death of Lyon favored following up the enemy. Sturgis, who succeeded Lyon in command, however, decided otherwise.

As colonel of the Fifty-second Illinois, Sweeny was attached to General Grant's army, and after the capture of Fort Donelson took charge of six thousand prisoners of war *en route* to Alton, Ill. At the battle of Shiloh (Pittsburg Landing), April 6 and 7, 1862, Sweeny commanded the Third Brigade of the Second Division, Army of the Tennessee, the brigade comprising about five thousand, five hundred men. Towards the close of the first day's battle, his command occupied a ravine near Gen. W. T. Sherman's left, known as the "Hornet's Nest."

Speaking of this battle General Sherman has said: "I remember well that Col. Thomas W. Sweeny, a one-armed officer who had lost an arm in the Mexican war and did not belong to my command, stood near by and quickly spoke up: 'I understand perfectly what you want; let me do it.' 'Certainly,' said I; 'Sweeny, go at once and occupy that ravine, converting it into a regular bastion.' He did it, and I attach more importance to that event than to any of the hundred achievements which I have since heard 'saved the day,' for we held that line and ravine all night, and the next morning advanced from there to certain victory."

In this battle Sweeny was again wounded, "receiving a minié ball in his remaining arm and another shot in his foot, while his horse fell riddled with seven balls. Almost fainting from loss of blood, he was lifted upon another horse and remained on the field through the entire day. His coolness and his marvelous escapes were talked of before many campfires throughout the army."

Capt. C. H. Fish, Fifty-second Illinois, speaking of the first day's battle at Shiloh, wrote of Sweeny: "Colonel Sweeny came riding up the line and reached our regiment, but not recognizing it, asked: 'What regiment is this?' On my telling him it was the Fifty-second Illinois, he said: 'Well, I am at home once more. I guess I will stay here.' Our colonel had only one arm—the left one; the other he lost in Mexico. When on drill or review he held the reins in his teeth and sword in left hand. The balls seemed to fill the air at this moment, the firing was so terrific, but our colonel [Sweeny] coolly sat on his horse, quietly smoking a cigar, ever and anon removing it and puffing forth vast quantities of smoke. Presently a minié ball came cutting through the air, struck his cigar, and cut it off at his teeth, doing some slight injury to his moustache. Yet not a muscle moved. He quietly replaced the cigar with a fresh one and smoked away."

After the battle of Shiloh, Sweeny was granted a leave of absence owing to disability resulting from wounds received. During this period he was presented an elegant sword by the city of Brooklyn, N. Y. At the expiration of his leave, he again took the field, returning in time to participate in the battle of Iuka and the siege of Corinth—Oct. 3 and 4, 1862,—where he was again wounded, and had a horse shot under him. Gen. Thomas A. Davies, commanding the Second Division, in his report of the battle of Corinth, states that "Colonel Sweeny, commanding First Brigade, behaved in the most gallant manner throughout, and should be immediately promoted."

Sweeny was commissioned brigadier-general of volunteers, Nov. 29, 1862. In the Atlanta campaign, he commanded the Second Division of the Sixteenth Corps, Army of the Tennessee. At Snake Creek Gap he took possession of the "Gap" with his division twenty-four hours before the arrival of supporting cavalry, and held it in spite of the desperate efforts of the enemy to dislodge him. Subsequently he took part in the battle of Resaca, and forced a passage across the Oostenaula river, at Lay's Ferry, where he fought a successful battle which resulted in Gen. "Joe" Johnston's retreat southward. He also took part in the battles of Dallas and Kennesaw Mountain, the actions at Nickajack Creek, Ruff's Mills, Rome Cross Roads, Calhoun's Ferry and other engagements.

At the battle before Atlanta, July 22, 1864, his division drove the enemy back with great slaughter, capturing four battle flags and nine hundred prisoners. This was the day that General McPherson was killed—he had shared Sweeny's tent the previous night. At the conclusion of the battle Gen. Frank P. Blair, commanding the Seventeenth Army Corps, who had witnessed the repulse by Sweeny's division, rode down at the head of his staff to where Sweeny stood and grasping him warmly by the hand, said: "Sweeny, I congratulate you. You have saved the army of the Tennessee!"

General Sweeny was one of the Guard of Honor in charge of the remains of President Lincoln when they lay in state in the city hall, New York. On Aug. 24, 1865, Sweeny was mustered out of the volunteer service, and was in command of the post at Nashville, Tenn., to October of that year.

An ardent lover of the land of his birth, General Sweeny longed for the day and the hour when, on the field of battle, he might meet the common foe of his adopted and of his native land. Even while lying disabled by his wounds in Mexico, he had made arrangements to cast himself into the then expected struggle for Irish independence, but the opportunity was not afforded him. In 1856, while he was stationed at Fort Pierre, Nebraska territory, he wrote to his family: "I see they are making another movement for Irish independence. I hope it will amount to something this time. E——, how would you like me to embark in such an undertaking? We might accomplish great things—do deeds that our children could point at on the page of history with pride—perhaps help to pull a sinewy tyrant from his throne, and raise a prostrate people from chains to liberty."

It was not, however, until after the close of the Civil War that the opportunity arrived. In 1865 the Fenian congress assembled in Philadelphia to decide upon the best means to adopt to obtain the liberation of Ireland. General Sweeny appeared before this convention and submitted to it his plan for the invasion of Canada. He also offered his services to aid in carrying out the plan, both plan and services being accepted. He was appointed secretary of war of the Fenian Brotherhood, and commander-in-chief of the Irish forces with the rank of major-general; William R. Roberts, a prominent merchant of New York and afterwards United States minister to Chili, was appointed president.

In 1866, General Sweeny was offered, by the Mexican government, the grade of general of division in the Mexican army, which he declined. He was finally retired from active service May 11, 1870, with the rank of brigadier-general, U. S. A. He was wounded so often in battle that on one occasion, after an engagement, General Grant met him and laughingly said : " How is it, Sweeny, that you have not been hit ? There must be some mistake. This fight will hardly count unless you can show another wound ! "

In a sketch of General Sweeny published some years ago, Junius Henri Browne, war correspondent of the *New York Tribune*, says : " Sweeny is, as his name indicates, an Irishman by birth, but an American to the backbone. No soldier was more devoted to the Union cause, or fought more valiantly for the integrity of the republic."

General Sweeny was twice married. His first wife was Eleanor Swain Clark of Brooklyn, N. Y., daughter of John and Hepsabeth (Paddock) Clark. In both the paternal and maternal line, she was descended from the Coffins, Barnards, Folgers, Husseys, Macys and Swains, who were among the ten purchasers of Nantucket in 1659. She was sixth in descent from John Swain, 2d, son of John Swain, 1st, and Mary (Weir) Swain, the first male white child born on the island (in 1664), and seventh in descent from Benjamin Franklin.

General Sweeny's second wife—who survives him—was Eugenia Octavia Reagan of Augusta, Ga., daughter of Dr. Francis Washington Reagan and Sarah Cecelia (Refo) Reagan. Her paternal ancestors were among the first settlers of the present states of Virginia, North Carolina, Georgia and Tennessee. Through her paternal great-grandmother, Mary Dandridge of Virginia, Mrs. Sweeny is descended from Dorothea Spotswood Dandridge, the second wife of Patrick Henry, and Martha Dandridge Custis, the wife of George Washington.

After retirement from the army General Sweeny virtually withdrew to private life. The last public act of his " long, varied and useful career," was to use his personal aid and influence to secure a fund for the erection of a home at Austin, Texas, for disabled Confederate veterans.

General Sweeny died at his residence, 126 Franklin street, Astoria, Long Island, April 10, 1892. He was buried in the family plot, Greenwood cemetery, with military honors, six batteries of the First U. S. Artillery furnishing the escort. The following are a few of the many tributes paid the deceased soldier :

Gen. W. T. Sherman : " One of my ' Old Guard.' "

Gen. J. M. Schofield : " General Sweeny was regarded by all who knew him as an exceedingly brave soldier and an ardent patriot."

Gen. F. Sigel: " He was an eminent soldier and a patriotic citizen."

Gen. Robert Nugent: " His gallant and unblemished record in the army is a matter of history."

Gen. John P. Hawkins : " He was a brave soldier and an honest man."

Army and Navy Journal: "As gallant, warmhearted and impulsive an officer as ever wore the uniform."

Archbishop Ryan of Philadelphia : " Many noble qualities distinguished that truly Christian soldier."

Harper's Weekly: " A distinguished soldier of three wars, whose conduct at Shiloh won Sherman's especial praise."

New York Recorder: " From lieutenant, to brigadier-general, he honored every position held by him during a period of service commencing with the Mexican War."

Military order of the Loyal Legion, Commandery of the State of New York : " General Sweeny was a man of noble heart and the highest aspirations."

PAPERS READ BEFORE THE SOCIETY, OR CONTRIBUTED FOR PUBLICATION.

Since its organization the Society has been favored with twenty-nine papers and many addresses, on topics within its line of work. Following is the list of papers:

By Thomas Hamilton Murray, Secretary-General of the Society: "The Irish Bacons who settled at Dedham, Mass., in 1640," one of whose descendants, John Bacon, was killed April 19, 1775, in the fight at West Cambridge (battle of Lexington).

By Hon. John C. Linehan, State Insurance Commissioner, Concord, N. H., a paper on "The Seizure of the Powder at Fort William and Mary," by Maj. John Sullivan and his associates, some of which powder was later dealt out to the patriots at Bunker Hill.

By Edward J. Brandon, City Clerk, Cambridge, Mass., a paper on the "Battle of Lexington, Concord and Cambridge," during which he read a list of Irish names borne by Minute-men or militia in the battle of the Nineteenth of April, 1775.

By Joseph Smith, Secretary of the Police Commission, Lowell, Mass., on "The Irishman, Ethnologically Considered."

By Dennis Harvey Sheahan, Providence, R. I., ex-Clerk of the Rhode Island House of Representatives, "The Need of an Organization such as the A. I. H. S., and its Scope."

By Thomas Hamilton Murray: "Matthew Watson, an Irish Settler of Barrington, R. I., 1722."

By Thomas Addis Emmet, M. D., New York city: "Irish Emigration During the Seventeenth and Eighteenth Centuries."

By Hon. John C. Linehan, Concord, N. H.: "Some Pre-Revolutionary Irishmen."

By Rev. John J. McCoy, P. R., Chicopee, Mass.: "The Irish Element in the Second Massachusetts Volunteers in the Recent War" (with Spain).

By Bernard Corr, Boston, Mass.: "The Ancestors of Gen. John Sullivan."

By Hon. Joseph T. Lawless, Secretary of State, Virginia: "Some Irish Settlers in Virginia."

By James F. Brennan, Peterborough, N. H.: "The Irish Pioneers and Founders of Peterborough."

By Joseph Smith, Lowell, Mass.: "Some Ways in which American History is Falsified."

By James Jeffrey Roche, Boston, Mass.: "The 'Scotch Irish' and 'Anglo-Saxon' Fallacies."

By Thomas Hamilton Murray: "Sketch of an Early Irish Settlement in Rhode Island."

By Edward Fitzpatrick, Louisville, Ky.: "Early Irish Settlers in Kentucky."

By Thomas Hamilton Murray: "Gen. John Sullivan and the Battle of Rhode Island, 1778."

By Martin Scully, Waterbury, Conn.: "An Early Irishman of Waterbury."

By Daniel M. O'Driscoll, Charleston, S. C.: "David Hamilton, a Soldier of the American Revolution."

By Hon. John C. Linehan, Concord, N. H.: "Irish Pioneers of Texas."

By Hon. Thomas J. Gargan, Boston, Mass.: Four papers outlining the field of the Society's work.

By Thomas Hamilton Murray: "The Irish Chapter in the History of Brown University."

By Joseph Smith, Lowell, Mass.: "The Whistlers—A Family Illustrious in War and Peace."

By Hon. John C. Linehan, Concord, N. H.: "Irish Pioneers and Builders of Kentucky."

By Michael E. Hennessy, of the *Daily Globe* staff, Boston, Mass.: "Men of Irish Blood who Have Attained Eminence in American Journalism."

By William Montgomery Sweeny, Astoria, L. I., N. Y.: "Brigadier-General Thomas W. Sweeny, U. S. A., A Biographical Sketch."

ADDRESSES DELIVERED.

Addresses have been delivered before the Society, or at events held under its auspices, by the following among others:

Hon. Thomas J. Gargan, Boston, Mass.

Hon. Hugh J. Carroll, Pawtucket, R. I.

Hon. John C. Linehan, Concord, N. H.
Charles A. DeCourcy, Lawrence, Mass.
Paul B. Du Chaillu, the traveler and author.
Osborne Howes, Boston, Mass.
James Cunningham, Portland, Me.
Robert A. Woods, Boston, Mass.
Gen. James R. O'Beirne, New York City.
John Mackinnon Robertson, London, England.
P. J. Flatley, Boston, Mass.
Rev. John J. McCoy, Chicopee, Mass.
Rev. Edward McSweeny, Bangor, Me.
Rev. P. Farrelly, Central Falls, R. I.
James Jeffrey Roche, Boston, Mass.
Edward A. Moseley, Washington, D. C.
Thomas B. Lawler, Worcester, Mass.
M. J. Harson, Providence, R. I.
Joseph Smith, Lowell, Mass.
Dennis H. Sheahan, Providence, R. I.
Rear-Admiral Belknap, U. S. N. (retired), Boston, Mass.
J. D. O'Connell, Washington, D. C.
Hon. Patrick A. Collins, ex-U. S. Consul-General to London.
Judge Wauhope Lynn, New York City.
Capt. Edward O'Meagher Condon, Washington, D. C.
Hon. Thomas Dunn English, Newark, N. J.
Dr. Thomas Addis Emmet, New York City.
Very Rev. M. C. O'Brien, V. G., Bangor, Me.
E. Benj. Andrews, President of Brown University.
Prof. Alonzo Williams, Brown University.
Rev. Arthur J. Teeling, Lynn, Mass.
Rev. T. P. Linehan, Biddeford, Me.
Mayor Tilton, Portsmouth, N. H.
Charles H. Clary, Hallowell, Me.
John Griffin, Portsmouth, N. H.
James F. Brennan, Peterborough, N. H.
Cornelius Horigan, Biddeford, Me.
Rev. James A. Flynn, Biddeford, Me.
Rev. John J. McGinnis, Sanford, Me.
Bernard Corr, Boston, Mass.
Dr. W. D. Collins, Haverhill, Mass.
John F. Doyle, New York City.

W. J. Kelly, Kittery, Me.
Dr. W. H. A. Lyons, Portsmouth, N. H.
James H. McGlinchey, Portland, Me.
Hon. John D. Crimmins, New York City.
Hon. Charles E. Gorman, Providence, R. I.
Hon. William McAdoo, New York City.
Charles McCarthy, Jr., Portland, Me.
Hon. Theodore Roosevelt, Governor of New York.
Hon. Patrick J. Boyle, Mayor of Newport, R. I.
Thomas F. O'Malley, Somerville, Mass.
Stephen J. Richardson, New York City.
Rev. S. Banks Nelson, Woonsocket, R. I.
Rev. Frank L. Phalen, Concord, N. H.
Rev. L. J. Deady, Newport, R. I.
Dennis H. Tierney, Waterbury, Conn.
John Jerome Rooney, New York City.
P. J. McCarthy, Providence, R. I.

MEMBERSHIP ROLL,

AMERICAN-IRISH HISTORICAL SOCIETY.[1]

[For officers of the Society see pages 9, 10, 11.]

Ackland, Thomas J., editorial department, *The Pilot,* 630 Washington Street, Boston, Mass.

Ahern, John, 5 Highland Street, Concord, N. H.

Ahern, John J., East Cambridge, Mass.

Ahern, William J., 64 Franklin Street, Concord, N. H.; has served as a member of the Legislature of New Hampshire.

Armstrong, Col. James, Charleston, S. C.

Aylward, James F., 347 Tremont Building, Boston, Mass.

Banigan, Hon. James E., Pawtucket, R. I., a State Senator.

Bannin, Michael E., 893 Lafayette Ave., New York City.

Barnes, James, Players' Club, New York City; grandnephew of Commodore Jack Barry.

Barrett, David L., Englewood, N. J.

Barrett, Thomas, 10 West 90th Street, New York City.

Barrett, Dr. Thomas J., 41 Wellington Street, Worcester, Mass.; member State Board of Dental Registration.

Barry, H. Nason, New York City.

Barry, Very Rev. John E., Vicar-General Roman Catholic Diocese of Manchester, N. H.; residence, Concord, N. H.

Barry, P. T., 93 South Jefferson Street, Chicago, Ill.

Bennett, Joseph M. (M. D.), 186 Broad Street, Providence, R. I.; a brother of Secretary of State Bennett of Rhode Island.

Betts, Rev. George C., Rector St. James's Protestant Episcopal Church, Goshen, N. Y.

Birmingham, Robert M. (M. D.), South Lawrence, Mass.

Black, Thomas, Berkley, Virginia.

Bodfish, Rev. Joshua P., Rector St. John's Roman Catholic Church, Canton, Mass.

Boland, Michael J., Biddeford, Me.

Bolton, Rev. J. Gray (D. D.) (Presbyterian), 1906 Pine Street, Philadelphia, Pa.

[1] This membership roll is brought down to February, 1900.

Boyle, Hon. Patrick J., Mayor of Newport, R. I.

Boyle, Thomas H., Lowell, Mass.

Bradley, Richard E., 122 Monument Street, Portland, Me.

Brady, Rev. Cyrus Townsend, Protestant Episcopal Archdeacon of Pennsylvania, Philadelphia, Pa.

Brady, Col. James D., Kellogg Building, Washington, D. C.; ex-Member of Congress from Virginia.

Brandon, Edward J., City Clerk, Cambridge, Mass.

Brannigan, Felix, Department of Justice, Washington, D. C.

Bree, James P., 820 Chapel Street, member of the Connecticut legislature, New Haven, Conn.

Breen, Hon. John, Lawrence, Mass.; served three terms as Mayor of Lawrence.

Brennan, James F., attorney and counselor-at-law, Peterborough, N. H.

Brennan, Michael, 2 West 75th Street, New York City; proprietor of the Hotel St. Remo, 74th and 75th Streets and Central Park West.

Brennan, Thomas S., 353 West 56th Street, New York City.

Broderick, James A., Opera Block, Manchester, N. H.

Broderick, Rev. Thos. W., Hartford, Conn.

Broe, James A., 478 Congress Street, Portland, Me.

Brogan, Rev. Farrah A., St. Vincent's Church, South Boston, Mass.

Brophy, John P. (Ph. D., LL. D.), 321 West 137th Street, New York City.

Brosnahan, Rev. Timothy, Rector St. Mary's Church, Waltham, Mass.

Brown, Col. William L., *Daily News,* New York City.

Bryson, John, 677 Elm Street, Manchester, N. H.

Buckley, Dennis T., 19 Bacon Street, Biddeford, Me.

Burke, Edmund, 377 Broadway, Milwaukee, Wis.

Burke, J. E., Superintendent of Public Schools, Lawrence, Mass.

Burke, Martin (M. D.), 147 Lexington Avenue, New York City.

Burke, Robert E., recently City Solicitor, Newburyport, Mass.

Burke, Tobias A., *Argus* office, Portland, Me.

Burke, William J., 119 Webster Street, East Boston, Mass.

Butler, Rev. Ellery C., Quincy, Mass.

Butler, Rev. Francis J., Brighton (Boston), Mass.

Butler, Rev. Thomas F., Lewiston, Me.

Butler, Hon. Matthew C., ex- U. S. Senator, Edgefield, S. C.

Buttimer, Thomas H., attorney-at-law, 27 Tremont Row, Boston, Mass.

Byrne, John, 45 Wall Street, New York City.

Byrne, Michael J., 147 Cook Street, Waterbury, Conn.

Byrne, Very Rev. William (V. G., D. D.), 6 Allen Street, Boston, Mass.

Cahill, John H., 15 Dey Street, New York City.

Cahill, M. J., dry-goods merchant, Essex Street, Lawrence, Mass.

Callaghan, Lawrence, manufacturer, 95 Locke Street, Haverhill, Mass.

Callahan, John A., School Principal, 79 Lincoln Street, Holyoke, Mass.

Callahan, John F., 202–206 Lincoln Street, Boston, Mass.

Callanan, E. J., of Marlier, Callanan & Co., 172 Tremont Street, Boston, Mass.

Calnin, James, 101–107 Lakeview Avenue, Lowell, Mass.

Campbell, James P., lawyer, 20 West 70th Street, New York City.

Cannon, James N., 240 Hamilton Street, New Haven, Conn.

Cantwell, John J., Brookline, Mass.

Canty, T. W., Chicopee, Mass.

Carey, Jeremiah J., office the *Sunday Star*, Lawrence, Mass.

Carmichael, James H., Lowell, Mass.

Carmody, John R., care U. S. Navy Department, Washington, D. C.

Carney, Matthew J., of M. Carney & Co., Lawrence, Mass.

Carney, Michael, of M. Carney & Co., Lawrence, Mass.

Carrigan, Thomas C., Worcester, Mass.

Carter, Richard A., Lawrence, Mass.

Carter, Hon. Thomas H., U. S. Senator, Helena, Mont.

Carroll, Edward, Cashier Leavenworth National Bank, Leavenworth, Kansas.

Carroll, Hon. Hugh J., Pawtucket, R. I., ex-Member of the Rhode Island General Assembly; ex-Mayor of Pawtucket.

Carroll, James B., lawyer, 50 Temple Street, Springfield, Mass.

Carroll, Thomas, director of the Public Library, Peabody, Mass.

Casey, Martin, Fort Worth, Texas.

Casey, Stephen J., lawyer, Providence, R. I.

Casey, William J., Palm Street, Bangor, Me.

Cashman, John, 30 Church Street, Manchester, N. H.

Casman, John P., 34 Howard Street, Springfield, Mass.

Cassidy, Patrick (M. D.), Norwich, Conn.

Cassidy, Patrick J. (M. D.), New London, Conn.

Cavanagh, Michael, 1159 Fourth Street, N. E., Washington, D. C.

Cavanaugh, John B., 924 Elm Street, Manchester, N. H.

Cavanaugh, Thomas Jeffrey, 54 Stark Corporation, Manchester, N. H.

Chittick, Rev. J. J., Hyde Park, Mass.

Clancy, Lawrence, Oswego, N. Y.

Clare, William F., 39 Cortlandt Street, New York City.

Clark, Joseph H., 13 Adam Street, Lowell, Mass.

Clark, Rev. James F., New Bedford, Mass.

Clarke, Rev. Michael, Rector Church of the Sacred Heart, East Boston, Mass.

Clary, Charles H., Hallowell, Me.

Clifford, James, El Paso, Texas.

Clune, John H., Springfield, Mass.

Coakley, Daniel H., 77 Arlington Street, Brighton (Boston), Mass.; Member of the Massachusetts House of Representatives in 1892–'94.

Coffey, John J., Neponset, Mass.
Coffey, Rev. Michael J., East Cambridge, Mass.
Cogan, D. S., 320 Congress Street, Portland, Me.
Coghlan, Rev. Gerald P., Church of Our Lady of Mercy, Philadelphia, Pa.
Cohalan, Daniel F., lawyer, 271 Broadway, New York City.
Coleman, Bernard F., 38 East 69th Street, New York City.
Coleman, Cornelius F., 162–164 Middle Street, Portland, Me.
Coleman, James S., 38 East 69th Street, New York City.
Collins, Rev. Charles W., the Cathedral, Portland, Me.
Collins, James M., 6 Sexton Avenue, South Main Street, Concord, N. H.
Collins, Hon. John S., Gilsum, N. H.
Collins, Hon. Patrick A., ex-Member of Congress; late United States Consul-General to London, England; Tremont Building, Boston, Mass.
Collins, Stephen J., 212 Main Street, Springfield, Mass.
Collins, Timothy J., *Daily Advertiser,* Quincy, Mass.
Collins, William D. (M. D.), 170 Winter Street, Haverhill, Mass.
Collison, Harvey N., member Massachusetts Legislature, 1887–'88; has also served on Boston School Board, 5 Tremont Street, Boston, Mass.
Conaty, Bernard, 30 Cypress Street, Providence, R. I.
Conaty, Rev. B. S., 340 Cambridge Street, Worcester, Mass.
Conaty, Rt. Rev. Thomas J. (D. D.), Rector of the Catholic University, Washington, D. C.
Concannon, John S., 19 Crystal Cove Avenue, Winthrop, Mass., or City Hall, Boston, Mass.
Condon, Edward O'Meagher, 98 5th Avenue, New York City.
Coney, Patrick H., attorney-at-law, Topeka, Kansas.
Conley, Henry, 7 Winthrop Street, Portland, Me.
Conley, John E., 87 Weybosset Street, Providence, R. I.; ex-Clerk of the Rhode Island House of Representatives.
Conlin, Rev. John F., Holyoke, Mass.
Conlin, Michael, 59 South Broadway, Lawrence, Mass.
Conlon, Michael, 15 Pool Street, Biddeford, Me.
Connellan, James A., 98 Exchange Street, Portland, Me.
Conners, Edward, 31 Hammond Street, Bangor, Me.; has been a member of the Board of Aldermen, and of the Police Examining Board.
Connery, William P., Pleasant Street, Lynn, Mass.
Connolly, James, Coronado, Cal.
Connolly, Michael J., Trustee of the Public Library, Waltham, Mass.
Connolly, Rev. Arthur T., Rector Church of the Blessed Sacrament, Center and Creighton Streets, Roxbury (Boston), Mass.
Connolly, Richard, 132 Boston Street, Salem, Mass.
Connor, J. F., of Connor & Tracy, Peabody, Mass.

12

Connor, John J., *Sunday Register* Office, Essex Street, Lawrence, Mass.

Connor, John W., 93 Main Street, Nashua, N. H.

Connor, Michael, 509 Beech Street, Manchester, N. H.

Conroy, Philip F., Newport Gaslight Co., Newport, R. I.

Cooke, Rev. Michael J., Fall River, Mass.

Corbett, Peter B., Tremont Building, Boston, Mass.

Corcoran, C. J., City Clerk, Lawrence, Mass.

Corcoran, John H., 587 Massachusetts Avenue, Cambridge, Mass.

Corcoran, Hon. John W., recently a Judge of the Superior Court; Tremont Building, Boston, Mass.

Corcoran, Dr. Luke, Springfield, Mass.

Corr, Bernard, Chamber of Commerce Building, Boston, Mass.

Corrigan, J. P. (M. D.), Benedict House, Pawtucket, R. I.

Costello, A. E., 4 East 119th Street, New York City.

Costello, John H., 40 East Brookline Street, Boston, Mass.

Coughlin, J. A., Manager, Essex Street, Lawrence, Mass.

Coughlin, John, 177 Water Street, Augusta, Me.

Coyle, Rev. James, Taunton, Mass.

Crane, John, 307 West 103d Street, New York City; member of the military Order of the Loyal Legion; vice-president of the Society of the Army of the Tennessee.

Cranitch, William, 841 West End Avenue, New York City.

Crimmins, Hon. John D., 40 East 68th Street, New York City.

Crimmins, Lieut. Martin L. (U. S. A.), care of Hon. John D. Crimmins, New York City, or War Department, Washington, D. C.

Cronin, Capt. William, Rutland, Vt.

Cronin, John H., druggist, 317 Broadway, Lawrence, Mass.

Croston, Dr. J. F., Emerson Street, Haverhill, Mass.

Crowe, Edward J., Lamoille, Winona County, Minn.

Crowell, Hon. Henry G., South Yarmouth, Mass.; a descendant of David O'Killia (O'Kelly), who settled on Cape Cod as early as 1657.

Crowley, Bartholomew, manufacturer, Haverhill, Mass.

Crowley, Hon. Jeremiah, Mayor of Lowell, Mass.

Crowley, John F., Standard Clothing Co., Bangor, Me.

Cuffe, Rev. John P., Quincy, Mass.

Cullen, Rev. John S., Watertown, Mass.

Cummins, Rev. John F., Roslindale, Mass.

Cummins, Thomas J., 65 First Place, Brooklyn, N. Y.

Cummings, Matthew J., Overseer of the Poor, Providence, R. I.

Cunningham, Christopher D., 178 Congress Street, Portland, Me.

Cunningham, Francis W., 167 Congress Street, Portland, Me.

Cunningham, James, 277 Congress Street, Portland, Me.

Cunningham, John E., Gardiner, Me.

Curran, Bartley J., 72 Exchange Street, Portland, Me.

Curran, James, President the James Curran Manufacturing Co., 512–514 West 36th Street, New York City.

Curran, Maurice J., of the Curran & Joyce Co., Lawrence, Mass.

Curran, William F., 38 Fern Street, Bangor, Me. ; has served several terms on the Board of Aldermen.

Curry, Capt. P. S., 1 Box Place, Lynn, Mass. ; superintendent of construction for the new Federal Building in that city.

Curtin, Jeremiah, Bristol, Vt. ; author of " Hero Tales of Ireland," " Myths and Folk-Lore of Ireland," " Myths and Folk-Tales of the Russians, Western Slavs and Magyars;" translator of works of Henryk Sienkiewicz.

Cusack, Peter, 38 Washington Street, Newburyport, Mass.

Cushnahan, Rev. P. M., Rector of St. Joseph's Roman Catholic Church, Ogden City, Utah.

Dailey, Peter, real estate, etc., 209 Washington Street, Boston, Mass.

Daly, Hon. Joseph F., New York City; recently Justice of the Supreme Court.

Daly, John, South Broadway, Lawrence, Mass.

Daly, John J., Salt Lake City, Utah ; one of the heaviest mine owners in the state.

Daly, Rev. Patrick J., Rector Church of St. Francis de Sales, Vernon Street, Roxbury (Boston), Mass.

Danaher, Hon. Franklin M., Albany, N. Y.

Danahy, Rev. J. T., Newton Upper Falls, Mass.

Danvers, Robert E., 17 West 65th Street, New York City.

Dasey, Charles V., 7 Broad Street, Boston, Mass.

Davidson, John A., 246 West 45th Street, New York City.

Davis, Charles E., 2 Park Square, Boston, Mass.

Davis, Dr. F. L., 253 Main Street, Biddeford, Me.

Davis, Hon. Robert T., Fall River, Mass. ; ex-Mayor ; ex-Member of Congress.

Davis, John J., Greenville, Pa.

DeCourcy, Charles A., of DeCourcy & Coulson, lawyers, Essex Street, Lawrence, Mass.

Delehanty, Dr. W. J., Trumbull Square, Worcester, Mass.

Dempsey, George C., Lowell, Mass.

Dempsey, Henry L., Stillwater, R. I. ; recently Postmaster; member Smithfield Town Council.

Dempsey, Patrick, Market Street, Lowell, Mass.

Dempsey, William P., Pawtucket, R. I.

Dennison, Joseph A., of law firm, Coakley & Dennison, Pemberton Square, Boston, Mass.

Desmond, J. J., 565 Broadway, Lawrence, Mass.

Desmond, Jeremiah J., Norwich, Conn.

Desmond, John F., civil engineer, 83 Merrimac Street, Haverhill, Mass.

Devine, P. A., 100 Central Street, Manchester, N. H.

Devlin, James H., 27 Farnsworth St., Boston, Mass.

Dignam, M. A. (D. D. S.), 295 Essex Street, Lawrence, Mass.

Dillon, Capt. Moses, El Paso, Texas.

Dillon, Thomas J. (M. D.), 121 Vernon Street, Roxbury (Boston), Mass.

Dixon, Richard, Equitable Life, 100 Broadway, New York City.

Doherty, James L., 131 Bowdoin Street, Springfield, Mass.

Doherty, Philip J., 23 Court Street, Boston, Mass.; lawyer; has served several terms in the Massachusetts Legislature; in 1886 was nominee for Speaker of the House.

Dolan, Patrick J., 901 Garfield Building, Cleveland, Ohio.

Donahoe, D. J., of Donahoe Brothers, manufacturers, Lynn, Mass.

Donahoe, Dr. Florence, 1134 Eighth Street, N. W., Washington, D. C.

Donahoe, Col. John P., Wilmington, Del.; National Commander, Union Veteran Legion; a member of the recent Constitutional Convention of the state.

Donahoe, Patrick, *The Pilot*, Boston, Mass.

Donahue, Dan A., Essex Street, Lawrence, Mass.

Donahue, Hugh (M. D.), 200 Winter Street, Haverhill, Mass.

Donahue, John J., Keene, N. H.

Donigan, Bernard E., 322 Essex Street, Lawrence, Mass.; formerly Postmaster at Orono, Me.

Donnellan, Col. John W., banker, Salt Lake City, Utah.

Donnelly, B. J., of Shea & Donnelly, Lynn, Mass.

Donnelly, Hon. Ignatius, St. Paul, Minn.; upholder of the Baconian theory regarding Shakespeare's works; twice elected Lieutenant-Governor of Minnesota; has been a Member of Congress.

Donnelly, Hugh J., 100 Central Street, Springfield, Mass.

Donoghoe, Dr. D. F., 240 Maple Street, Holyoke, Mass.; member School Board.

Donovan, D. D., Brown & Sharpe Manufacturing Co., Providence, R. I.

Donovan, Daniel, 21 High Rock Street, Lynn, Mass.; an authority on heraldry, armorial bearings, etc., particularly as the same relate to Ireland.

Donovan, Daniel A., of D. A. Donovan & Co., manufacturers, 47–51 Willow Street, Lynn, Mass.

Donovan, Col. Henry F., Chicago, Ill.; late Inspector-General Illinois National Guard; served five terms as President of the County Board of Education; proprietor of the *Chicago Eagle.*

Donovan, Dr. James A., Lewiston, Me.

Donovan, Joseph, Central Building, Lawrence, Mass.

Donovan, M. F., of D. A. Donovan & Co., 47–51 Willow Street, Lynn, Mass.

Donovan, Michael R. (M. D.), 128 South Common Street, Lynn, Mass.
Donovan, Timothy, of D. A. Donovan & Co., 47–51 Willow Street, Lynn, Mass.
Donovan, William H., Lawrence, Mass.
Doogue, Luke J., East Cottage Street, Dorchester (Boston), Mass.
Doogue, William, Superintendent of public grounds, Boston, Mass.
Doogue, William J., 154 East Cottage Street, Dorchester (Boston), Mass.
Doolittle, James G., Salt Lake City, Utah.
Doran, John, of the law firm, McGuinness & Doran, Providence, R. I.
Doran, Patrick L., Salt Lake City, Utah.
Dore, John P., 374 Dudley Street, Roxbury (Boston), Mass.
Dowd, Frederick C., Tremont Building, Boston, Mass.
Dowd, Michael, Tacoma, Wash.
Dowd, Michael J., 31–39 Merrimack Street, Lowell, Mass.
Dowd, Peter A., 95 Milk Street, Boston, Mass.
Dowling, M. J., Renville, Minn.
Dowling, Rev. Austin, Providence, R. I.
Downey, Dr. Charles J., Springfield, Mass.
Downey, Daniel, 50 Piedmont Street, Worcester, Mass.
Doyle, Alfred L., 14 West 87th Street, New York City.
Doyle, James, 50 Front Street, New York City.
Doyle, John F., 45 William Street, New York City.
Doyle, Col. John F., Jr., 14 West 87th Street, New York City.
Doyle, John M., 14 South Third Street, Philadelphia, Pa.
Driscoll, Hon. C. T., Mayor of New Haven, Conn.
Driscoll, Florence F., 56 Adams Street, Portland, Me.
Drum, John D., Pemberton Square, Boston, Mass.
Drummond, Michael J., 148 West 76th Street, New York City.
Duff, Dr. John, 5 Dexter Row, Charlestown (Boston), Mass.
Duff, John, 35 Purchase Street, New Bedford, Mass.
Duffy, Arthur E., 39 Ash Street, New Bedford, Mass.
Duggan, John T. (M. D.), Worcester, Mass.
Dunn, Edward P., 12 Lincoln Street, Augusta, Me.
Dunn, Hon. Robert C., State Auditor, Capitol Building, St. Paul, Minn.; publisher, Princeton, Minn., *Union.*
Dunne, F. L., 328 Washington Street, Boston, Mass.
Dunnigan, D. G., publisher, New Bedford, Mass.
Durac, Patrick H., Barstow, Ward County, Texas.
Dwyer, M. J., Boston, Mass.
Dyer, Dr. William H., Dover, N. H.
Dyer, Hon. Elisha, Governor of Rhode Island.
Early, James, Deputy Sheriff, Worcester, Mass.
Egan, James T., of the law firm, Gorman & Egan, Banigan Building, Providence, R. I.

Egan, Maurice F. (LL. D.), Catholic University, Washington, D. C.

Egan, Rev. M. H., Rector Church of the Sacred Heart, Lebanon, N. H.

Ellard, George W., 180 Lisbon Street, Lewiston, Me.

Elston, A. A., Preston Street, Somerville, Mass.

Emmet, Dr. J. Duncan, 89 Madison Avenue, New York City.

Emmet, Robert, 89 Madison Avenue, New York City.

Emmet, Dr. Thomas Addis, 89 Madison Avenue, New York City; grand-nephew of Robert Emmet, the Irish patriot.

English, Hon. Thomas Dunn (LL. D.), 57 State Street, Newark, N. J.; ex-Member of Congress.

Esler, Frederic B., Union Surety Co., Dun Building, 290 Broadway, New York City.

Fahey, Rev. John T., Fall River, Mass.

Fallon, Hon. Joseph D., 789 Broadway, South Boston, Mass.

Fallon, Hon. Joseph P., 170 East 121st Street, New York City

Fallon, Michael F. (M. D.), 9 Portland Street, Worcester, Mass.

Farrell, Edward D., 329 West 50th Street, New York City.

Farrell, Henry W. (M. D.), 1913 Westminster Street, Providence, R. I.

Farrell, J. T. (M. D.), 1913 Westminster Street, Providence, R. I.

Farrell, John F., 45 Lake Avenue, Albany, N. Y.

Farrell, John P., 230 Grove Street, New Haven, Conn.

Farrell, Joseph A., 598 Madison Avenue, Albany, N. Y.

Farrell, William, Carnation Street, Pawtucket, R. I.

Farrelly, Frank T., 424 Main Street, Springfield, Mass.

Farrelly, Patrick, American News Co., New York City.

Farrelly, Stephen, American News Co., New York City.

Fay, Martin, 55 Bainbridge Street, Roxbury (Boston), Mass.

Feehan, Rev. Daniel F., Fitchburg, Mass.

Feeley, William J., treasurer of The W. J. Feeley Co., silversmiths and manufacturing jewelers, 185 Eddy Street, Providence, R. I.

Feenan, Bernard, 85 Harbor Street, Salem, Mass.

Ferguson, Dr. Farquhar, 20 West 38th Street, New York City.

Field, Hon. John H., 27 High Street, Nashua, N. H.; State Senator.

Finerty, Hon. John F., 69 Dearborn Street, Chicago, Ill.; Editor of *The Citizen*; ex-Member of Congress.

Finn, Rev. Thomas J., St. Mary's Roman Catholic Church, Derby, Conn.

Finnigan, James C., 139 Broad Street, Bangor, Me.

Finnigan, Patrick J. (M. D.), 361 Cambridge Street, East Cambridge, Mass.

Finnigan, Thomas J., 121 Somerset Street, Bangor, Me.; member of the Park Commission.

Fitzgerald, David E., 179 Church Street, New Haven, Conn.

Fitzgerald, Rev. E. J., Chicopee, Mass.

Fitzgerald, Edmund P., 88 Bank Street, Waterbury, Conn.

Fitzgerald, Patrick J., 44 Nichols Street, Haverhill, Mass.

Fitzgerald, William T., High Street, Nashua, N. H.

Fitzmaurice, Charles R., Rossland, British Columbia.

Fitzpatrick, Daniel E., Waterbury, Conn.

Fitzpatrick, Edward, editorial department of *The Times*, Louisville, Ky.

Fitzpatrick, J. M., 120 West 59th Street, New York City.

Fitzpatrick, John B., 23 Court Street, Boston, Mass.; was for several years an officer of the Massachusetts Supreme Court.

Fitzpatrick, Thomas B., of the wholesale dry goods firm of Brown, Durrell & Co., Boston, Mass.

Fitzpatrick, Rev. William H., 2221 Dorchester Avenue, Boston, Mass.

Fitzsimons, Hon. James M., Chief Justice of the City Court, New York.

Flaherty, Thomas H., 62 Gray Street, Portland, Me.

Flanagan, Dr. Andrew J., 29 George Steeet, Springfield, Mass.

Flannery, Capt. John, Savannah, Ga.; of John Flannery & Co., cotton factors and commission merchants.

Flatley, Joseph P., 916 Beacon Street, Boston, Mass.

Flatley, P. J., lawyer, Tremont Building, Boston, Mass.

Flatley, Rev. John, Rector St. Peter's Roman Catholic Church, Cambridge, Mass.

Flynn, Hon. Joseph J., Opera House, Lawrence, Mass.; a State Senator.

Flynn, Rev. James A., Biddeford, Me.

Flynn, Thomas J., 18–20 Essex Street, Boston, Mass.

Fogarty, James A., New Haven, Conn.

Fogarty, Jeremiah W., assessors' department, City Hall, Boston, Mass.; Secretary of the Charitable Irish Society (founded 1737).

Foley, Bernard, 39 Edgewood Street, Roxbury (Boston), Mass.

Foley, Frank W., 284 Grand Avenue, New Haven, Conn.

Foy, Julius L., 408–409 Continental Bank Building, St. Louis, Mo.

Frawley, John P., 73 Main Street, Bangor, Me.

Gaffney, T. St. John, 40 Wall Street, New York City.

Gallagher, Cornelius J., 271 State Street, Bangor, Me.

Gallagher, Hugh T., 11 Birch Street, Bangor, Me.

Galligan, Edward F. (M. D.), 63 Washington Street, Taunton, Mass.

Gallivan, Maurice, 58 Dracut Street, Dorchester, Mass.

Galvin, Rev. John B., Rector St. Ann's Church, Somerville, Mass.

Galvin, John E., 14 Bailey Street, Dorchester, Mass.

Gargan, Thomas J., ex-President Boston Charitable Irish Society (founded 1737); delivered the oration for the city, July 4, 1885; served several terms in the Massachusetts Legislature; member of the law firm, Gargan & Keating, Pemberton Square, Boston, Mass.

Garrigan, Rev. Philip J., Catholic University, Washington, D. C.

Garvan, Hon. Patrick, President Park Commission, 236 Farmington Avenue, Hartford, Conn.

Garvey, Patrick J., lawyer, Holyoke, Mass.

Gavegan, Matthew, 57 Prospect Street, New Haven, Conn.

Gavin, Michael, of M. Gavin & Co., wholesale grocers and cotton factors, 232–234 Front Street, Memphis, Tenn.

Geoghegan, Charles A., 537–539 West Broadway, New York City.

Geoghegan, Joseph, Salt Lake City, Utah.

Geoghegan, Joseph G., 20 East 73d Street, New York City.

Geoghegan, Stephen J., 20 East 73d Street, New York City.

Gibbons, T. F., with Theodore M. Roche & Co., 203 Broadway, New York City.

Giblin, William, Mercantile Safe Deposit Co., 120 Broadway, New York City.

Gilbride, Patrick, of O'Donnell & Gilbride, Lowell, Mass.

Gilligan, Rev. Michael, Medford, Mass.

Gilman, John E., 28 Court Square, Boston, Mass.

Gilroy, Hon. Thomas F., New York City.

Gleason, Joseph J., 142 West 76th Street, New York City.

Glynn, John W., Manager the Mansion House, Springfield, Mass.

Glynn, Thomas H., Water and Federal Streets, Newburyport, Mass.

Goggin, John F., 57 Locust Street, New Bedford, Mass.

Goodwin, John (life member), 70–72 West 23d Street, New York City.

Goff, Hon. John W., 319 West 104th Street, New York City.

Gorman, Hon. Charles E., Banigan Building, Providence, R. I. ; ex-Speaker of the Rhode Island House of Representatives; ex-U. S. District Attorney; member of the recent Commission to Revise the State Constitution of Rhode Island.

Gorman, Dennis J., 62 Forest Street, Roxbury (Boston), Mass.

Gorman, James J., 406 Spring Street, Fall River, Mass.

Gorman, William, Stephen Girard Building, Philadelphia, Pa.

Graham, Andrew M., 27 Middle Street, Newburyport, Mass.

Graham, Rev. John J., St. James's Roman Catholic Church, Haverhill, Mass.

Grainger, William H. (M. D.), 408 Meridian Street, East Boston, Mass.

Gregg, Matthew C., 213 Water Street, Lawrence, Mass.

Griffin, John, 110 State Street, Portsmouth, N. H.

Griffin, Martin I. J., 711 Sansome Street, Philadelphia, Pa.

Griffin, Rt. Rev. Mgr. (D. D.), St. John's Church, Worcester, Mass.

Griffis, Rev. William Elliot (D. D.), Ithaca, N. Y. ; formerly pastor of the First Reformed Church, Schenectady, N. Y., and subsequently of the Shawmut Congregational Church, Boston, Mass. ; some years ago went to Japan to organize schools on the American plan; held chair of physics in the Imperial University at Tokio; an author of note.

Grimes, Robert W., Pawtucket, R. I.

Guiney, John, 9 Harvey Street, Biddeford, Me.

Hall, Edward A., member of the Connecticut Valley Historical Society, 66 Spring Street, Springfield, Mass.

Halley, William, publisher of *The Vindicator*, Austin, Ill.

Haltigan, Patrick J., Government Printing Office, Washington, D. C.

Hanley, Frank L., Olneyville, R. I.

Hanlon, Marcus, Room 234, 641 Washington Street, New York City.

Hanrahan, Dr. John D., Rutland, Vt., Surgeon in U. S. Navy during Civil War; ex-Postmaster of Rutland; first President Rutland County Medical and Surgical Society.

Hanrahan, William J., 200 Essex Street, Lawrence, Mass.

Harney, Hubert J., of the manufacturing firm Harney Bros., 103 Washington Street, Lynn, Mass.

Harney, Patrick J., of Harney Bros., 103 Washington Street, Lynn, Mass.

Harney, Thomas F., of Harney Bros., 103 Washington Street, Lynn, Mass.

Harrigan, M. R., *Bangor Commercial*, Bangor, Me.

Harriman, Dr. Patrick H., Norwich, Conn.

Harrington, Rev. J. C., Rector of St. Joseph's Roman Catholic Church, Lynn, Mass.

Harrington, Rev. John M., Lewiston, Me.

Harrington, Thomas F. (M. D.), Lowell, Mass.

Harris, Charles N., 229 Broadway, New York City.

Harson, M. Joseph, Providence, R. I.; a founder of Phi Kappa Sigma Fraternity; member of the Rhode Island Historical Society.

Hart, Frank M., Passaic, N. J.

Hart, James A., Orange, N. J.

Hart, J. G., 965 Second Avenue, Brooklyn, N. Y.

Harty, Rev. John, Rector of the Church of the Sacred Heart, Pawtucket, R. I.

Hastings, Hon. Daniel H., recently Governor of Pennsylvania, Harrisburg, Pa.

Haverty, Frank, 14 Barclay Street, New York City.

Hayes, John, Concord Street, Manchester, N. H.

Hayes, Dr. John F., Waterbury, Conn.; member of the Board of Education.

Hayes, Hon. John J., 8 Oliver Street, Boston, Mass.; has been a member of the Boston School Board and a State Senator.

Hayes, Dr. S. W., New Bedford, Mass.

Heagney, Michael J., 2 Hancock Street, Linden district, Malden, Mass.

Healey, Col. D. F., Manchester, N. H.; served on the staff of Governor Goodell of New Hampshire; was high sheriff of Hillsborough County, N. H., for over twelve years; supervisor of census, 1900, for N. H.

Healey, Jere, Newburyport, Mass.

Healy, John F., Davis, Tucker County, W. Va.

Healy, Col. John G., 117 Sherman Avenue, New Haven, Conn.; served in Ninth Connecticut Regiment during Civil War; has been first Vice-President of the Nineteenth Army Corps Association.

Healy, John A., 85 West Hollis Street, Nashua, N. H.

15

Healy, Richard, President Bay State Savings Bank, Worcester, Mass.

Hearn, Edward L., State Deputy Knights of Columbus, South Framingham, Mass.

Heery, Col. Luke, 99 Fairmount Street, Lowell, Mass.; recently on the staff of Governor Waller of Connecticut.

Heery, James, 99 Fairmount Street, Lowell, Mass.

Heffern, Peter J. (D. D. S.), 255 Main Street, Pawtucket, R. I.; member of the State Board of Registration in Dentistry.

Hegerty, Stephen J., Hallowell, Me.

Henebry, Rev. Richard (Ph. D.), Catholic University, Washington, D. C.

Hennessy, Dr. Daniel, 5 High Street, Bangor, Me.

Hennessy, M. E., *Daily Globe*, Boston, Mass.

Henry, Charles T., 120 Liberty Street, New York City.

Hickey, James G. (life member), Manager U. S. Hotel, Boston, Mass.

Hickey, Michael J., 80 Emerson Street, Haverhill, Mass.

Hickey, Rev. William A., Holyoke, Mass.

Hicks, Michael, 147 West 121st Street, New York City.

Higgins, Francis, 12 East 34th Street, New York City.

Hogan, Capt. Thomas J., 225 Middle Street, Portland, Me.

Hogan, Daniel W., 40 Cushing Street, Medford, Mass.

Hogan, John W., 4 Weybosset Street, Providence, R. I.

Hogan, Very Rev. John B. (S. S., D. D.), President of St. John's Ecclesiastical Seminary, Brighton (Boston), Mass.

Holland, D. A., Opera Block, Manchester, N. H.

Holland, Dennis J., Industrial Trust Building, Providence, R. I.

Holland, John P., 65 Nelson Place, Newark, N. J.; inventor of the submarine torpedo boat.

Hopkins, William, Assistant Day Editor *Boston Globe*; the talented '' Bud Brier.''

Horigan, Cornelius, Biddeford, Me.; ex-Member Maine Legislature.

Howard, Rev. J. J., St. Peter's Roman Catholic Church, Worcester, Mass.

Howard, T. J., Manchester, N. H.

Howes, Osborne, Secretary of the Board of Fire Underwriters, 55 Kilby Street, Boston, Mass.

Howley, Edward B., El Paso, Texas.

Hoye, John A., 40 Third Street, Dover, N. H.

Hughes, Rev. Christopher, Fall River, Mass.

Hurley, Rev. E. F., Rector of St. Dominic's Roman Catholic Church, Portland, Me.

Hurley, John E., care of Remington Printing Co., Providence, R. I.

Hyde, William A., U. S. Custom House, Boston, Mass.

Johnson, James G., 301 West End Avenue, New York City.

Jordan, M. J., lawyer, 42 Court Street, Boston, Mass.

Kane, Dr. John H., Lexington, Mass.

Kane, John P., Central Building, Lawrence, Mass.

Kavanagh, Rev. Patrick J., Lexington, Mass.

Keating, James E. (M. D.), 143 Pine Street, Portland, Me.

Keating, Patrick M., of the law firm, Gargan & Keating, Pemberton Square, Boston, Mass.

Keating, William H., 15 Vaughn Street, Portland, Me.

Keefe, Dennis F. (D. D. S.), Butler Exchange, Providence, R. I.

Keefe, Patrick H. (M. D.), 257 Benefit Street, Providence, R. I.

Keegan, Rev. James J., Woburn, Mass.

Keely, George, 270 Brackett Street, Portland, Me.

Kehoe, John B., Portland, Me.

Keleher, T. D., Disbursing Clerk for office of auditor to the Post-office Department, Washington, D. C.

Kelley, Daniel B., 21 Windsor Street, Haverhill, Mass.

Kelley, J. D. Jerrold, Lieutenant-Commander U. S. N.; was recently attached to the battleship *Texas*; address, care Navy Department, Washington, D. C.

Kelley, Patrick, 19 Davidson Street, Lowell, Mass.

Kelliher, Michael W. (M. D.), Pawtucket, R. I.

Kelly, James, 13 Greenleaf Street, Portland, Me.

Kelly, James E., Ogdensburg, N. Y.

Kelly, John F., 284 West Housatonic Avenue, Pittsfield, Mass.

Kelly, John P. (D. D. S.), 12 Essex Street, Newburyport, Mass.

Kelly, Michael F. (M. D.), Fall River, Mass.

Kelly, William J., 9 Dove Street, Newburyport, Mass.

Kelly, William J., Kittery, Me.

Kendricken, Hon. Paul H., 75 Maple Street, Roxbury (Boston), Mass.; ex-State Senator; member of the Military Order of the Loyal Legion.

Kenefick, Owen A., Essex Street, Lawrence, Mass.

Kennedy, Charles F., Brewer, Me.

Kennedy, Dr. Francis M., 446 County Street, New Bedford, Mass.; trustee of Public Library.

Kennedy, Joseph P., 311 South Water Street, New Bedford, Mass.

Kennedy, Hon. P. J., 165 Webster Street, East Boston, Mass.; has been a State Senator.

Kennedy, P. J., 322 and 324 Nicollet Avenue, Minneapolis, Minn.

Kenney, James W., Treasurer Union Brewing Co., Roxbury (Boston), Mass.

Kent, Pierce, 356 East 57th Street, New York City; recently lieutenant in the 69th Regiment.

Kerr, Dr. James, 1711 H Street, N. W., Washington, D. C.

Kiernan, Rev. Owen, Rector Church of the Immaculate Conception, Fall River, Mass.

Kiernan, Patrick, 18 East 83d Street, New York City.

Kiley, Daniel F., Essex Street, Lawrence, Mass.

Killoren, Hon. Andrew, Dover, N. H.; ex-State Senator.
Kilroy, Patrick, 475 Main Street, Springfield, Mass.
Kilroy, Philip (M. D.), Glen-Rath, Springfield, Mass.
King, Thomas E., 104 Howard Street, Springfield, Mass.
Kinsela, John F., 509 Gorham Street, Lowell, Mass.
Kirby, John P., Chicopee, Mass.
Kirmes, Victor C., Melrose, Mass.
Kivel, Hon. John, Dover, N. H.
Lally, Frank, 161 Saratoga Street, East Boston, Mass.
Lamb, Matthew B., 516 Main Street, Worcester, Mass.
Lamson, Col. Daniel S., Weston, Mass.
Lane, Rev. Florence A., Chicopee, Mass.
Lane, Thomas J., 120 Havre Street, East Boston, Mass.
Lannan, P. H., *The Tribune* Office, Salt Lake City, Utah.
Lappin, J. J., 7 Grant Street, Portland, Me.
Larkin, Very Rev. Thomas J. (S. M.), President of All Hallows College,
    Salt Lake City, Utah.
Lavelle, John, Inquiry Division, Post-office, Cleveland, Ohio.
Lawler, Thomas B., 70 Fifth Avenue, New York City; with Ginn & Co.,
    publishers ; Librarian and Archivist of the Society; member, American
    Oriental Society and of the Archæological Institute of America.
Lawless, Hon. Joseph T., Secretary of State, Richmond, Va.
Leahey, Dr. George A., Lowell, Mass.
Leary, Daniel E., Springfield, Mass.
Leary, Denis F., 254 Central Street, Springfield, Mass.
Lee, Hugh J., on staff of *The Times*, Pawtucket. R. I.
Lee, Rev. Robert F., 156 Danforth Street, Portland, Me.
Lee, Thomas C., 277 Central Street, Lowell, Mass.
Lenehan, John J., 165 Broadway, New York City.
Lenihan, Rev. M. C., Marshalltown, Iowa.
Lennox, George W., manufacturer, Duncan Street, Haverhill, Mass.
Leonard, James F., Lawrence, Mass.
Leonard, Thomas F., musical director, Essex Street, Lawrence, Mass.
Linehan, James C., 18 Foster Street, Peabody, Mass.
Linehan, Hon. John C., State Insurance Commissioner, Concord, N. H.
Linehan, John J., Springfield, Mass.
Linehan, Rev. Timothy P., Rector of St. Mary's Roman Catholic Church,
    Biddeford, Me. ; was for ten years Rector of the Cathedral, Port-
    land, Me.
Linehan, Timothy P., Wolfe Tavern, Newburyport, Mass.
Littleton, Stephen F., 10 Riverside Street, Worcester, Mass.
Long, M. D., O'Neill, Neb.
Lovell, David B. (M. D.), 32 Pearl Street, Worcester, Mass. ; member
    New England Ophthalmological Society.

Lowe, Hon. Robert A., Waterbury, Conn.

Lowery, Dr. James E., Sopris, Las Animas County, Colorado.

Lowery, William H., 86 Adams Street, Portland, Me.

Lowney, Rev. T. B., Marlborough, Mass.

Lucey, Rev. Thomas P., Northampton, Mass.

Lyman, William, 51 East 122d Street, New York City.

Lynch, Charles E., 367 Main Street, Springfield, Mass.

Lynch, Cornelius J., 331 Pine Street, Bangor, Me.

Lynch, J. H., Fort Hamilton, N. Y.

Lynch, James M., *Daily Democrat,* Waterbury, Conn.

Lynch, John E., Principal Thomas Street School, Director Free Public Library, Worcester, Mass.

Lynch, Gen. John J., 145 Spring Street, Portland, Me.

Lynch, Dr. M. H., Chicopee Falls, Mass.

Lynch, Thomas J., Augusta, Me.; treasurer Augusta Board of Trade.

Lynn, Hon. Wauhope, 280 Broadway, New York City.

Lyons, Rev. Francis X., Laconia, N. H.

Lyons, Rev. John J., Manchester, N. H.

Lyons, Michael R., 243 Main Street, Fitchburg, Mass.

Lyons, Dr. W. H. A., Portsmouth, N. H.

MacDonnell, John T. F., Holyoke, Mass.

MacGoldrick, Rev. D. J., St. Thomas College, Scranton, Pa.

Mack, Hon. William A. M., 36 Third Street, Elizabeth, N. J.

Macguire, Constantine J. (M. D.), 120 East 60th Street, New York City.

Magee, John A. (M. D.), 203 Haverhill Street, Lawrence, Mass.

Magenis, James P., care of Dickson & Knowles, 53 State Street, Boston, Mass.

Magner, Thomas, Sup't Metropolitan Life Insurance Co., Rutland, Vt.

Magrane, P. B., dry goods merchant, Lynn, Mass.

Maguire, John, Butte City, Montana.

Maguire, John C., Brooklyn, N. Y.

Maher, James J., Augusta, Me.

Maher, Dr. Stephen J., 212 Orange Street, New Haven, Conn.

Mahoney, Daniel D., of D. D. Mahoney & Son, Essex Street, Lawrence, Mass.

Mahoney, James, Hotel Nottingham, Boston, Mass.

Mahoney, James V., Commissioner of the Commercial Association, Sioux City, Iowa.

Mahoney, John P. S., Central Building, Lawrence, Mass.; recently President of the Common Council.

Mahoney, Rev. Martin, Mendota, Minn.

Mahoney, M. J., Hampshire and Bradford Streets, Lawrence, Mass.

Mahoney, Dr. Michael P., 63 East Street, Providence, R. I.

Malloy, Gen. A. G., El Paso, Texas; a veteran of the Mexican and Civil Wars; during the latter conflict he was successively Major, Colonel, and Brigadier-General; has been Collector of the Port of Galveston.

Malone, John, Actors' Society of America, 1432 Broadway, New York City.

Maloney, Cornelius, publisher, *Daily Democrat*, Waterbury, Conn.

Maloney, Dr. M. W., Woonsocket, R. I.

Maloney, Dr. Thomas E., 278 Franklin Street, Fall River, Mass.

Maneely, John, 309-311 Arch Street, Philadelphia, Pa.

Mangan, John J. (M. D.), 55 North Common Street, Lynn, Mass.

Manning, Timothy T., care of James & Marra, Springfield, Mass.

Mannix, Cornelius A., 40 Sheridan Street, Portland, Me.

Marshall, Rev. George F., Rector of St. Paul's Roman Catholic Church, Milford, N. H.

Martin, Rev. Farrell (D. D.), Waterbury, Conn.

Martin, Dr. James F., Springfield, Mass.

Martin, Hon. John B., 762 Fourth Street, South Boston, Mass.

May, Henry A., Roslindale, Mass.

McAdoo, Hon. William, Assistant Secretary of the Navy (under Cleveland). New York City.

McAleer, George, Treasurer Bay State Savings Bank, Worcester, Mass.

McAlevy, John F., 26-50 North Main Street, Pawtucket, R. I.

McAuliffe, John F., with the Livermore & Knight Co., Westminster Street, Providence, R. I.

McCaffrey, Hugh, Fifth and Berks Streets, Philadelphia, Pa.

McCann, Daniel E., 37 Preble Street, Portland, Me.

McCarrick, James W., Clyde's Steam Lines, Norfolk, Va.

McCarthy, Charles, Jr., Portland, Me.

McCarthy, Eugene T., 343 Union Street, Lynn, Mass.

McCarthy, Rev. Jeremiah, Gardiner, Me.

McCarthy, John H., 8 West 125th Street, New York City.

McCarthy, Joseph, Editorial Department *Daily Globe*, Boston, Mass.

McCarthy, Patrick J., Industrial Trust Building, Providence, R. I.

McCarthy, T. A. (D. D. S.), Main Street, Nashua, N. H.

McCaughey, Bernard, 93-105 North Main Street, Pawtucket, R. I.

McClallen, Edward C., Rutland, Vt.; of the fifth American generation.

McCluskey, James J., 34 School Street, Boston, Mass.

McConnell, James E., Fitchburg, Mass.; candidate for Lieutenant-Governor of Massachusetts, 1896.

McConway, William, manufacturer, Pittsburg, Pa.

McCoy, Rev. John J., Permanent Rector of the Church of the Holy Name, Chicopee, Mass.

McCrystal, Maj. Edward T., 69th Regiment Infantry, N. G. N. Y., New York City.

McCullough, Edward (M. D.), 123 Union Street, Bangor, Me.

McCullough, John, 55 Maxfield Street, New Bedford, Mass.

McCusker, John F. (M. D.), 96 Broad Street, Providence, R. I.

McDermott, Rev. William A., Redwood, N. Y. ; under the *nom-de-plume* " Walter Lecky " he has produced much literary work.

McDermott, Thomas J., Biddeford, Me. ; proprietor of Biddeford Iron and Brass Works.

McDonald, Dr. Edward W., Waterbury, Conn.

McDonald, Dr. J. A., 116 Main Street, Charlestown (Boston), Mass.

McDonald, John, 70 Leicester Street, Boston, Mass.

McDonald, Mitchell C., Paymaster U. S. N. ; recently attached to the battleship *Texas* ; address, care Navy Department, Washington, D. C.

McDonnell, Thomas F. I., 17 Custom House Street, Providence, R. I.

McDonnell, Thomas H., School Street, Quincy, Mass.

McDonough, Edward J. (M. D.), 333 Congress Street, Portland, Me.

McDonough, Hon. John J., Fall River, Mass.

McDonough, Rev. M. C., Bath, Me.

McEleney, William, 45 Cedar Street, Portland, Me.

McElroy, Rev. Charles J., Rector St. Mary's Roman Catholic Church, Derby, Conn.

McEvoy, John W., 137 Central Street, Lowell, Mass.

McGauran, Michael S. (M. D.), Lawrence, Mass.

McGillicuddy, Hon. D. J., Lewiston, Me. ; Mayor 1887–'90.

McGinnis, Rev. John J., Sandford, Me.

McGinniss, Lieut.-Col. John R., ordnance corps, U. S. A. ; care War Department, Washington, D. C.

McGlinchy, J. H., 128 Danforth Street, Portland, Me.

McGoey, J., 78 Worth Street, New York City.

McGolrick, Rev. E. J., 84 Herbert Street, Brooklyn, N. Y.

McGovern, Joseph P., 193 Green Street, New York City.

McGowan, James, 6 Wall Street, New York City.

McGowan, Joseph A., 263 Congress Street, Portland, Me.

McGowan, P. F., Board of Education, New York City.

McGrath, Rev. Christopher, 264 Washington Street, Somerville, Mass. ; Rector St. Joseph's Church.

McGuinness, Bernard, 32 Westminster Street, Providence, R. I.

McGuinness, Hon. Edward D., Providence, R. I. ; has served two terms as Mayor of Providence, and two as Secretary of State of Rhode Island.

McGuire, Edward J., 62 Wall Street, New York City.

McGuire, Rev. Francis D., The Cathedral, Albany, N. Y.

McGurk, Charles J., City Auditor, New Bedford, Mass.

McGurrin, Frank E., Salt Lake City, Utah.

McIntyre, John F., lawyer, 220 Broadway, New York City.

McKechnie, Rev. James H., Worcester, Mass.

McKechnie, William G., 366 Walnut Street, Springfield, Mass.

McKellegett, George F., 27 Tremont Row, Boston, Mass.

McKeon, Francis P., Millbury Street School, Worcester, Mass.

McLaughlin, Edward A., 16 Pemberton Square, Boston, Mass.; was for several years clerk of the Massachusetts House of Representatives.

McLaughlin, Henry V. (M. D.), 29 Kent Street, Brookline, Mass.

McLaughlin, James M., 56 Bowdoin Street, Dorchester (Boston), Mass.; Supervisor of Music in Boston Public Schools; author of " The Educational Music System."

McLaughlin, Marcus J., 250 West 25th Street, New York City.

McLaughlin, Thomas, Hallowell, Me.

McLaughlin, William H., 24 C Street, Knightville, Portland, Me.

McLaughlin, William I., State Mutual Building, Worcester, Mass.

McMahon, Edward J., Walker Building, Worcester, Mass.

McMahon, James, 51 Chambers Street, New York City.

McMahon, James H., 17 Main Street, Fitchburg, Mass.

McMahon, Rev. John W. (D. D.), Rector St. Mary's Church, Charlestown (Boston), Mass.

McManus, Col. John, 145-147 Westminster Street, Providence, R. I.; served on the staff of Governor Davis of Rhode Island.

McManus, Michael, of McManus & Co., clothiers, 670 Washington Street, Boston, Mass.

McManus, Gen. Thomas, 333 Main Street, Hartford, Conn.

McManus, Rev. Michael T., Rector St. Mary's Church, Brookline, Mass.

McMunn, R. H., Roxbury (Boston), Mass.

McNamee, John H. H., 51 Frost Street, North Cambridge, Mass.

McNeely, Richard, 309 East 42d Street, New York City.

McNeirny, Michael J., Gloucester, Mass.

McNulty, Rev. John J., 92 West 6th Street, South Boston, Mass.

McQuade, E. A., 75-77 Market Street, Lowell, Mass.

McQuaid, Rev. William P., Rector St. James Church, Harrison Avenue, Boston, Mass.

McQueeney, Henry J., of the Post-office staff, Lawrence, Mass.

McSweeney, Edward F., Assistant U. S. Commissioner of Immigration, Ellis Island, N. Y.

McSweeny, Rev. Edward, Rector St. John's Roman Catholic Church, Bangor, Me.

McVey, Edward D., 519 Westford Street, Lowell, Mass.

McVicar, P. A., Auburndale, Mass.

McWilliams, Daniel A., 16 Hamilton Street, New Haven, Conn.

Meany, Thomas J., New Bedford, Mass.

Mehan, Charles, El Paso, Texas.

Mehegan, Daniel J. (M. D.), 31 Broadway, Taunton, Mass.

Melden, P. M., Rutland, Vt.

Mellen, Hon. W. M. E., ex-Mayor, Chicopee, Mass.

Milholland, John E., Tubular Despatch Co., Tribune Building, New York City.

Millea, William H., 154 Washington Street, Salem, Mass.

Minahan, Hon. T. B., Board of Trade, Columbus, Ohio.

Miskella, James, 10 Chase Street, Lowell, Mass.

Molloy, Hugh J., State Normal School, Lowell, Mass.

Moloney, T. W., of Butler & Moloney, counselors-at-law, Rutland, Vt.

Monaghan, Rt. Rev. John J. (D. D.), Bishop of Wilmington, Del.

Monohan, Michael, 874 Broadway, New York City.

Mooney, J. G., 154 Exchange Street, Bangor, Me.

Mooney, John A., 353 West 27th Street, New York City.

Moore, Dr. James A., 223 Grand Avenue, New Haven, Conn.

Moore, O'Brien, recently of the Washington (D. C.) bureau of the *St. Louis Republic*; publisher of the *Daily Gazette*, Charleston, W. Va.

Moran, Col. James, Providence, R. I.; served in the Fifth R. I. Heavy Artillery during the Civil War; recently commanded the Second Regiment, Rhode Island Militia.

Moran, Dr. James, 333 West 51st Street, New York City.

Moran, Thomas, Jr., Biddeford, Me.

Moran, William, Biddeford, Me.

Morrissey, William T., Portsmouth, N. H.

Morrissey, Very Rev. Andrew (C. S. C.), president of the University of Notre Dame, Notre Dame, Ind.

Morrison, Francis M., 492 Main Street, Worcester, Mass.

Moseley, Edward A., Secretary of the Interstate Commerce Commission, Washington, D. C.

Moses, George H., editor *The Monitor*, Concord, N. H. (U. S. Senator Chandler's paper.)

Moyes, Rev. David (D. C. L.), Ashburnham, Mass.

Moynahan, Bartholomew, 120 Broadway, New York City.

Moynihan, Michael A., Portsmouth, N. H.; U. S. Internal Revenue Office.

Mulcahy, Rev. John, Arlington, Mass.

Mulholland, Gen. St. Clair A., U. S. Pension Agent, Philadelphia, Pa.

Mullaney, Rev. John F., Rector Church of St. John the Baptist, Syracuse, N. Y.

Mullen, Hugh, of Brown, Durrell & Co., Boston, Mass.

Mullen, John T., 23 Aborn Street, Providence, R. I.

Mulligan, B. J., 37 Warren Street, Salem, Mass.

Mundy, Rev. John F., 55 Norfolk Street, Cambridgeport, Mass.

Murphy, Chas. B., Augusta, Me.

Murphy, D. P., Jr., 31 Barclay Street, New York City.

Murphy, Daniel D. (M. D.), Amesbury, Mass.

Murphy, David E., 8 Perley Street, Concord, N. H.

Murphy, Edward J., 327 Main Street, Springfield, Mass.

16

Murphy, Frank J., lock box 161, Olean, N. Y.

Murphy, Fred C., Dickinson Building, Springfield, Mass.

Murphy, J. H., attorney-at-law, Portland, Oregon.

Murphy, Hon. John R., Boston, Mass.; ex-State Senator of Massachusetts.

Murphy, James, real estate and insurance, Essex Street, Lawrence, Mass.

Murphy, James, 42 Westminster Street, Providence, R. I.

Murphy, James R., lawyer, 27 School Street, Boston, Mass.

Murphy, John A., 276 Union Street, Springfield, Mass.

Murphy, Thomas, 144 Elm Street, Biddeford, Me.

Murphy, William, 2 Lewis Park, Roxbury (Boston), Mass.

Murray, Capt. John F., police department, Cambridge, Mass.; residence, 9 Avon Street.

Murray, Frank E., 47 Park Street, Worcester, Mass.

Murray, Joseph T., 131 Pearl Street, Manchester, N. H.

Murray, Michael J., attorney-at-law, 27 School Street, Boston, Mass.

Murray, Thomas Hamilton, Secretary-general of the Society, editor *The Evening Call,* 77 Main Street, Woonsocket, R. I.

Nammack, Dr. Charles E., 42 East 29th Street, New York City.

Naphen, Hon. Henry F., 42 Court Street, Boston, Mass.; member of Congress.

Neagle, Rev. Richard, Malden, Mass.

Neagle, Thomas J., 66 Franklin Street, Haverhill, Mass.

Neilon, John F., Saco, Me.

Nicholson, George, 40 Oak Street, Lynn, Mass.

Nolan, Frank F., 224 Thames Street, Newport, R. I.

O'Beirne, Gen. James R., 357 West 117th Street, New York City.

O'Brien, Capt. Lawrence, New Haven, Conn.

O'Brien, Charles J., 670 Washington Street, Boston, Mass.

O'Brien, Frank J., of Donigan & O'Brien, 322 Essex Street, Lawrence, Mass.; late a member of the City Council.

O'Brien, Hon. C. D., 212 Globe Building, St. Paul, Minn.; ex-Mayor of St. Paul.

O'Brien, James W., lawyer, 23 Court Street, Boston, Mass.

O'Brien, John D., Bank of Minnesota Building, St. Paul, Minn.; of the law firm Stevens, O'Brien, Cole & Albrecht.

O'Brien, Hon. Morgan J., 42 West 44th Street, New York City; a Justice of the Supreme Court.

O'Brien, Patrick, 399 South Broadway, Lawrence, Mass.

O'Brien, Rev. James J., Somerville, Mass.; a son of the late Hon. Hugh O'Brien, Mayor of Boston.

O'Brien, Rev. Michael, Rector St. Patrick's Church, Lowell, Mass.

O'Brien, Thomas, 155 Main Street, Pawtucket, R. I.

O'Brien, Very Rev. Michael C., 30 Cedar Street, Bangor, Me.; Vicar-General of the Roman Catholic Diocese of Portland.

O'Byrne, J. J., 206 57th Street, Brooklyn, N. Y.

O'Byrne, M. A., 370 West 118th Street, New York City.

O'Callaghan, John, editorial department, *Daily Globe*, Boston, Mass.

O'Callaghan, P. J., Lawrence, Mass.

O'Callaghan, Rev. Denis (D. D.), Rector St. Augustine's Roman Catholic Church, South Boston. Mass

O'Connell, Dr. J. C., U. S. Pension Office, Saginaw, Mich.

O'Connell, J. D., Bureau of Statistics, U. S. Treasury Department, Washington, D. C.

O'Connell, John, 302 West End Avenue, New York City.

O'Connell, Timothy, 140 State Street, Newburyport, Mass.

O'Connor, Charles A., 135 Lawrence Street, Manchester, N. H.; member State Constitutional Convention; two terms in the State Legislature.

O'Connor, Charles J., 4 Weybosset Street, Providence, R. I.

O'Connor, D. F., 341 Central Street, Manchester, N. H.

O'Connor, Dr. Joseph M., 204 Main Street, Biddeford, Me.

O'Connor, Edward DeV., 4 Weybosset Street, Providence, R. I.

O'Connor, Francis, 531 Washington Street, Boston, Mass.

O'Connor, James, 37 Prospect Street, Biddeford, Me.

O'Connor, John D., The Washington Press, 18 Essex Street, Boston, Mass.

O'Connor, Patrick, 99 Mill Street, New Haven, Conn.

O'Conor, P. H., Washington Street, Peabody, Mass.

O'Donnell, Rev. James H., Watertown, Conn., author of a recently published history of the Catholic diocese of Hartford, Conn.

O'Donnell, James J., 65 Taylor Street, Holyoke, Mass.

O'Donnell, Hon. John B., ex-Mayor, Northampton, Mass.

O'Donnell, Rev. Philip J., 887 Shawmut Avenue, Boston, Mass.

O'Doherty, Hon. Matthew, Louisville, Ky.

O'Doherty, Rev. James, Rector St. James Roman Catholic Church, Haverhill, Mass.

O'Donoghue, Col. D. O'C., 75 Emery Street, Portland, Me.

O'Dowd, Michael, 922 Elm Street, Manchester, N. H.

O'Driscoll, Daniel M., Western Union Telegraph Co., Charleston, S. C.

O'Dwyer, Hon. E. F., 37 West 76th Street, New York City.

O'Farrell, Charles, 173 Devonshire Street, Boston, Mass., an earnest, scholarly worker in the Irish language movement.

O'Farrell, Col. P. A., Spokane, Wash.

O'Farrell, Patrick, of O'Farrell, Fowler & O'Farrell, lawyers, Solicitors of American and Foreign Patents, 1425 New York Avenue, N. W., Washington, D. C.

O'Farrell, Rev. Denis J., 7 North Square, Boston, Mass.; Rector St. Stephen's Church.

O'Flaherty, John (M. D.), Hartford, Conn.; served during the Civil War in Corcoran's Legion as a member of the 170th Regiment, New York Volunteers.

O'Flynn, Thomas F., 25 Grosvenor Street, Worcester, Mass.

O'Gorman, Hon. J. A., 312 West 54th Street, New York City.

O'Hart, John, 1 Woodside, Vernon Avenue, Clontarf, Ireland; author of " O'Hart's Irish Pedigrees," " The Last Princes of Tara," etc.

O'Hearn, William H. (M. D.), 283 Essex Street, Lawrence, Mass.

O'Keefe, Daniel T. (M. D.), 183 Green Street, Jamaica Plain (Boston), Mass.

O'Keefe, Edmund, Inspector Buildings, New Bedford, Mass.

O'Keefe, John A., lawyer, 25 Exchange Street, Lynn, Mass.; formerly Principal of the High School in that city; recently candidate for Attorney-General of Massachusetts.

O'Kennedy, J. J. Karbry (LL. D.), 77 Broadway, New York City.

O'Loughlin, Patrick, lawyer, 23 Court Street, Boston, Mass.

O'Mahoney, Daniel J., Essex Street, Lawrence, Mass.; ex-Superintendent of Streets.

O'Mahoney, Michael, of Moulton & O'Mahoney, contractors, Lawrence, Mass.

O'Malley, Rev. John, Greenfield, Mass.

O'Malley, Thomas F., law office, 7 Hill Building, Somerville, Mass.

O'Neil, Hon. Joseph H., Boston, Mass.

O'Neil, James, 521 7th Street, N. W., Washington, D. C.

O'Neil, James, Hampshire and Common Streets, Lawrence, Mass.

O'Neil, Rev. J. L. (O. P.), 871 Lexington Avenue, New York City. This is a life membership standing to the credit of " The Editor of *The Rosary Magazine*." Father O'Neil was the first to represent the magazine in the organization.

O'Neill, Rev. Daniel H., 935 Main Street, Worcester, Mass.

O'Neill, Rev. D. P., Westchester, N. Y.

O'Neill, Eugene C., 51 Lee Avenue, Newport, R. I.

O'Neill, James L., Franklin Street, Elizabeth, N. J.

O'Neill, John, 131 Cook Street, Waterbury, Conn.

O'Neill, John E., 53 Lee Avenue, Newport, R. I.; member of the Board of Aldermen; cashier New York and Boston Despatch Express Company.

O'Neill, Thomas J., The Aquidneck, Newport, R. I.

O'Neill, William F., Chicopee Falls, Mass.

O'Reilly, F. C., Orange, N. J.

O'Reilly, Luke F., 825 7th Street, N. W., Washington, D. C.

O'Reilly, Rev. James T. (O. S. A.), Rector St. Mary's Church, Lawrence, Mass.

O'Reilly, Thomas B., Salt Lake City, Utah.

O'Rourke, Timothy, 91 Scoville Street, Waterbury, Conn.

O'Shea, J. F. (M. D.), 116 Union Street, Lynn, Mass.

O'Sullivan, Hon. Edward F., City Engineer's Office, Lawrence, Mass.; an ex-Senator.

O'Sullivan, Humphrey, 105 Butterfield Street, Lowell, Mass.

O'Sullivan, James, of O'Sullivan Bros., Merrimack Street, Lowell, Mass.

O'Sullivan, James T., real estate and insurance, Lawrence, Mass.; ex-City Marshal.

Palmer, Rev. Edmund B., 4 Peter Parley Street, Jamaica Plain (Boston), Mass.

Patterson, Rev. Geo. J., Rector St. Vincent's Church, South Boston, Mass.

Payne, William E., New York City.

Penney, William M., 34 West 26th Street, New York City.

Perry, Dr. Charles, P. O. Box 2977, New York City.

Phalen, Rev. Frank L., pastor Unitarian Church, Worcester, Mass.; chaplain of the First New Hampshire Regiment, U. S. Volunteers (war with Spain).

Phelan, Dr. Daniel J., 123 West 94th Street, New York City.

Phelan, James J., 66 West 85th Street, New York City.

Phelan, Rev. J., Rector St. Mary's Roman Catholic Church, Rock Valley, Iowa; recently editor of the *Northwestern Catholic*.

Philpott, Anthony J., *Daily Globe*, Boston, Mass.

Piggott, Michael, 1634 Vermont Street, Quincy, Ill.

Pigott, Hon. James P., 179 Church Street, New Haven, Conn.; ex-Member of Congress.

Plunkett, Thomas, 257 6th Street, East Liverpool, Ohio.

Power, James D., U. S. Custom House, New York City.

Power, Rev. James W., 47 East 129th Street, New York City.

Powers, Patrick H., President Emerson Piano Co., 110 Boylston Street, Boston, Mass.

Pulleyn, John J., Treasurer Catholic Club, 171 West 94th Street, New York City.

Quinlan, Daniel J., 53 East 127th Street, New York City.

Quinlan, Prof. Francis J. (M. D., LL. D.), 33 West 38th Street, New York City; President New York Celtic Medical Society; late surgeon in the U. S. Indian service.

Quinlan, Col. James, 116 Liberty Street, New York City.

Quinn, Hon. John, 66 Broadway, New York City.

Quinn, Joseph F., 6 Broad Street Court, Salem, Mass.

Quinn, William H., Hallowell, Me.

Quinton, Major William, U. S A., care of War Department, Washington, D. C.

Radikin, Edward F., Pawtucket, R. I.

Rafferty, Dr. James J., Worcester, Mass.

Ratigan, John B., Walker Building, Worcester, Mass.

Reardon, Edmund, 24 Commerce Street, Boston, Mass.; residence, Cambridge, Mass.; Member Boston Chamber of Commerce; Director Commercial National Bank.

Reddy, Hon. W. F., 23 Schafer Building, Richmond, Va.; member of the State Legislature.

Redican, Rev. J. F., Leicester, Mass.

Reed, Henry E., Portland, Ore.; care of *The Oregonian.*

Regan, W. P., architect, Lawrence, Mass.

Reilly, James C., Clement Building, Rutland, Vt.

Reilly, John M., Box 122, Columbus, Ind.

Reilly, Robert J., Cedar Street, Bangor, Me.

Reynolds, James F., 12 Belmont Place, Somerville, Mass.

Rice, James D., 39 Hammond Street, Bangor, Me.

Rice, John H., Eastern Trust and Banking Co., Bangor, Me.

Richardson, Stephen J., 1785 Madison Avenue, New York City.

Riddle, Patrick E., East Cottage Street, Dorchester (Boston), Mass.

Riley, James Whitcomb, Indianapolis, Ind.

Riordan, John H., 136 Fort Hill Avenue, Lowell, Mass.

Robinson, Thomas W., Main Street, Pawtucket, R. I.

Roche, James Jeffrey, (LL. D.), editor of *The Pilot,* 630 Washington Street, Boston, Mass.

Roche, Martin J., 23 City Square, Charlestown (Boston), Mass.

Rock, Thomas H., Main Street, Pawtucket, R. I.

Roe, James V., Harbor View, East Boston, Mass.

Rodwaye, Alfred J., 44 Kingston Street, Boston, Mass.; a member of the Jacobite Order of the White Rose; Fellow of the Royal Historical Society, England; Fellow of the Royal Society of Northern Antiquarians, Denmark; member of the Royal Italian Heraldic Academy.

Ronayne, Thomas H., 5 Beekman Street, New York City.

Rooney, John J., of Rooney & Spence, customs brokers, 66, 68, and 70 Beaver Street, New York City.

Rorke, James, 40 Barclay Street, New York City.

Rossa, Jeremiah O'Donovan, New York City.

Roosevelt, Hon. Theodore, Governor of New York, Albany, N. Y.

Ruggles, Henry Stoddard (ninth American generation), Wakefield, Mass.; a member of the Sons of the Revolution and of the Sons of the American Revolution.

Rush, John, 16th and Farnham Streets, Omaha, Neb.

Ryan, Charles V., Springfield, Mass.

Ryan, Felix L., 47 Main Street, Bangor, Me.

Ryan, John, 789 Westfield Street, Lowell, Mass.

Ryan, John J., 204 Merrimack Street, Haverhill, Mass.

Ryan, John J., 59 South Broadway, Lawrence, Mass.

Ryan, John J., 158 East 95th Street, New York City.

Ryan, Patrick H., 789 Westfield Street, Lowell, Mass.

Ryan, Philip, 79 Portland Street, Worcester, Mass.

Ryan, Richard, Rutland, Vt.

Ryan, Sylvester A., 565 Chestnut Street, Springfield, Mass.

Sanders, Col. C. C., Gainesville, Ga.; President of the State Banking Co.; commanded the 24th Georgia Regiment in the Civil War.

Scanlan, John F., 4333 Indiana Avenue, Chicago, Ill.

Scanlan, Rev. M. A., 1276 Woodland Avenue, Cleveland, Ohio.

Scully, Martin, *Daily Democrat*, Waterbury, Conn.

Scully, Rev. Thomas, Cambridgeport, Mass.

Sexton, Sergt. Patrick G., Augusta, Me.

Shahan, Rev. Thomas H., Malden, Mass.

Shahan, Rev. Thomas J. (D. D.), Catholic University, Washington, D. C.

Shanahan, Rev. Edmund T. (Ph. D., D. D.), Catholic University, Washington, D. C.

Shea, C. J., of Shea & Donnelly, Lynn, Mass.

Shea, John, 99 Georgia Street, Dorchester (Boston), Mass.

Shea, John T., 119 3d Street, East Cambridge, Mass.; member of the Board of Aldermen.

Shea, M. J., Piedmont Street, Canton, Ohio.

Shea, Richard J., City Hall, Lawrence, Mass.; clerk of the Council; City Auditor.

Sheahan, Dennis H., Providence, R. I.; ex-clerk of the Rhode Island House of Representatives.

Sheahan, Dr. Joseph M., 6 School Street, Quincy, Mass.

Sheehan, John A., Pickering Building, Manchester, N. H.

Sheehan, Joseph, southwest corner 6th and Market Streets, Philadelphia, Pa.

Sheran, Hugh F., 46 Woodbine Street, Roxbury (Boston), Mass.

Sheridan, Bernard H., principal of the Oliver School, Lawrence, Mass.

Shortell, Joseph P., 28 Cabot Street, Salem, Mass.

Shuman, A., 440 Washington Street, Boston, Mass.

Slattery, James A., Boston, Mass.

Sloane, Prof. William M., Columbia College, New York City; author of a "Life of Napoleon."

Slocum, Rev. Wm. J., Waterbury, Conn.

Smith, Rev. James J., 88 Central Street, Norwich, Conn.

Smith, Joseph, Secretary of the Police Commission, Lowell, Mass.; a clear, vigorous writer, and author of many articles of an ethnological and historical nature.

Smith, Dr. Thomas B., Wyman's Exchange, Lowell, Mass.

Smith, Rev. Thomas M., East Liverpool, Ohio.

Smyth, Eneas, Brookline, Mass.

Smyth, Philip A., 11 Pine Street, New York City.

Smyth, Rev. Hugh J., New Bedford, Mass.

Smyth, Rev. Hugh P., Rector St. Joseph's Church, Roxbury (Boston), Mass.

Smyth, Rev. Thomas, Springfield, Mass.

Somers, James F., 83 West 132d Street, New York City.

Somers, P. E., 17 Hermon Street, Worcester, Mass.

Somers, Thomas F., 349 Broadway, New York City.

St. Gaudens, Augustus, sculptor, New York City.

Steele, N. C. (M. D.), Chattanooga, Tenn. ; four generations removed from Ireland.

Stevens, Walter F., 176 Winter Street, Haverhill, Mass.

Sullivan, Eugene M., Chicopee, Mass.

Sullivan, Dr. James E., 254 Wayland Avenue, Providence, R. I.

Sullivan, James J., 18 Margaret Street, Springfield, Mass.

Sullivan, James O., 245 Main Street, Biddeford, Me.

Sullivan, Jeremiah D., 431 Purchase Street, New Bedford, Mass.

Sullivan, John D., 113 Palm Street, Nashua, N. H.

Sullivan, John J., 140 Chestnut Street, Nashua, N. H.

Sullivan, John J., 61–63 Faneuil Hall Market, Boston, Mass. ; of Doe, Sullivan & Co.

Sullivan, Hon. M. B., Dover, N. H., ex-State Senator.

Sullivan, M. F. (M. D.), Oak Street, Lawrence, Mass.

Sullivan, M. J., of Buckley, McCormack & Sullivan, Lawrence, Mass.

Sullivan, Patrick F., of Sullivan Bros., 9 School Street, Boston, Mass.

Sullivan, Patrick H., Opera Block, Manchester, N. H.

Sullivan, Hon. Richard, Hemingway Building, Boston, Mass.

Sullivan, Roger G., 803 Elm Street, Manchester, N. H.

Sullivan, Timothy P., Concord, N. H. ; furnished granite from his New Hampshire quarries for the new National Library building, Washington, D. C.

Sullivan, William J. (M. D.), Lawrence, Mass.

Supple, Rev. James N., Rector St. Francis de Sales Church, Charlestown (Boston), Mass.

Sweeny, William Montgomery, 120 Franklin Street, Astoria, L. I., N. Y.

Swords, Col. Henry Leonard, The Florence, 4th Avenue and 18th Street, New York City.

Swords, Joseph Forsyth, Room 500, Bank of Commerce Building, Nassau and Cedar Streets, New York City.

Tally, Philip, 353 Westminster Street, Providence, R. I.

Teeling, Rev. Arthur J., Rector St. Mary's Roman Catholic Church, Lynn, Mass.

Tennian, Rev. John C., Rector Church of the Assumption, Potter's Avenue, Providence, R. I.

Thomas, Robert J., Water Department, Lowell, Mass.

Thompson, Robert Ellis (Ph. D., S. T. D.), President Central High School, Philadelphia, Pa. ; recently a professor in the University of Pennsylvania.

Tierney, Dennis H., 167 Bank Street, Waterbury, Conn.

Tierney, Rev. John D., Salem, Mass.

Tierney, Myles, 317 Riverside Drive, New York City.

Tigh, Frederick (M. D.), 132 High Street, Newburyport, Mass.

Timmins, Patrick J. (M. D.), 487 Broadway, South Boston, Mass.

Toland, M. A., *The Pilot* Office, 630 Washington Street, Boston, Mass.

Toomey, Daniel J., manager *Donahoe's Magazine*, Washington Street, Boston, Mass.

Toomey, R. A., with Forbes & Wallace, Springfield, Mass.

Tracy, James J., Archives Division, State Capitol, Boston, Mass.

Travers, Ambrose F., 107 Duane Street, New York City.

Travers, F. C., President of Travers Brothers Co., 107 Duane Street, New York City, cordage manufacturers.

Travers, Vincent P., 107 Duane Street, New York City.

Treanor, J. O., 211 Union Street, Nashville, Tenn.

Tuckey, James F., 26 Grove Street, New Haven, Conn.

Vail, Roger, associate editor *The Irish Standard*, Minneapolis, Minn.

Vance, Thomas F., Main Street, Pawtucket, R. I.

Waldron, Thomas F., 74 Washington Street, Haverhill, Mass.

Wallace, Rev. T. H., Lewiston, Me.

Wallace, Rev. Thomas W., 437 West 51st Street, New York City.

Waller, Hon. Thomas M., ex-Governor of Connecticut, 15 Wall Street, New York City.

Walsh, Henry Collins, care of the *New York Herald*, New York City; a descendant of Gen. Stephen Moylan of the American Revolution.

Walsh, James A., Lewiston, Me.; agent Lewiston Bleachery.

Walsh, Michael (LL. D., Ph. D.), editor of the *Sunday Democrat*, 32 Park Row, New York City.

Walsh, William P., 247 Water Street, Augusta, Me.

Ward, Edward, Kennebunk, Me.

Ward, John T., Kennebunk, Me.

Ward, Michael J., Hotel Ilkley, Huntington Avenue, Boston, Mass.

Ward, Patrick, 13 Casco Street, Portland, Me.

Ware, Alfred, Lowell, Mass.

Weadock, Hon. Thomas A. E., Detroit, Mich.; member of the 52d and of the 53d Congresses.

Welsh, John P., Portland, Me.

Whalen, Maurice H., 8 Vetromile Street, Biddeford, Me.

Whalen, Nicholas J., 97 Merrimack Street, Manchester, N. H.

Whall, William B. F., 57 Monmouth Street, East Boston, Mass.

White, Hon. Andrew J., 6 Mount Morris West, New York City.

Williams, Hon. George Fred, 209 Washington Street, Boston, Mass.

Willis, John R., 1164 Elm Street, Manchester, N. H.

Wilson, Hon. Thomas, St. Paul, Minn.; care of Chicago, St. Paul, Minneapolis & Omaha R. R.

Wilson, William Power, Exchange Building, 53 State Street, Boston, Mass.

Winters, Lawrence, 350 West 120th Street, New York City.

Woods, John J., 54 Federal Street, Newburyport, Mass.

Woods, Robert J., treasurer University Settlement, 6 Rollins Street, Boston, Mass.

Woods, William S., City Solicitor, Taunton, Mass.

Wright, John B., editor of *The Gazette*, Haverhill, Mass.

Wynne, Peter, 301 East 105th Street, New York City.

THE DEAD OF THE SOCIETY.

"Memory, gray old warder, throw open thy portals in welcome
Wide to the dead—our dead"— they loved us well in their lifetime.

Col. Jeremiah W. Coveney.

Born in Cambridge, Mass., 1840; during the Civil War enlisted in 28th Massachusetts Regiment; was successively commissioned Lieutenant, Captain, Major, and Lieutenant-Colonel; seriously wounded in 1864, while Brigade Inspector of the Second Brigade, First Division, Second Corps; member of the Massachusetts Legislature; surveyor of the port of Boston; private secretary to Governor Russell; postmaster of Boston; admitted to the Society March 29, 1897; died in Cambridge, Mass., April 29, 1897.

Rear-Admiral Richard Worsam Meade, U. S. N.

Born in New York City, 1837; appointed Midshipman Oct. 2, 1850; first sea service in sloop-of-war *Preble*, 1851; warrant as Master and commission as Lieutenant, 1858; Lieutenant-Commander, 1862; was a Commander in 1870; commissioned Captain in 1880; became a Commodore in 1892, and Rear-Admiral in 1894; admitted to the Society at its organization, Jan. 20, 1897, and chosen President-General of the same, being the first to hold the office; died in Washington, D. C., May 4, 1897.

Henry V. Donovan, M. D.

Born in Lawrence, Mass., 1868; graduated from Harvard University; was elected to the school board of Lawrence, and rendered excellent service; admitted to the Society May 25, 1897; died in Lawrence, Mass., Aug. 4, 1897.

Gen. John Cochrane.

Descendant of an officer who served under Washington; President of the N. Y. Society of the Cincinnati; from 1857 to 1861 was a Congressman from New York City; was commissioned Colonel of the First U. S. Chasseurs, June 11, 1861; Brigadier-General of Volunteers, July 17, 1862; in 1864 was nominated at Cleveland, O., for Vice-President of the United States; had previously been Attorney-General of New York state; admitted to the Society on its organization, Jan 20, 1897; died in New York City, Oct. 7, 1897.

Mr. Laurence J. Smith.

Born in County Meath, Ireland, 1850; member of City Council, Lowell, Mass., 1881–'86; member Lowell Public Library Board; was made a License Commissioner of Lowell, 1894; Police Commissioner, 1895; attained the highest rank in the Foresters of America, having been Supreme Chief Ranger of the United States; admitted to the Society Feb. 27, 1897; died in Lowell, Mass., Oct. 23, 1897.

Hon. Owen A. Galvin.

Born in Boston, Mass., 1852; admitted to the bar, 1876; elected to the Massachusetts House of Representatives, 1881; a State Senator from Boston during 1882, 1883, and 1884; candidate for President of the Senate, 1884; candidate for Mayor of Boston, 1889; was U. S. District Attorney, 1887–'89; admitted to the Society July 15, 1897; died in Boston, Mass., Dec. 18, 1897.

Hon. Charles B. Gafney.

Born in Ossipee, N. H., 1843; enlisted Sept. 27, 1862, as Second Lieutenant of Co. B, 13th New Hampshire Volunteers; promoted to First Lieutenant, June 1, 1863, and to Captain, May 30, 1865; severely wounded in the thigh at Petersburg, June 15, 1864; was Clerk to the National Senate Committee on Naval Affairs for eight years; went to Rochester, N. H., in 1871, and formed a law partnership with Joseph H. Worcester, which firm became Worcester, Gafney & Snow; was appointed Judge of Probate for Strafford county; admitted to the Society Feb. 9, 1897; died in Rochester, N. H., Jan. 25, 1898.

Mr. Andrew Athy.

Born in County Galway, Ireland, 1832; filled public offices of trust and responsibility in Worcester, Mass., almost continuously during more than thirty years; was first elected to the Common Council in 1865, and served thirteen years; represented the city in the Legislature of 1874 and 1875; was a member of the Board of Aldermen from 1881 to 1886, and a member of the commission to build the new City Hall; candidate for mayor in 1886. He was a member of the old Jackson Guards at the time of disbandment, during the Know-Nothing administration of Governor Gardner; admitted to the Society as a life member March 5, 1898; died in Worcester, Mass., May 15, 1898.

Mr. John R. Alley.

Born in Dublin, Ireland, 1822; a prominent Boston brewer; life member of the Society. His grandfather, John Alley, was at one time lord mayor of Dublin, and his father was a graduate of Cambridge University, England. Mr. Alley, our deceased associate, had warm Irish sympathies, and it has been truly said of him that few men in Boston or New England did more for the Irish cause than he. His purse and voice were always at the disposal of his fellow-countrymen in the various phases of Irish movements in this country for the past thirty years. He was an ardent lover of Ireland, and took a lively interest in her history and literature. Admitted to the Society June 24, 1897; died in Boston, Mass., June 21, 1898.

Joseph H. Fay, M. D.

A graduate of the University of Vermont; admitted to the Society March 3, 1898; died in Fall River, Mass., June 25, 1898.

Capt. John Drum.

Born in Ireland, 1840; a veteran of the Civil War; later, commissioned Lieutenant in the regular army; saw much service in campaigns against the Indians; military instructor at St. Francis Xavier's College, New York City; on the outbreak of hostilities with Spain he was a captain in the Tenth U. S. Infantry; went with his regiment to Cuba, where he met a soldier's death; admitted to the Society July 20, 1897; killed in action before Santiago de Cuba, July 1, 1898. (The date of his death is given on page 29 of this volume as July 2. It should read July 1, as here stated.)

Mr. John E. Conner.

Born in Bradford, Vt., 1852; chief of police of Chicopee, Mass., 1885 to 1894 and in 1896 and 1897; city marshal of Chicopee at the time of his death; admitted to the Society June 22, 1898; died in Chicopee, Mass., Aug. 25, 1898.

Rev. Philip Grace, D. D.

Born in County Kilkenny, Ireland, 1838; ordained to the Roman Catholic priesthood at Hartford, Conn., 1862; was attached to various churches in the diocese of Providence, R. I.; was made a doctor of divinity by Pope Leo XIII; became rector of St. Mary's church, Newport, R. I., and passed away while occupying that position; admitted to the Society March 14, 1898; died in Newport, R. I., Sept. 23, 1898.

Capt. John M. Tobin.

Born in Waterford, Ireland, 1836; was commissioned First Lieutenant in the Ninth Massachusetts at outbreak of the Civil War; became Adjutant of the regiment; participated in the battles of Yorktown, Hanover Court House, Gaines' Mill, |Malvern Hill, and many other engagements; was wounded at the Battle of the Wilderness; at Malvern Hill he voluntarily took command of the regiment while Adjutant, and bravely fought it from 3 P. M. until dusk, rallying and reforming the regiment under fire, and twice picking up the regimental flag—the color-bearers having been shot down—

and placing it in safe hands. In 1863–'64 he was Inspector-General of a brigade in the First Division of the Fifth Corps, at Bealton, Va. He was severely wounded at the Battle of Laurel Hill, Va. For twenty-five years he was engaged as editor and publisher of weekly papers, and also did much work upon the Boston dailies. In the recent war with Spain, Captain Tobin was Quartermaster in the First Brigade, Second Division, First Army Corps; admitted to the Society Jan. 20, 1897; died in Knoxville, Tenn., December, 1898.

Hon. Patrick Walsh.

Born in Ireland, 1840; became editor and proprietor of *The Chronicle*, Augusta, Ga.; was also manager of the Southern Associated Press; in 1894 he became United States senator from Georgia; was elected mayor of Augusta, and held the office at the time of his death; admitted to the Society January 20, 1897; died in Augusta, Ga., March 19, 1899.

Col. Patrick T. Hanley.

Born in Roscommon, Ireland, 1831; was an officer in the Ninth Massachusetts regiment during the Civil War, being successively commissioned Lieutenant, Captain, Major, and Lieutenant-Colonel; took command of the regiment at the Wilderness on the fall of Colonel Guiney; prominent in Boston business circles; admitted to the Society, November 29, 1898; died in Boston, Mass., March 31, 1899.

Hon. John H. Sullivan.

Born in County Cork, Ireland, 1848; a prominent citizen of Boston, Mass.; state senator of Massachusetts; member of the Governor's Council; sinking fund commissioner of Boston; president of the Columbia Trust and Safety Deposit Company; died in East Boston, Mass., April 9, 1899.

Hon. Eli Thayer.

Born in Mendon, Mass., 1819; descended from John Alden of Mayflower fame; elected to congress from the Worcester, Mass., district in 1856; author of "A History of the Kansas Crusade;" admitted to the Society, 1898; died in Worcester, Mass., April 15, 1899.

William F. Cummings, M. D.

Born in Rutland, Vt., 1870; graduated in medicine at the University of Vermont, 1893; treasurer of the Rutland County Medical and Surgical society; admitted to the Society, August 3, 1898; died in Rutland, Vt., April 16, 1899.

Mr. Joseph J. Kelley.

Born in Ireland, 1844; served as a member of the school board of Cambridge, Mass., and in various other positions of honor in that city; member of the Massachusetts legislature; admitted to the Society, March 29, 1898; died in East Cambridge, Mass., April 29, 1899.

Mr. William Slattery.

Born in Ireland, 1849; graduated from the law school of Harvard University; became a prominent lawyer of Holyoke, Mass.; associate justice of the city court; admitted to the Society, June 23, 1898; died in Holyoke, Mass., July 22, 1899.

Rev. George W. Pepper.

Born in County Down, Ireland, 1833; was ordained to the Methodist Episcopal ministry in this country; a member of the North Ohio conference for a period of forty years; commanded a company in the Eightieth Ohio regiment during the Civil War and later served as a chaplain; in 1890 was appointed U. S. consul to Milan, Italy, by President Harrison; admitted to the Society on its organization, January 20, 1897; died in Cleveland, O., August 6, 1899.

Rev. Denis Scannell.

Born in County Kerry, Ireland, 1846; was ordained to the Roman Catholic priesthood at Alleghany, N. Y., 1870; appointed rector of St. Anne's church, Worcester, Mass., 1872, having previously had charge of the parish in Blackstone, Mass.; served two terms of three years each on the school board of Worcester; admitted to the Society, November 3, 1898; died in Worcester, Mass., August 20, 1899.

Mr. Edmund Phelan.

Born in Ireland 31 years ago; at the time of his death he was president of Newspaper Mailers' Union, No. 1, Boston, Mass. He was known throughout the state as a temperance worker in Catholic circles, and also took much interest in the work of our Historical Society. He died at his home, 32 Adams street, Roxbury (Boston), Mass., November 29, 1899.

GENERAL INDEX.

ANALYTICAL INDEX.

Lower Dublin, Pa., 183.

Loyal Legion, Military Order of the, 16, 43, 201, 210, 219.

Ludwig, William, the Irish Baritone, Sings before the Society, 118.

Lyon County (Ky.), 141.

Lyon, Hon. Chittenden, 152.

Lyon, Hon. Matthew, 141, 142.

Lyons, Judge Peter, of Virginia, 163

Lynch, Aide-de-camp to the Chevalier de Chastellux, 115.

Lynch, Thomas J., Augusta, Me., 29, 221.

Lynn, Hon. Wauhope, of New York, 25, 46, 221.

Lynn, Maj. B. W., of Virginia, 164.

Macdonough, United States Torpedo-boat Destroyer, 28, 37, 45.

Machias, Me., The O'Briens of, 35, 39.

Macroom (Ireland), 193.

Mac Sparran, Rev. James, of Rhode Island, 180, 181.

Mac Sweeny of Banagh, 193.

Mac Sweeny of the Battle Axes, 193.

Mac Sweeny of Fanad, 193.

Mac Sweeny na D'Tuagh, 197.

Mac Sweeny na D'Tuatha, 193.

Mac Sweeny of the Territories, 193.

Mac Sweenys, Standard Bearers to the O'Donnells, 194.

Mac Sweenys Anciently Famous for Hospitality, 194.

Magill, Col. William, Commanded a Georgia Regiment during the Civil War, 178.

Magills of Florida, The, 178.

Maginnis, John Sharp (D. D.), of Providence, R. I., and Rochester, N. Y., 186.

Mahone, Gen. William, 164.

Maine Legislature, 218.

Maine, United States Battleship, Resolution of Sorrow Adopted on the Loss of the, 25.

Malloy, Gen. A. G., of Texas, 137, 222.

Malvern Hill, Battle of, 44, 237.

Manning, President, of Rhode Island College, 184, 185.

"Man Without a Country," Edward Everett Hale's, 120.

Many Irish Emigrate to France, 62.

Marion and Sumpter, 176.

Marmion on the Irish Exodus, 67.

Martha Dandridge Custis, 200.

Mary Dandridge of Virginia, 200.

Mary Nunn of Cork, Ireland, 186.

Marye's Heights, Irish Valor at, 103.

Maryland, Catholic Irishmen from, at Siege of Boston, 68.

Maryland, Governor Bradford of, 98.

Massachusetts Bay, General Court of, 63.

Massachusetts, Governor Andrew of, 98.

Massachusetts House of Representatives, 208.

Massachusetts Legislature, 208, 209, 212, 215, 224, 235, 236, 239.

Massachusetts Patriots, Honor Roll of, 40.

Massachusetts Revolutionary Records, 176.

Massachusetts Superior Court, 210.

Massachusetts Supreme Court, 215.

Masters Knox and Crocker, "Natives of Ireland" and Early School Teachers in Rhode Island, 182.

Matthew Thornton, Monument to, 22.

Matthew Watson, A Settler of Barrington, R. I., 189.

Maxwell, Gen. William, of the American Revolution, 79, 81.

May, Henry A., of Roslindale, Mass., a Descendant from James Butler, who Immigrated from Ireland in 1653, 19, 222.

Mayflower, John Alden of the, 238.

Mayflower, The, 65, 238.

Mayor Boyle of Newport, R. I., 25, 38, 40, 116, 205, 207.

Mayor Crowley of Lowell, Mass., 210.

Mayor Driscoll of New Haven, Conn., 213.

Mayor O'Brien of Boston, Mass., 117.

McAdoo, Gen. A. G., of Texas, 137, 222.

McAdoo, Hon. William, of New Jersey and New York, 17, 42, 51, 100, 102, 205, 222.

McCaffery, Hugh, of Philadelphia, Pa., 17, 222.

McCarthy, Dr. T. A., of Nashua, N. H., 29.

McCarthys of Desmond, The, 194.

McCarty, a Naval Officer who came over with our French Allies in the American Revolution, 115.

McCarty, Captain Page, of Virginia, 165.

McCarty, Daniel, Speaker of the Virginia House of Burgesses (1715), 165.

McCarty of Glenclare, 165.

McCarty, Major Richard, of the Revolution, 165.

McClanahan, Colonel, of the Revolution, 165.

McClellan Rifles, The, 190.

McCoy, Rev. John J., Chicopee, Mass., 12, 27, 32, 42, 47, 50, 85, 202, 204.

McConway, William, of Pittsburg, Pa., 22, 222.

McCormick, David, of Texas, 127.

McCracken, the Presbyterian Minister, 109.

McElroy, James, a Soldier of the Revolution, 81.

McGee, Thomas D'Arcy, 16, 64.

McGovern, James, of New York, 32.

McGuinness, Hon. E. D., of Rhode Island, 17, 105, 191, 223.

McGuire, Dr. Hunter, of Virginia, 165.

EDITOR'S NOTE : To the membership roll herein contained should be added the names : James McGovern, New York City, John E. Maguire, Haverhill, Mass., and John Goggin, Nashua, N. H. In answer to inquiries, I desire to state that the edition of Vol. I of the JOURNAL has been exhausted. A second edition of the same may be issued later when the funds of the Society warrant. It will be noticed that each volume is complete and independent in itself. New members who have not Vol. I, will find in the Chronological Record in the present volume a comprehensive outline of the work thus far done by the Society.

Kane, John P., Central Building, Lawrence, Mass.

Kavanagh, Rev. Patrick J., Lexington, Mass.

Keating, James E. (M. D.), 143 Pine Street, Portland, Me.

Keating, Patrick M., of the law firm, Gargan & Keating, Pemberton Square, Boston, Mass.

Keating, William H., 15 Vaughn Street, Portland, Me.

Keefe, Dennis F. (D. D. S.), Butler Exchange, Providence, R. I.

Keefe, Patrick H. (M. D.), 257 Benefit Street, Providence, R. I.

Keegan, Rev. James J., Woburn, Mass.

Keely, George, 270 Brackett Street, Portland, Me.

Kehoe, John B., Portland, Me.

Keleher, T. D., Disbursing Clerk for office of auditor to the Post-office Department, Washington, D. C.

Kelley, Daniel B., 21 Windsor Street, Haverhill, Mass.

Kelley, J. D. Jerrold, Lieutenant-Commander U. S. N.; was recently attached to the battleship *Texas*; address, care Navy Department, Washington, D. C.

Kelley, Patrick, 19 Davidson Street, Lowell, Mass.

Kelliher, Michael W. (M. D.), Pawtucket, R. I.

Kelly, James, 13 Greenleaf Street, Portland, Me.

Kelly, James E., Ogdensburg, N. Y.

Kelly, John F., 284 West Housatonic Avenue, Pittsfield, Mass.

Kelly, John P. (D. D. S.), 12 Essex Street, Newburyport, Mass.

Kelly, Michael F. (M. D.), Fall River, Mass.

Kelly, William J., 9 Dove Street, Newburyport, Mass.

Kelly, William J., Kittery, Me.

Kendricken, Hon. Paul H., 75 Maple Street, Roxbury (Boston), Mass.; ex-State Senator; member of the Military Order of the Loyal Legion.

Kenefick, Owen A., Essex Street, Lawrence, Mass.

Kennedy, Charles F., Brewer, Me.

Kennedy, Dr. Francis M., 446 County Street, New Bedford, Mass.; trustee of Public Library.

Kennedy, Joseph P., 311 South Water Street, New Bedford, Mass.

Kennedy, Hon. P. J., 165 Webster Street, East Boston, Mass.; has been a State Senator.

Kennedy, P. J., 322 and 324 Nicollet Avenue, Minneapolis, Minn.

Kenney, James W., Treasurer Union Brewing Co., Roxbury (Boston), Mass.

Kent, Pierce, 356 East 57th Street, New York City; recently lieutenant in the 69th Regiment.

Kerr, Dr. James, 1711 H Street, N. W., Washington, D. C.

Kiernan, Rev. Owen, Rector Church of the Immaculate Conception, Fall River, Mass.

Kiernan, Patrick, 18 East 83d Street, New York City.

Kiley, Daniel F., Essex Street, Lawrence, Mass.